Thank you, Vance Christie, for yo
remarkable Christian women in history. Your book, ~~ ~~~~
Faith and Courage, shows in a beautifully-written and fascinating style, the faithful devotion of these women for Christ, and allows us to look deeply into their lives and ministries. I can highly recommend this book, and I hope women around the world will study it for personal spiritual growth and also in a group Bible study setting. Truly, these five women are role models for all of us today!

Denise George
Birmingham, Alabama

Women of Faith and Courage aptly describes Vance Christie's five subjects in this well-researched account. In days when sacrifice for Christ's sake is often sadly lacking in our churches there is much here to challenge and even disturb us.

Faith Cook
Derbyshire, England

Women of Faith and Courage, biographies of five women who faced daunting difficulties, both inspires and challenges. Whether confronted with poverty, a self-centered husband, endless debt, physical disabilities, perennial illness, government persecution, destructive fires, or loneliness, they all found faith in Christ gave them a courage to overcome every obstacle and serve Him. Whatever our own trials or difficulties, the stories of Susanna Wesley, Fanny Crosby, Catherine Booth, Mary Slessor, and Corrie ten Boom are certain to strengthen our own Christian faith and courage.

Diana Lynn Severance
Spring, Texas

Seeing the names of these five women missionaries, I felt a sense of 'déjà vu'. They were all women whose stories I knew (or thought I knew) fairly well. Then, as I read, I became more and more 'hooked'. By the time I reached Mary Slessor, I could not put it down. The whole book has fascinated and intrigued me, and I am so grateful to Vance for putting so much hard work into the research, bringing to light so much 'new' material. He has written each life story in such a vibrant way, truly making each of the five women come alive. May many young women (and not so young!) be stirred, challenged and inspired by what God has done through these women, each in their own circumstances and differing situations. Indeed, may we all be challenged to keep 'going for God' to the end of our journeys – as these five did; and may we live with one passion 'to please our Lord and Saviour Jesus'.

Helen Roseveare
Holywood, Northern Ireland

Nothing inspires me like reading about the lives of women who lived and died serving the Lord Jesus. Vance Christie has done a wonderful job of opening the lives of five women--sharing their strengths and weaknesses as well as their victories and tragedies. I came away knowing that all I must do is to please God and the affirmation that the key to doing that is obedience, standing under Scripture without being swayed by my own logic or perceived giftedness or even by the opportunities presented! Indeed for God to take ordinary women and use them in such extraordinary ways should give every woman a mandate to serve the Lord faithfully even if in the most humble circumstances!

Dorothy Patterson
Fort Worth, Texas

Women

of

Faith and Courage

VANCE CHRISTIE

CHRISTIAN
FOCUS

Copyright © Vance Christie 2011

ISBN 978-1-84550-686-5

10 9 8 7 6 5 4 3 2 1

Published in 2011
by
Christian Focus Publications,
Geanies House, Fearn,
Ross-shire, IV20 1TW, Scotland
www.christianfocus.com

Cover design
by
Paul Lewis

Printed by
Bell and Bain, Glasgow

CONTENTS

To my sisters, Debbie and Vicki,
with fond memories of our childhood together
and sincere prayers for God's continued blessings on you

Introduction

Ever since Bible days devout women have played an indispensable role in helping to support and advance the work of God's kingdom on earth. In Old Testament times such women as Sarah, Miriam, Deborah, Ruth and Esther were strategically used of the Lord to serve His people and help bring about His purposes. A number of women in the Gospels provided Christ and His Disciples with financial and moral support (Luke 8:1-3; 10:38-40; 23:27, 49, 55-56). In Acts and the epistles Dorcas, Lydia, Phoebe, Priscilla, Euodia, Syntyche and other women received high commendation for their service of the saints and their work in the cause of the Gospel (Acts 9:36-39; 16:14-15; Rom.16:1-6, 12; Phil. 4:2-3).

From the pages of church history, especially following the Reformation, numerous examples can be cited of women who (without intending to do so) gained renown for their exceptional Christian piety and service. The current volume presents abbreviated biographical accounts of the lives and ministries of five such outstanding women from the past three centuries – Susanna Wesley, Fanny Crosby, Catherine Booth, Mary Slessor and Corrie ten Boom.

Susanna Wesley (1669-1742) was the godly mother of John and Charles Wesley, key players in England's evangelical revival and founders of the Methodist movement in the eighteenth century. She faithfully supported and helped to strengthen the ministry of her oftentimes-difficult husband, Samuel, a clergyman in the Church of England. Susanna also poured her life into the educating and scrupulous spiritual upbringing of her numerous children. Her life models the shaping of an exceptional character through assorted trials, including religious persecution, financial deprivation, family heartache and poor health.

In an era filled with prominent Gospel song composers, Fanny Crosby (1820-1915) became the world's premiere hymnwriter. Blind from six weeks of age, she wrote nearly 9,000 hymns in her lifetime, including a number that are still sung today – to name but a few, 'All the Way My Savior Leads Me', 'Blessed Assurance', 'He Hideth My Soul', 'I Am Thine, O Lord', 'Jesus, Keep Me Near the Cross', 'Redeemed', 'Rescue the Perishing', 'Tell Me the Story of Jesus' and 'To God Be the Glory'. A Presbyterian by upbringing, Fanny ministered in various denominational settings as an adult. Well into her eighties, she traveled widely, ministering in churches, Bible conferences, rescue missions, YMCAs, patriotic rallies and various other settings.

Catherine Booth (1829-1890) is commonly thought of as the mother of the Salvation Army, having co-founded it with her husband, William. Before that time they were involved in itinerant evangelistic ministry with the Methodists. The Salvation Army, which experienced explosive growth and spread to a number of countries in the Booths' lifetime, emphasized ministry to the spiritual and material needs of the lower classes of society. For over three decades Catherine carried on a powerful public speaking ministry, becoming the pre-eminent female preacher of her generation. The pronounced influence she and her husband had on their nine children (including an adopted son) resulted in all of them growing up to become devoted believers, most entering vocational Christian service.

Mary Slessor (1848-1915), a Scottish Presbyterian, overcame a difficult childhood that included coping with an alcoholic father, grinding family poverty and exhausting labor in a textile mill as the primary provider for her mother and siblings. She went on to invest thirty-eight years of her life in carrying the Gospel to savage, degraded tribes in the dense forests of Calabar (southern Nigeria), West Africa. Mary courageously pioneered in areas that other missionaries and even traders avoided, planting churches and schools in several locations. Through her efforts, a variety of unthinkable pagan practices were eliminated or greatly reduced, and many individuals were led to saving faith in Christ.

Corrie ten Boom (1892-1983) is well known as one of the brave Dutch Reformed Christians who assisted and sheltered Jewish people and other fugitives during the German occupation of Holland in World War 2. After being arrested for their underground work, Corrie and her sister, Betsie, carried out a phenomenal ministry of Christian witness and mercy in the Nazi concentration camps where they were incarcerated. Following her providential release, Corrie returned to Holland where she established a recovery ministry to victims of the war. She devoted the final three decades of her life to itinerant evangelistic ministry in more than sixty countries throughout the world.

The examples of these women have tremendous potential to inspire and instruct contemporary believers – male and female, younger and older – in various aspects of the Christian life. They model devotion to Christ and sacrificial service of His kingdom. They show how to balance one's family and ministry responsibilities. Susanna, Fanny, Catherine, Mary and Corrie exemplify a compassionate and practical response to the spiritual and physical needs of others. These women earnestly evangelized perishing unbelievers who needed the Savior. They exercised steadfast faith in God to supply their material needs, to help them carry out their ministries and to see them through overwhelming circumstances.

By no means were they nearly perfect. They wrestled with fears, frustrations, discouragements and temptations. All were well aware of their personal weaknesses, shortcomings and failures. Such personal struggles and inadequacies helped keep them from pride, gave them increased gentleness in ministering to fellow strugglers and caused them to lean more heavily on the Lord for His grace and enablement. The fact that they were less than perfect encourages other Christians by reminding them how greatly God is able to use deficient individuals who are thoroughly consecrated to Him. Susanna Wesley, Fanny Crosby, Catherine Booth, Mary Slessor and Corrie ten Boom also serve as a reminder that when God accomplishes significant things through imperfect people, He (rather than they) deserves the glory.

1

Susanna Wesley

ONE

Following the christening service of yet another of the Reverend Samuel Annesley's numerous children, someone asked, 'How many olive branches [children] does Doctor Annesley have?'

'I am not sure,' came the response of the minister who had officiated the service, 'but it is either two dozen or a quarter of a hundred.'

The christened infant was Susanna Annesley, born in London on January 20, 1669. She was the twenty-fifth and, as it turned out, final of Doctor Annesley's children.

Her father, a devout Puritan, attended Queen's College, Oxford University, and in 1644 graduated with a Master of Arts degree. He was ordained in the Church of England and became the rector of a church in Cliffe, Kent, southeast of London. The young clergyman could not avoid being swept up in the tumultuous religious and political events that engulfed England in the 1640s. For decades the Puritans (so named because of their desire to 'purify' the Church of England) had been pressing for reforms in both the church and government. Some thought there were vestiges of Roman Catholicism that needed to be eliminated from Anglican Church practices. Others believed the Church of England's episcopal form of governance could not be supported by Scripture and ought to be replaced by a presbyterian or congregational polity. The Puritans disapproved of the lax standards Anglicans had concerning acceptable Lord's Day activities. Other more radical Puritans, known as Separatists, desired to establish their independence from the Church of England and called for a separation of church and state.

Escalating tensions finally erupted in bloody civil war in the 1640s. The Royalist army fought for King Charles I and the Church of England while the forces of the Parliamentarians, led by Oliver Cromwell, demanded a Puritan form of government. The Parliamentarians were victorious and for several years Puritan ideals held sway in England's church and government. Eventually, however, the majority of the population wearied of the strict Puritan lifestyle and, after the death of Cromwell, recalled Charles II to be their ruler in 1660. The Church of England returned to episcopacy.

By then the capable Annesley was serving as vicar of London's St Giles Church, Cripplegate. There he received a generous salary of £700 per year. But in 1662 the English parliament passed the Act of Uniformity, requiring all England's ministers to conform to Anglican beliefs and practices. Samuel Annesley was among the 2,000 ministers who could not in good conscience agree to that condition. In what came to be known as the Great Ejection, these men were removed from their positions in the churches and universities. They and their families were turned out of their parsonages.

These ministers, labeled thereafter as Nonconformists or Dissenters, were not allowed to preach. Their activities were closely monitored by the authorities. Any attempt to hold a religious service could lead to a heavy fine, a jail sentence of several years or even banishment to semi-slavery in a foreign country.

Annesley lost his pastoral position and salary at St Giles. In addition, he lived with the strain of being constantly under surveillance. The threat of being seized and imprisoned always hung over him and was likely a continual strain on his family members.

Such stressful conditions still prevailed when Susanna was born into the Annesley household. But three years after her birth, in 1672, King Charles II relaxed some of the laws restricting the Dissenters. Doctor Annesley immediately returned to active pastoral ministry. He leased a meeting place on Bishopsgate Street in London's Little St Helen's district and soon had a flourishing congregation. Nonconformists looked to him as one of their most prominent leaders.

Susanna's mother, whose name has not been preserved, was said to be a woman of superior understanding and earnest piety who spared no labor in seeking to promote the religious welfare of her children. She was Samuel Annesley's second wife, his first wife and child having both died while he was pastoring in Cliffe, Kent. The second Mrs Annesley bore twenty-four children. Of that number, Susanna and at least nine of her siblings are known to have reached adulthood.

While pastoring in Little St Helen's, Doctor Annesley was able to move his family to Spital Yard, one of London's well-to-do neighborhoods. Susanna's upbringing there was likely comfortable, though not luxurious.

In an age when many girls and women, even among the upper class, never learned to read and write, Susanna had the blessing of receiving a good education as a child. Since it was not common for girls to receive a formal education, she probably was taught at home, under the supervision of a parent, sibling or private tutor. An avid reader, she spent much time digesting good books. With access to her father's library, Susanna likely studied a number of theological treatises written by the earlier Reformers or by the Puritans of her own era. Her writings as an adult reveal not only an excellent command of the English language, but also a breadth of biblical and theological knowledge rivaling that of many ministers in that day or this.

She developed a strict religious discipline early in life. Many years later she wrote in a letter to her son John: 'I will tell you what rule I observed ... when I was young, and too much addicted to childish diversions, which was this – never to spend more time in mere recreation in one day than I spent in private religious devotions.'[1] This became a guiding principle which she followed the rest of her life.

A number of prominent, learned leaders from among the Dissenters were regular guests in the Annesley home. Among them were Richard Baxter, author of such Puritan classics as *The Reformed Pastor* and *The Saint's Everlasting Rest*, as well as John Owen, Vice Chancellor of Oxford University until his expulsion in the Great Ejection. Even today Owen is esteemed as the 'Prince of Puritans,' and his voluminous works continue to be studied.

---

1   Arnold A. Dallimore, *Susanna Wesley, The Mother of John and Charles Wesley* (Grand Rapids: Baker, 1996), p. 15.

These and other Nonconformist leaders met regularly with Samuel Annesley in his home to discuss a variety of theological and ecclesiological issues. Quite naturally much discussion was devoted to the differences between Anglicanism and Dissent. Young Susanna listened intently to many such conversations and through them gained a clear perspective of the differing convictions that separated the two groups. Even before she became a teenager, she devoted serious thought to the matter. Her contemplations led her to take a stunning step, especially for one so young, as she related in a letter to one of her children years afterward:

> Because I was educated among the Dissenters, and there was something remarkable in my leaving them at so early an age, not being full thirteen, I had drawn up an account of the whole transaction, under which I had included the main of the controversy between them and the Established Church, as far as it had come to my knowledge.[2]

Unfortunately the document in which Susanna recorded her reasons for siding with the Church of England was destroyed in a fire that razed the Epworth rectory where she lived as an adult. Just as amazing as young Susanna's determination to leave her father's church to join an Anglican congregation was his willingness to allow her to do so. Having suffered so much in order to be true to his Dissenting convictions, he could not have helped but be grieved over his daughter's contrary conclusions. His treatment of her in this matter shows that he gave his children the freedom to stand on their own convictions.

---

2   Ibid., p. 16.

For her part, this incident showed not only the strength of Susanna's convictions but also her determination to follow them. Doubtless her decision to join the Anglican Church was a difficult one for her to make. She stood alone in doing so, as none of her family joined her. She had to be somewhat aware, likely more so as time went on, of the disappointment this decision caused her parents. But having made up her mind, she never turned back. To the end of her life she remained loyal to the Church of England.

Among those who attended Samuel Annesley's church were a number of young men from the Dissenting schools located around London. One such student, John Dunton, married Susanna's sister, Elizabeth. One of their wedding guests was a friend and fellow student of Dunton's named Samuel Wesley. As his wedding gift Wesley had composed a romantic poem which he read before the assembled guests as a tribute to the bride and groom.

At the time of this wedding Samuel Wesley was a young man of nineteen while Susanna Annesley was a girl of thirteen. It is not known whether this was the first time they met or if they had been previous acquaintances. What is clear is that a relationship developed between them that resulted in their marriage to each other six years later.

Like Susanna, Samuel Wesley was of staunch Puritan stock. His father, John, studied at Oxford University where he was known for his piety and academic excellence. Following his graduation he returned to his home area of Dorset, along England's southern coast, where he became the pastor of Winterbourn Whitchurch and was married.

Four years later he and his pregnant wife were turned out of their church and parsonage, victims of the Great

Ejection. Not one to allow his convictions to be silenced, John moved around from town to town and continued preaching nearly every day. It was under such trying circumstances, just four months after their dismissal from Winterbourn Whitchurch, that Samuel Wesley was born in November of 1662.

As the ensuing years passed, John was arrested and imprisoned four times. During his final incarceration he became sick and died at age forty-two. Mrs Wesley was left a destitute widow with four young children to care for. Friends from among the Dissenters assisted her by providing funds so that Samuel could pursue an education. He showed excellent academic potential and it was supposed he might well enter the Dissenting ministry. At age fifteen or sixteen he was placed in one of the Nonconformist academies in London. These institutions had been established because while Dissenting students could attend the universities, which were under the auspices of the Church of England, they were not permitted to graduate from them.

During the course of his studies Wesley was required to research all the reasons for supporting Dissent. The assignment left him unsettled, for through it he came to realize he did not share many of the political and religious views of the Nonconformists. Around that same time a close friend supplied him with a number of arguments against Dissent that further troubled him. After a period of intense soul-searching he concluded that he 'lived in groundless separation from the Established Church.'

It is not known how much influence, if any, Samuel Wesley and Susanna Annesley had on each other's thinking about Dissent and the Church of England. If Wesley had contact with the Annesley family prior to John and Elizabeth Dunton's wedding, then he could have played a part in influencing Susanna's thinking on the issue or vice versa. It is also entirely possible that Susanna and Samuel reached their conclusion in favor of the Church of England completely independently of each other and then discovered that they shared similar convictions. Doubtless they discussed the issue at considerable length during the years of acquaintance that preceded their marriage.

Wesley is known to have played a key role in steering Susanna away from a heresy that threatened her faith some time after she joined the Established Church. For a brief season she was adversely influenced by the teaching of Socinianism (the forerunner of Unitarianism) that was then well established in England. Socinianism denied the doctrines of original sin, the Trinity, the deity of Christ, His atoning death for sin, and predestination. Having been exposed to this teaching, Susanna was shaken in her faith and for a short time she doubted the Gospel.

While still a student at a dissenting academy, Wesley gained a familiarity with Socinian beliefs and doctrines when he was hired to translate the writings of John Biddle, the father of English Socinianism. After realizing the nature of Biddle's beliefs, he refused to finish the job. But he was later able to use his knowledge of the heresy in guiding Susanna away from its deadly spiritual influence.

In August 1683, at age twenty, Wesley left his mother's home in London and walked to Oxford where he enrolled in Exeter College. There he quietly joined the membership of an Anglican church. Having done so, he was able to pursue his higher education as a fully-fledged member of the university. He was able to support himself by being a servitor (carrying out various menial tasks for students who were better positioned financially), by tutoring and by doing some important translation work for the university's Bodleian Library.

In June of 1688 he graduated from Oxford University with a Bachelor of Arts degree. He immediately returned to London where, a short while later, he was ordained as a minister of the Church of England and was given a curacy. In that position, which paid only £28 per year, he served as the assistant to the rector of a parish.

Nothing is known of Samuel Wesley's courtship of Susanna Annesley. Probably they corresponded during his years at Oxford and perhaps he was able to visit her occasionally at her parents' home in London. It is not hard to understand how the couple came to be attracted to each other. They shared not only a common Puritan heritage but also the same strong convictions that led them to join the Church of England. In addition to their deep earnestness about spiritual matters, they both possessed a keen mind, a strong personality and an attractive physical appearance. Susanna was described by her contemporaries as being a very beautiful woman. Considerably taller than the five foot, four inch Wesley, she was slender and carried herself in a dignified fashion.

They were married on November 11, 1688. He had just turned twenty-six and she was nineteen. The exact location of their wedding is unknown, but likely they were married in an Anglican church. Wesley would later confess in a written autobiographical account of his life and ministry that perhaps he should not have married until he had more firmly established his financial fortunes. He divulged of his marriage to Susanna before such time,

'I have no excuse, unless a most passionate love may be taken for one.'

TWO

After only a few months in his London curacy, Samuel Wesley accepted an offer to serve as chaplain aboard a naval vessel on the Irish Sea, a position that promised him an annual salary of £70. But the new situation proved most unsatisfactory and he left the ship half a year later. Returning to London, he joined Susanna who had been living in a boarding house.

Before long, the couple moved into the home of Susanna's parents, where she gave birth to their first child on February 10, 1690. The newborn was named Samuel after his father and grandfather. Several weeks later Wesley was offered the position of rector of St Leonard's Church in South Ormsby, Lincolnshire, and promptly accepted.

By this time he was already in debt, a condition that would plague him and his family throughout his life. Money was owed to the owner of the boarding house, and further finances needed to be borrowed to cover the cost of moving to South Ormsby and furnishing their home there.

The Wesleys began their ministry in South Ormsby, a village of 260 residents located about thirty miles east of Lincoln, in June 1690. Samuel's salary was a modest £50 per year, and their rectory was a primitive dwelling 'composed of reeds and clay'. As all but the poorest families of that era did, the Wesleys employed a servant girl to help with the endless household chores, all of which needed to be done by hand.

Seven months after settling in South Ormsby, Susanna gave birth to a daughter. As was fairly common in that day, the baby girl was named Susanna after her mother. Just one year later, in January 1692, another daughter, Emilia, was born. Unfortunately, as would be the case throughout her childbearing years, Susanna often experienced extended periods of weakness and poor health in connection with her pregnancies and deliveries. Not uncommonly she was largely incapacitated for months at a time. Even at this young age she also began to suffer recurring bouts of rheumatism.

Samuel and Susanna cherished the hope that their son, Sammy, would grow up to be a clergyman. But that hope seemed to be dashed when, by the time he was three or four years old, the boy had never spoken a single word, leading his parents to conclude he was a mute. One morning Sammy was nowhere to be found, and Susanna went through the house and out into the yard looking for him. Fearing that some harm might have come to him, she began repeatedly calling his name. Presently she heard a child's voice clearly state, 'Here I am, Mamma.' Looking under a table, she was amazed and overjoyed to find Sammy, the youngster who had spoken, sitting with his favorite cat in his arms. From then on he talked as normally as any other child.

That same year the Wesleys experienced the loss of a child, a sorrowful experience that would be all too common in the years to follow. After a lingering illness of several months, their daughter, Susanna, died at age two or three. Eventually, nine of the nineteen children Susanna bore died in infancy or early childhood.

While ministering at South Ormsby, Wesley was able to continue his university studies and eventually received a Master of Arts degree from Cambridge. After he had been at South Ormsby four years, in hopes of advancing his ministerial career, he requested and gained permission to dedicate a volume of poetry he had recently written to England's Queen Mary. The book was entitled *The life of our blessed Lord and Saviour Jesus Christ, a heroic poem.* The dedication addressed the Queen in highly flattering language and declared Wesley's loyalty both to her and to her husband, William of Orange, as the king. (As will be seen shortly, many Englishmen were not willing to accept William, a member of the Dutch royal family, as their sovereign.) This had the desired result of bringing Wesley to the Queen's attention and commending him to her. To gain her goodwill was a great benefit, for numerous privileges and positions within the Church of England were under her command.

Interestingly, in that same work Wesley included several lines of verse as a tribute to his wife:

> She graced my humble roof, and blest my life,
> Blest me by a far greater name than wife;
> Yet still I bore an undisputed sway,
> Nor was't her task, but pleasure, to obey:
> Scarce thought, much less could act, what I denied.
> In our low house there was no room for pride;
> Nor need I e'er direct what still was right,
> She studied my convenience and delight.
> Nor did I for her care ungrateful prove,
> But only used my power to show my love:
> Whate'er she asked I gave, without reproach or grudge,
> For still she reason asked, and I was judge.
> All my commands, requests at her fair hands,
> And her requests to me were all commands.
> To others' thresholds rarely she'd incline:

Her house her pleasure was, and she was mine;
Rarely abroad, or never, but with me,
Or when by pity called, or charity.[3]

These lines are significant in that they reveal the loving, albeit lordly, way in which Wesley related to his wife. Susanna is seen to be a submissive, attentive wife who sought to please her husband and care for his needs. While tending to her own household was her primary focus, she also is seen to have carried out missions of mercy to needy individuals in the community.

Sorrow again visited the Wesley household late in 1694 or early in 1695. Susanna bore twin boys – Annesley and Jedediah – but they lived only one month. Later in 1695, however, she gave birth to a healthy baby girl, whom she also named Susanna, after herself and in memory of her deceased daughter. This new daughter commonly went by the nickname Sukey. The following year yet another daughter, Mary, was born.

The benefit that Samuel Wesley had hoped to gain in dedicating a book to the Queen was realized early in 1697. He was appointed as rector of Epworth, in western Lincolnshire. This charge came with a greatly increased salary of £200 per annum. 'Queen Mary gave me this benefice,' Wesley stated. But subsequent research has shown he actually received the gift as a favor from King William.[4]

Epworth was a market town of about 2,000 residents located some thirty miles northwest of Lincoln. It was the principal town on what was called the Isle of Axholme.

---

3   Kathy McReynolds, *Susanna Wesley* (Minneapolis: Bethany, 1998), p. 35.

4   Dallimore, *Susanna Wesley*, p. 38.

That portion of land, about fourteen miles in length, was so named because it was surrounded by the rivers Trent, Don and Idle. Susanna was doubtless pleased with the larger rectory that awaited them there. It was a three-storied, five-gabled home built of timber, plastered and having a thatched roof.

Shortly after their arrival at Epworth, Susanna gave birth to a daughter, Mehetabel, to whom was given the nickname Hetty. Another child was born the following year, 1698, but lived only a short time. Neither its name nor gender has survived. A son was born in May of 1699 and named John. But he, too, died in infancy. Another son, Benjamin, arrived the next year.

Besides carrying out clerical duties, Wesley took up farming upon his arrival at Epworth. He cultivated the parish glebe and acquired cows, pigs, chickens and ducks. He likely did so in an effort to reduce his debts. But due to expenses incurred from the unforeseen collapse of his barn, his agrarian endeavors actually had the opposite effect.

In his early Epworth years Wesley was selected to serve as a representative of the diocese of Lincoln at the convocation of the Church of England. The convocation, which was held in London, was basically an ecclesiastical parliament that legislated concerning the affairs of the Anglican Church. While this was an honor for Wesley, he was not remunerated for his services. In fulfilling these responsibilities he was sometimes required to stay in London for several weeks and had to cover all related expenses out of his own salary. This, too, increased his indebtedness.

In fact, Wesley's debts had so increased by the end of 1700, three years after his coming to Epworth, that he was forced to appeal to Dr Sharpe, the Archbishop of York, for aid. Wesley's letter, dated December 28, detailed the string of financial woes he had faced throughout his ministerial career:

> I must own that I [am] ashamed ... to confess that I [am] three hundred pounds in debt, when I have a living of which I have made two hundred pounds per annum, though I could hardly let in now for eight score.

> I doubt not one reason of my being sunk so far is my not understanding worldly affairs, and my aversion to law ...

> 'Twill be no great wonder that when I had but fifty pounds per annum for six or seven years together [while at South Ormsby], and nothing to begin the world with, one child at least per annum, and my wife sick for half that time, that I should run one hundred and fifty pounds behindhand ...

> When I had the rectory of Epworth given me, my Lord of Sarum was so generous as to pass his word to his goldsmith [banker] for one hundred pounds which I borrowed of him. It cost me very little less than fifty pounds of this in my journey to London, and getting into my living ...; and with the other fifty pounds I stopped the mouths of my most importunate creditors.

> When I removed to Epworth I was forced to take up fifty pounds more, for setting up a little husbandry ... and buying some part of what was necessary towards furnishing my house, which was larger, as well as my family ...

> The next year my barn fell, which cost me forty pounds in rebuilding ... and having an aged mother who must have gone to prison if I had not assisted her, she cost me upwards of forty pounds, which obliged me to take up another fifty pounds. I have had but three children born since I came hither, about three years since; but another coming, and my wife incapable of any business in my family, as she has been for

almost a quarter of a year; yet we have but one maidservant, to retrench all possible expenses …

Fifty pounds interest and principal I have paid my Lord of Sarum's goldsmith. All which together keeps me necessitous, especially since interest money begins to pinch me … Humbly asking pardon for this tedious trouble,

I am your grace's most obliged and humble servant,

S. Wesley[5]

The archbishop responded with financial assistance of his own for Wesley. He also appealed to a number of titled individuals in the rector's behalf, with the result that gifts totaling £185 were given to the hard-pressed clergyman.

By the following May, with Susanna due to deliver a child any day, the pastor couple again found themselves financially straitened. Pooling their meager resources one Wednesday evening, they came up with a mere six shillings with which to buy some coal to help heat their house. The next morning Wesley received a gift of £10 from the Countess of Northampton, who had learned of his difficulties through Dr Sharpe. 'Never came anything more like a gift from heaven,' the relieved rector commented.

That very night Susanna gave birth to twins, a boy and a girl. Regrettably, like her first set of twins, this latter pair survived only a short while. Their names have not been preserved. To make matters worse, not many months after the birth of these twins, Benjamin passed away.[6] Of the

---

5   Ibid., pp. 44-5.

6   A helpful record of several of the children born to Samuel and Susanna in their early years at Epworth is found in: Eliza Clarke, *Susanna Wesley* (London: Allen, 1886), pp. 26-7.

thirteen children born to Susanna up to that point, eight had died as babies or very young children.

Beginning late in the winter of the following year, 1702, a most unfortunate estrangement occurred between Samuel and Susanna. Though John Wesley himself later recorded this regrettable development, some Wesley biographers of the past called into question that these events ever took place. But in 1953 a series of letters that Susanna wrote during this troubled time came to light and were published in the *Manchester Guardian*, confirming the estrangement and providing considerably more detail about the difficult period.[7]

The historic backdrop for the difficulties dated back to 1688 when England's King James II was exiled for favoring the Roman Catholic Church over the Church of England. His daughter Mary became queen, and her husband, William of Orange, a member of the Dutch royal family, came from Holland and was declared England's king. Many of the English thought William had no rightful claim as their monarch and refused to give him their allegiance. As has already been seen, Samuel Wesley was an ardent supporter of both Queen Mary and King William, though his devotion was far from altruistic. Before God, Susanna thought her allegiance should be given to Mary as queen but not to William as king.

The painful consequence to which that difference of conviction led was shared by Susanna in a letter to Lady Yarborough, a noblewoman to whom she appealed for advice. The missive, written on Saturday, March 7, stated in part:

---

7   Dallimore, *Susanna Wesley*, pp. 46-54, provides an extended account of this period including excerpts from several of Susanna's letters during that time.

I must tell your ladyship that you have somewhat mistaken my case. You advise me to continue with my husband, and God knows how gladly I would do it, but there, there is my supreme affliction, he will not live with me. 'Tis but a little while since he one evening observed in our family prayers that I did not say Amen to his prayer for KW [King William] as I usually do to all others; upon which he retired to his study, and calling me to him asked the reason of my not saying Amen to the prayer. I was a little surprised at the question and don't know well what I answered, but too well I remember what followed: he immediately kneeled down and imprecated the divine vengeance upon himself and all his posterity if ever he touched me more or came into a bed with me before I had begged God's pardon and his for not saying Amen to the prayer for the king.

This, madam, is my unhappy case. I've unsuccessfully represented to him the unlawfulness and unreasonableness of his oath; that the man in that case has no more power over his own body than the woman over hers; that since I'm willing to let him quietly enjoy his opinions, he ought not to deprive me of my little liberty of conscience. But he has opened his mouth to the Lord and what help? ... I have no resentment against my master [husband], so far from it that the very next day I went with him to the Communion, though he that very night forsook my bed, to which he has been a stranger ever since.[8]

Though King William died the day after Susanna wrote that letter, Samuel would not be persuaded to set aside his oath. Nor could Susanna, in good conscience, say that she had sinned by not affirming her husband's prayer for the King. Wesley continued in Epworth throughout the remainder of that month. But he refrained from sleeping with his wife, and there is some indication he may have not lived in the house with her and the children during that time.

8   Ibid., p. 48.

On April 5 he left for London where he hoped to obtain a chaplaincy on a naval ship. In that way he could continue to support his family financially while at the same time having a seemingly valid reason for being away from home. (The care of his parish would be left in the hands of a curate.)

In June, with her husband still away, Susanna bore a daughter whom she named Anne. Samuel did not return to Epworth till late in July. At that time Susanna suggested they refer their situation to an arbitrator, presumably a bishop, in an effort to work out a solution to their impasse, but Samuel refused. After just two days in Epworth, he left early one morning with the determination never to see her again.

At that point, however, Providence intervened. That very morning, shortly after Wesley left, a servant accidentally set the house on fire. Susanna, though far from well, took a child under each arm and ran through the smoke and fire to safety. In the haste and confusion of the moment one of the little girls was left behind. When her cries were heard, some of the neighbors entered the house and brought her out through the flames. Two thirds of the home was destroyed in the fire and most of the family's belongings were ruined.

The rector was just at the southern outskirt of town when word came to him that his house was on fire. Borrowing a horse, he hurried home, where he learned 'that my wife, children and books were saved'.

After that, Wesley remained in Epworth and once again lived with Susanna and the children. Doubtless he realized the injustice it would be to desert his family under such desperate circumstances. Perhaps the shock of nearly losing his wife and children finally brought him to his senses. Though there is no record of this, he may have interpreted this tragedy as an indication of Divine displeasure over how he had been treating his family.

Some have suggested that Samuel probably feared his wife's perceived disloyalty to the King would weaken his opportunity for obtaining ecclesiastical advancement from the monarchy. By dealing firmly with such lack of allegiance, he might succeed in retaining royal favor. While such motivation is possible, it is not known definitely to have been the case. These unfortunate events likely expose, more simply, some of Samuel's noticeable character flaws, including impetuousness, imperiousness, implacability and inability to acknowledge personal faults and wrongdoings.

Wesley's conduct in this affair likely led to his forfeiting the opportunity for professional advancement he seemed so eager to gain. The remainder of his career was spent at Epworth, apparently without his being considered for more prominent ministry opportunities elsewhere.

Susanna's responses to her husband in all this are both remarkable and highly commendable. Despite his glaring faults, she continued to show him respect and was desirous, even eager, to be reunited with him. She was willing to forgive his considerable collection of transgressions against her. There is no indication that afterwards she ever reminded him of his shortcomings in these events or sought to hold them over him.

THREE

After the rebuilding of the Epworth rectory in 1702, Susanna began to devote six hours per day to educating her children at home. She had already given considerable time and attention to educating her older children before that time, but beginning that year her efforts along that line became even more pronounced. For the next two decades that became the primary focus of her life.

As an adult, her son John repeatedly asked her to provide him with an account of her methods in rearing and educating her children. She was hesitant to do so, explaining:

> It cannot, I think, be of service to anyone to know how I, who have lived such a retired life for so many years, used to employ my time and care in bringing up my children. No one can, without renouncing the world, in the most literal sense, observe my method; and there are few, if any, that would entirely devote above twenty years of the prime of life in hopes to save the souls of their children, which they think may be saved without so much ado; for that was my principal intention, however unskillfully and unsuccessfully managed.[9]

In July of 1732, however, at the age of sixty-three, Susanna finally did comply with John's request.[10] She revealed that training of her children started from the time they were infants:

> The children were always put into a regular method of living, in such things as they were capable of, from their birth; as in dressing and undressing, changing their linen, etc. The first quarter [of their life] commonly passes in sleep.

---

9   Clarke, *Susanna Wesley*, pp. 29-30.

10   A complete copy of the letter to John in which Susanna outlined her parental and educational methodologies is preserved in: McReynolds, *Susanna Wesley*, pp. 75-82.

After that they were, if possible, laid into their cradle awake, and rocked to sleep, and so they were kept rocking till it was time for them to awake. This was done to bring them to a regular course of sleeping, which at first was three hours in the morning, and three in the afternoon; afterwards two hours till they needed none at all.

When turned a year old (and some before) they were taught to fear the rod and to cry softly, by which means they escaped abundance of correction which they might otherwise have had, and that most odious noise of the crying of children was rarely heard in the house, but the family usually lived in as much quietness as if there had not been a child among them.[11]

Religious training included learning the Lord's Prayer as soon as they could speak then reciting it when rising in the morning and retiring at night. They were also taught other brief prayers, a short catechism and portions of Scripture. The Christian Sabbath was carefully observed by being devoted exclusively to religious activities. 'Taking God's name in vain, cursing and swearing, profanity, obscenity, rude ill-bred names' were never tolerated.

She placed great stress on the importance of conquering a child's will from an early age:

In order to form the minds of children, the first thing to be done is to conquer their will, and bring them to an obedient temper. To inform the understanding is a work of time and must with children proceed by slow degrees as they are able to bear it; but the subjecting the will is a thing which must be done at once; and the sooner the better.

For by neglecting timely correction, they will contract a stubbornness and obstinacy, which is hardly ever after conquered; and never, without using such severity as would

---

11 Ibid., p. 75.

be as painful to me as to the child. In the esteem of the world they pass for kind and indulgent, whom I call cruel, parents who permit their children to get habits, which they know must be afterward broken. ... Whenever a child is corrected, it must be conquered; and this will be no hard matter to do, if it be not grown headstrong by too much indulgence.

And when the will of a child is totally subdued, and it is brought to revere and stand in awe of the parents, then a great many childish follies and inadvertences may be passed by. Some should be overlooked and taken no notice of, and others mildly reproved; but no willful transgression ought ever be forgiven children; without chastisement less or more, as the nature and circumstances of the offense require.[12]

Each of the Wesley children were taught to read when they turned five years old. 'The day before a child began to learn, the house was set in order, everyone's work appointed them, and a charge given, that none should come into the room [where the child was learning the alphabet] from nine till twelve, or from two till five, which ... were our school hours.' All but two of the children learned the entire alphabet, upper and lower case letters, in a single day. As soon as they knew the letters, they began reading from the first chapter of Genesis, spelling out and reading one word then verse at a time.

Susanna testified of the success of these educational methods: 'And it is almost incredible what a child may be taught in a quarter of a year by a vigorous application, if it have but a tolerable capacity and good health. Every one of these ... could read better in that time than most women can do as long as they live.'

The Wesleys saw to it that each of their sons received a first-rate university education. Susanna took care that

---

12   Ibid., pp. 76-7.

her daughters' education, while confined to their home, was given top priority. She related one of her cardinal rules of education:

> That no girl be taught to work till she can read very well; and then that she be kept to her work with the same application and for the same time that she was held to reading. This rule also is much to be observed; for the putting children to learn sewing before they can read perfectly is the very reason why so few women can read fit to be heard, and never to be well understood.[13]

Samuel Wesley, after watching her teach one of the children, once complimented her: 'I wonder at your patience; you have told that child twenty times the same thing.'

'If I had satisfied myself by mentioning it only nineteen times,' she responded, 'I should have lost all my labor. It was the twentieth time that crowned it.'

Susanna's most famous son, John, the future founder of Methodism, was born on June 28, 1703. He was named John Benjamin in memory of two older siblings who had died earlier. Among family members, he commonly went by the nicknames Jack or Jacky.

A month or two before John's birth, the eldest Wesley son, Samuel, was placed in a school at Epworth run by a Mr John Holland. As it turned out, he was the only of the Wesley boys to receive any schooling other than what they gained at home before leaving to enter a public school in London. That move came for Samuel the following year when, at age fourteen, he was enrolled in the celebrated St Peter's Classical School adjoined to Westminster Abbey.

---

13   Ibid., pp. 81-2.

As she would with several of her children when they were later away from home, Susanna continued to watch out for Samuel's welfare by writing him letters full of instruction and advice concerning a variety of spiritual, moral and practical matters. Some of those letters were nothing less than theological treatises. Her first letter to him, for instance, took up the subjects of divine revelation and the law of reason, and stretched out over several large foolscap pages. She explained her motivation to him: 'I shall be employing my thoughts on useful subjects for you when I have time, for I desire nothing in this world so much as to have my children well instructed in the principles of religion, that they may walk in the narrow way which alone leads to happiness.'[14]

The controversial role Susanna's husband played in a bitterly contested federal election brought marked grief to the Wesleys in 1705. Four men – two Tories and two Whigs – were running for election, and Samuel Wesley initially indicated his support of one man from each party. But when it became clear that the Tories supported the church and the crown while the Whig candidates did not, Wesley publicly threw his support to the two Tories. This incensed many people in Epworth and the Isle of Axholme who favored the Whigs. Even on the steps of his own church Wesley was denounced as a 'rascal and scoundrel'.

Early in May Susanna bore a son whose name has not been preserved. In a letter to Archbishop Sharpe, Samuel described the tragic events that unfolded at the end of that month, less than three weeks after Susanna delivered the infant:

---

14 Clarke, *Susanna Wesley*, p. 47.

I went to Lincoln on Tuesday night, May 29th, and the election began on Wednesday, 30th. A great part of the night our Isle people kept drumming, shouting and firing of pistols and guns under the window where my wife lay, who had been brought to bed not three weeks. I had put the child to nurse over against my own house; the noise kept his nurse waking till one or two in the morning. Then they left off and his nurse, being heavy with sleep, overlaid the child. She waked, and finding it dead, ran over to my house almost distracted, and calling my servants, threw it into their arms. They, as wise as she, ran with it to my wife, and before she was well awake, threw it cold and dead into hers. She composed herself as well as she could, and that day got it buried.

A clergyman met me in the castle yard [at Lincoln], and told me to withdraw, for the Isle men intended me mischief. Another told me he had heard near twenty of them say, 'If they got me in the castle yard they would squeeze my guts out' … I went [home] by Gainsbro' and God preserved me.

When they knew I was got home, they sent the drum and mob, with guns etc., to compliment me till after midnight. One of them, passing by on Friday evening and seeing my children in the yard cried out, 'O ye devils! we will come and turn ye all out of doors a-begging shortly.' God convert them and forgive them!

All this, thank God, does not in the least sink my wife's spirits. For my own, I feel them disturbed and disordered …[15]

Samuel's estimation of how his wife was processing all these trials was very likely too optimistic. And the adversities deepened in the weeks to follow. Political opponents used their influence to keep Wesley from receiving first an army chaplaincy, then a prebend (a stipend granted out of the estate of a cathedral), both of which had been promised to him and would have helped reduce his debts. Late in

---

15   Dallimore, *Susanna Wesley*, p. 67.

June a relative of one of the Whigs Wesley had opposed in the election had the clergyman arrested for a debt of less than £30 he owed him. This man, a Mr Pinder, refused Wesley's attempts to negotiate a peaceful settlement, and because he could not pay the entire debt immediately, had him imprisoned at Lincoln Castle.

Of his concern for his family Wesley wrote to Archbishop Sharpe:

> I thank God, my wife was pretty well recovered, and churched some days before I was taken from her; and hope she'll be able to look to my family, if they don't turn them out of doors, as they have often threatened to do. One of my biggest concerns was my being forced to leave my poor lambs in the midst of so many wolves. But the great Shepherd is able to provide for them, and to preserve them. My wife bears it with that courage which becomes her, and which I expected from her.[16]

Susanna and the children were sorely tried in the ensuing months. The Wesleys' flax crop was destroyed by arson. Their milking cows were stabbed, causing them to dry up. The family dog, a mastiff, was attacked and one of its legs was nearly severed.

While investigating the Wesleys' state of affairs for himself, Archbishop Sharpe asked Susanna: 'Tell me, Mrs Wesley, whether you ever really wanted bread?'

'My Lord,' she responded candidly, 'I will freely own to your Grace that, strictly speaking I never did want bread. But then I had so much care to get it before it was eat, and to pray for it after, as has often made it very unpleasant to me. And, I think, to have bread on such terms is the next degree of wretchedness to have none at all.'

---

16   Ibid., p. 68.

'You are certainly right,' he replied. The next day he gave her a generous monetary gift.

She sent her wedding rings to her husband, hoping he could sell them to eliminate his debt more quickly and end his incarceration. He did not hesitate to return them to her. Others came to Samuel's aid, contributing donations to reduce his debt. Before the year ended he was able to return home.

FOUR

The three years to follow passed in relative calm for the Wesleys. Susanna birthed a daughter, Martha, late in 1706. A son, Charles, who like his brother John would play a prominent role in the founding of Methodism, was born on December 18, 1707. He arrived quite prematurely, and for several weeks was a frail infant who neither cried nor opened his eyes. But in time he thrived well enough. Then in February of 1709, just one month before Susanna bore her nineteenth and final child, crisis again befell the Wesley household.

On Wednesday, February 9, some time after 11 p.m., fire broke out, probably in the fireplace chimney, and quickly spread to the thatched roof. When family members awakened they found flames spreading throughout the house. Samuel pushed open the front door but a strong northeast wind immediately blew fierce flames into the house, driving them all back. A servant and two Wesley daughters escaped through the parlor window. Samuel led three of his daughters and the maid, who carried Charles, to safety through the small back door that led into the garden.

Susanna, unable to climb out the window in her advanced stage of pregnancy, also found herself cut off by fire from the back door. Three times she tried to force her way through the flames at the front door but each time was driven back. She thought she might be about to die but, praying to Christ for help, found new strength. Having nothing on but her shoes, a nightgown and a coat wrapped around her upper body, she waded through three yards of flame, with the fire on the ground reaching to her knees. Her face and hands were scorched and her legs sustained minor burns, but she was not otherwise harmed.

In all the commotion, five-year-old Jacky (John) had been accidentally left behind in the upstairs nursery that he shared with the maid and some of his siblings. Samuel reentered the house and tried to mount the stairs but they collapsed under his weight. Kneeling momentarily in the flaming hallway, he commended his son's soul to the Lord. Thankfully, some neighbors spotted the distressed youngster and rushed to his rescue. One man climbed on the shoulders of another and snatched John from an upstairs window just as the entire roof collapsed inward.

Susanna, doubtless seriously dazed, sat out in the yard alone for several minutes. With the entire house engulfed in flames and seeing none of her family, she feared they may have all perished. She never looked up or spoke till Samuel made his way to her. Discovering that she and all his children were still alive and relatively unharmed, he cried out: 'Come, neighbors, let us kneel down; let us give thanks to God! He has given me all my eight children; let the house go. I am rich enough.'

The entire rectory was consumed within a mere fifteen minutes. Lost in the inferno were all the Wesleys' furnishings and personal belongings, Samuel's entire library, all his sermons and literary manuscripts, as well as the Epworth parish records.

While the rectory was being rebuilt, Samuel and Susanna, along with their toddler, Charles, lived in the home of some of their parishioners. While there, barely a month after the fire, Susanna bore her last child, a daughter named Kezia. Other Wesley children were placed in various homes while Sukey and Hetty went to live with their uncle, Matthew Wesley, a prosperous physician in London.

The oldest Wesley daughter, Emilia, then eighteen years old, stayed with her parents in order to help care for her mother and two youngest siblings. A close bond developed between mother and daughter, and a year later Susanna wrote a sixty-page treatise entitled *A religious conference between Mother and Emilia*. The work, intended for the spiritual nurture not only of Emilia but of all her children, was based on Galatians 4:19: 'My little children, of whom I travail in birth again until Christ be formed in you.'

Samuel immediately set about arranging for the construction of a new rectory. The new home was built of solid brick and was large enough to accommodate his sizeable family. While the costs were partly supplied by the Ecclesiastical Commissioners, £400 of the expense fell to him, thus increasing his indebtedness considerably.

Sammy entered Oxford University that same year at age nineteen. Susanna continued to write him letters filled with fervent spiritual counsel. She also penned a lengthy exposition on the Apostle's Creed to Sukey in London.[17]

---

17 Susanna's introductory remarks on and exposition of the Apostle's Creed are included in their entirety in McReynolds, *Susanna Wesley*, pp. 87-97, 122-46.

That work, like the one sent to Emilia, was doubtless intended for the spiritual benefit of all her children. In it she expounded on the need for the divine revelation of Scripture (without which people are unable to ascertain the truths and realities it sets forth), commented on angels and the entrance of sin into the world, and expanded on each phrase in the creed. Her introductory remarks to that letter reveal how earnestly she desired to benefit the daughter spiritually, even during their enforced separation:

> Since our misfortunes have separated us from each other, and we can no longer enjoy the opportunities we once had of conversing together, I can no other way discharge the duty of a parent, or comply with my inclination of doing you all the good I can but in writing.
>
> You know very well how I love you. I love your body, and do earnestly beseech Almighty God to bless it with health, and all things necessary for its comfort and support in this world. But my tenderest regard is for your immortal soul, and for its spiritual happiness, which regard I cannot better express than by endeavoring to instill into your mind those principles of knowledge and virtue that are absolutely necessary in order to your leading a good life here, which is the only thing that can infallibly secure your happiness hereafter.[18]

Within about a year after the fire, basic rebuilding work on the rectory was completed, though the house was still in quite an unfinished condition. Samuel hoped to have the rest of the work done as soon as his finances allowed. Susanna was delighted to have her family back together under one roof again. But much to her dismay, she discovered that while her children had been living

---

18 Ibid., pp. 87-8.

in other homes, their piety and manners in general had greatly declined. Years later she wrote:

> Never were children better disposed to piety, or in more subjection to their parents, till that fatal dispersion of them, after the fire, into several families. In those they were left at full liberty to converse with servants, which before they had always been restrained from; and to run abroad, and play with any children, good or bad. They soon learned to neglect a strict observation of the Sabbath, and got knowledge of several songs and bad things, which before they had no notion of. That civil behavior, which made them admired when at home by all that saw them, was in great measure lost; and a clownish accent and many rude ways were learned, which were not reformed without some difficulty.[19]

To correct that state of affairs Susanna undertook 'a strict reform'. She initiated the custom of their singing psalms at the beginning and ending of each school day. She also began pairing up older siblings with younger children and having them read some Psalms and a chapter from the Old Testament before breakfast as well as further Psalms and a New Testament chapter at afternoon's end. Between the morning Scripture reading and breakfast the children were also sent to their private prayers.

The Wesleys' financial hardships continued to deepen throughout those years. With a degree of cynicism, Emilia later wrote of that period:

> I began to find out that we were ruined. Then came on London journeys, [ecclesiastical] convocations of blessed memory, that for seven winters my father was at London, and we at home in intolerable want and afflictions. ... Thus we went on growing worse and worse; all of us children in scandalous want of

---

19 Ibid., p. 80.

necessaries for years together; vast income, but no comfort or credit with it.[20]

During 1711 and 1712 Samuel was assisted in the care of his parish by a curate named Inman. The curate preached during Wesley's not infrequent absences. Quite astonishingly, Inman often used his occasions to preach as opportunities to indirectly criticize the rector by decrying the evil of being in debt! Once, to test him, Wesley asked the curate to preach on the text 'without faith it is impossible to please God' (Heb. 11:6) on an occasion when he would be present to hear him. Inman began: 'Friends, faith is a most excellent virtue, and it produces other virtues also. In particular it makes a man pay his debts.' He continued railing against debt for fifteen more minutes.

Around that same time, during one of Samuel's extended absences, Susanna initiated a practice with her own household that, surprisingly, came to have a profound positive effect on the entire Epworth congregation. Inman did not hold an afternoon church service. Ever a strong believer in devoting the Christian Sabbath to sacred focuses, she concluded it was her duty to spend part of the day instructing her family since they had so much time available for such activities. She read them sermons from Samuel's library and led them in a time of family prayer. Shortly after she started doing so, others heard of the Sunday evening gatherings in Susanna's kitchen and asked if they might attend as well. Soon between thirty and forty people were present each week.

Just then Emilia discovered in her father's study an account of Danish missionaries who had risked their lives

---

20 Dallimore, *Susanna Wesley*, p. 132.

and sacrificed all the world holds dear in order to advance the honor of Christ by taking His Gospel to foreign lands. Susanna was greatly inspired by their example and concluded, '… if my heart were sincerely devoted to God, and if I were inspired with a true zeal for His glory, and did really desire the salvation of souls, I might do somewhat more than I do.'

Susanna resolved to begin with her own children, and thereafter took some time each evening to meet with one of them to discuss that child's spiritual condition and concerns. By meeting with one child each day and two on Sunday, she was able to provide all her children with individualized spiritual guidance every week. She also began discoursing more freely and fervently with the neighbors who attended the Sunday evening gatherings. 'I chose the best and most awakening sermons we had, and I spent more time with them in such exercises.' The results were amazing, for in a short time over 200 people per week were attending the Sunday night readings, which doubtless had to be moved to a larger venue.

Learning of the meetings, Samuel wrote from London to express some concerns about them. When, early in February 1712, Susanna provided him with a full written account of the gatherings and answered his initial objections, he gave his approval for the gatherings to continue. But Inman was envious and annoyed because more people were attending Susanna's evening readings than his own morning sermons. He and a couple of other men wrote the rector, accusing his wife of holding a conventicle, an illegal religious meeting. Alarmed, Samuel again wrote, this time asking Susanna to stop her meetings.

In her earnest but measured written response toward the end of February, Susanna pointed out her primary reasons for thinking the Sunday evening gatherings should continue. No more than three or four individuals were objecting to the meetings. Whereas twenty to twenty-five people used to attend evening services at the church, now between two and three hundred people were coming out for the readings. Some families who formerly seldom went to church were now attending church services regularly, including one person who had not attended for seven years. Many people were 'very much reformed in their behavior on the Lord's Day'. Through this ministry Susanna had 'an opportunity of exercising the greatest and noblest charity, that is, charity of their souls.' Very significantly for the Wesleys, given their history of sometimes strained relations with their own parishioners, 'our meeting has wonderfully conciliated the minds of this people toward us, so that we can now live in the greatest amity imaginable'.

Susanna closed that letter with these compelling words:

> If you do, after all, think fit to dissolve this assembly, do not tell me that you desire me to do it, for that will not satisfy my conscience; but send me your positive command, in such full and express terms as may absolve me from all guilt and punishment, for neglecting this opportunity of doing good, when you and I shall appear before the great and awful tribunal of our LORD JESUS CHRIST.[21]

Samuel raised no further objections, and the meetings continued till his return. At that time he found the moral and spiritual condition of his congregation remarkably improved. Through Susanna's Spirit-led ministrations nothing less than a touch of revival had come to Epworth.

---

21 Ibid., pp. 79, 81.

FIVE

Two years later, in 1714, John, aged eleven, left home for London, where he began attending Charterhouse School. Both the education he had received from his mother and the instruction his father had given him in Latin and Greek grammar and literature left him well prepared for his future course of studies. Just one year later, Charles, at the tender age of eight, was taken to London and enrolled in the Westminster School. By that time his oldest brother, Samuel, had graduated from Oxford with a Master of Arts degree, been ordained and returned to Westminster as a teaching assistant. Brother Samuel agreed to board Charles at his own home, adjacent to the abbey, leaving father Samuel responsible to provide only the young boy's clothes.

For a period of just over two months at the end of 1715 and the beginning of 1716, a series of strange, inexplicable events took place in the Epworth rectory that led the Wesleys to conclude their house was haunted. Wesley biographers have suggested a number of explanations, both natural and supernatural, for the unusual sounds and sights witnessed by family members and household servants during that time. The Wesleys, like many people of that day, definitely believed in ghosts, apparitions and hauntings. This incident in the Wesley family history, while intriguing, proved to be quite temporary and of no lasting significance.[22]

---

22   The incident is mentioned in this account of Susanna's life merely as an acknowledgement of the considerable attention normally paid these events in accounts of Wesley family history. Full accounts (that offer contrasting explanations for the phenomena) of the reported haunting can be found in Dallimore, *Susanna Wesley*, pp. 81-86, and McReynolds, *Susanna Wesley*, pp. 52-56.

Susanna had a brother, Samuel Annesley, who spent his career in India working with the East India Company. He indicated his intention to provide well for Susanna and her daughters, especially Sukey, when he returned to England after making his fortune. Through many years of poverty the Wesley girls had comforted themselves with dreams of the day when Uncle Samuel would return to relieve them. Against Susanna's advice, Annesley hired her husband to manage his affairs in England. As Susanna feared, Samuel Wesley proved inefficient in business decisions and financial matters. Annesley ended up entrusting his affairs to another manager and, indeed, was so provoked that he announced he would reconsider his intention to assist Susanna and her girls.

The serious disappointment and shock of this news led Sukey to throw herself into a hasty and imprudent marriage. Her husband, Richard Ellison, belonged to a wealthy family from which he received a considerable inheritance. But in addition to being severely domineering, he was 'coarse, vulgar and immoral'. Of her daughter's marriage to him, Susanna wrote her brother Samuel:

> Sukey, a pretty woman, and worthy a better fate, when, by your last unkind letters, she perceived that all her hopes in you were frustrated, rashly threw herself upon a man (if a man he may be called who is little inferior to the apostate angels in wickedness) that is not only her plague, but a constant affliction to the family.[23]

Apparently after an exchange of letters between Susanna and her brother in 1722, their relationship was mended. He encouraged her to meet him in London upon his

---

23 Dallimore, *Susanna Wesley*, p. 102.

arrival there by ship, which he anticipated in the near future. With hope revived, Susanna made her way to London where Charles reported she was delighted to see again the areas she had known in childhood. But tragic news awaited her when she made her way to the boat that had brought Annesley back from India. His personal belongings were in his cabin but he was missing. The officers of the ship claimed to know nothing about the cause of his disappearance. Susanna had to return to Epworth not only with her financial hopes once again dashed, but also realizing that her brother may have been murdered and his body disposed of at sea.

Around that same time, Emilia, then about thirty years of age, taught at a girls' school in Lincoln for two years. But not long after the disappointment and tragedy involving Samuel Annesley, Emilia returned home, knowing her mother was in great need of her help. While teaching she had a few possessions of her own; back home that was not the case. Of this period she divulged:

> I found what a condition I was in – every trifling want was either not supplied, or I had more trouble to procure it than it was worth. I know not when we have had so good a year, both at Wroot and Epworth, as this year; but instead of saving anything to clothe my sister and myself, we are just where we were. A noble crop has almost gone, beside Epworth living, to pay some part of those infinite debts my father has run into.[24]

The Wroot to which she referred was a village about five miles west of Epworth. Samuel Wesley secured the rectorship of the Wroot parish in 1724, and the family moved there that same year. By hiring a curate to assist

---

24   Ibid., p. 132.

him, Wesley was able to serve both parishes. Doubtless the main motivation for this change was financial. In addition to receiving £50 a year as Wroot's rector, for a time he was able to rent out the Epworth rectory to Ellison and Sukey. That rental arrangement, however, proved to be a trial, for the Wesleys were constantly pained by Ellison's foul language, and the son-in-law scorned Samuel's formerly undisputed domination of his family.

The schoolteacher at Wroot was John Romley, an Oxford graduate whose father had previously served as curate at Epworth. A romantic relationship began to develop between him and Hetty, who was then twenty-seven years old. She was said to be the 'wittiest, cleverest, mirthfullest' of all the Wesley sisters. She was also highly intelligent, being the only one of his daughters whom Samuel had taught Greek and Latin. In addition, she possessed her father's gift of composing poetry.

Romley had a good voice and one evening was asked to sing for a small gathering at the Wroot rectory. He chose a popular satirical song of the day about a clergyman who sought, by constantly changing his allegiance, to retain the monarchy's favor and gain preferment. Samuel Wesley felt ridiculed and took offense. He angrily ordered Romley out of the house and forbade Hetty to see him further. When it was later discovered that Romley and Hetty were still carrying on a private correspondence, Samuel decided Hetty must be sent somewhere away from her would-be suitor. Without telling his daughter, the rector visited the Granthams, a well-to-do family in the village of Kelstern, some thirty miles to the east. He offered Hetty's services as a companion to Mrs Grantham, apparently indicating she would not need to be compensated.

When he announced this arrangement to Hetty she protested vigorously. But Samuel and Susanna were agreed this was a necessary course of action, so the daughter was taken to Kelstern. There the Granthams told her they would never have desired her company but had not known how to refuse her father's offer of her services. Feeling betrayed by her parents, heartbroken over Romley and unwanted by her employers, she ran away to London. There is no record of where or with whom she lived during the next several months. But when she returned to her parents' home in early October 1725, it was discovered, to her family's horror and anguish, that she was five months pregnant though still unmarried.

Again without Hetty's knowledge, Wesley quickly arranged for her to be married to William Wright, a journeyman plumber who happened to be working in the area at that time. While appearing to be industrious, he was unlearned, boorish and given to excessive drink. Each of Hetty's brothers, her sister Mary and likely Susanna sided with her in objecting to this obvious matrimonial mismatch. But Samuel would not be dissuaded, and less than two weeks after Hetty's return to Wroot the couple were wed in a ceremony at which he refused to officiate.

Hetty gave birth the following February but the baby quickly weakened and died. At that point Matthew Wesley, the London physician, came to the young couple's aid with a gift of £500. That allowed them to move to London where William was able to establish a plumbing business.

A few months after Hetty's child was born John was elected to a fellowship in Lincoln College, part of Oxford University. This provided him with a stipend of £45 per year. Charles, then nineteen years of age, began his studies at Oxford. Before that year (1726) ended, Samuel, aged sixty-four, suffered a stroke that permanently paralyzed his right hand.

Two years later the rector was involved in a hazardous boating accident while traveling with John Whitelamb, a young man who assisted him in his ministries. They were ferrying across a 'fierce stream' when their boat was slammed broadside against a barge. Humans and horses were thrown into the river. 'I was just preparing to swim for life,' Wesley afterward related, 'when John Whitelamb's long legs and arms swarmed up into the keel, and lugged me in after him.'

Whitelamb first went to work for Wesley at the Epworth rectory in 1723, performing such chores as carrying wood and drawing water. He proved to be intelligent and wrote with a good hand. So the rector taught him Latin and Greek and used him in transcribing some of his literary works. Perhaps partially out of gratitude for having saved his life, Wesley sent Whitelamb to Oxford in 1730.

Samuel was involved in another serious accident early in June 1731. He and Susanna were sitting on chairs in the back of a wagon when the horses unexpectedly broke into a gallop. Wesley and his chair flew out of the wagon; he landed on his head and was rendered unconscious. By the time their hired man got the wagon stopped and they rushed back to Samuel his face was turning black from lack of oxygen. Back at home a doctor was summoned who wrapped his badly bruised head. He also had considerable soreness in his shoulder and side. The accident occurred on a Friday. Two days later Wesley insisted on preaching twice and serving Communion, then fell ill and slept nearly all the next day.

After that incident the aging clergyman began to consider more seriously the need to make arrangements for the ongoing support of his family in the event of his death. Consequently, in 1733 he approached his oldest son Samuel about replacing him as rector of Epworth. That way Susanna could continue to live there and be provided for following the death of her husband. When Samuel declined his father's proposal, the rector made the same offer to his son John the following year. John anticipated a teaching career at Oxford rather than pastoral ministry, so he, too, declined. Charles had obtained a Master of Arts degree from Oxford in 1733 but was not yet ordained.

In 1734, however, John Whitelamb graduated from Oxford, was ordained and became Samuel's curate at Epworth. A short while later he and Mary Wesley, who, at thirty-eight, was likely several years older than he, were married. Due to an accident when she was just a baby, Mary had grown up crippled and shorter than the rest of her sisters. She was convinced she would never find a man who would marry her. Happily, that proved not to be the case.

Wesley's recommendation was approved that Whitelamb be appointed to the Wroot parish. So Samuel and his family moved back to Epworth after a decade of living at Wroot. John and Mary joyfully entered into married life and their new ministry responsibilities. The future looked bright for them. Tragically, however, less than a year later Mary died in childbirth.

Shortly after the Wesleys returned to Epworth, Samuel was laid low by serious illness. For six months he was confined to the rectory and was unable to preach or perform many of his ministerial duties. The following April, Susanna wrote to John and Charles, urging them to come immediately to Epworth as their father was nearing death. He died peacefully early in the evening on April 25, 1735, at the age of seventy-two. For several days before Samuel's death Susanna often broke down after entering his room and had to be helped away. But when the actual time of her husband's passing came she was 'far less shocked' than her children had anticipated. According to Charles, she told them 'now she was [her prayers were] heard, in his having so easy a death, and her being strengthened to bear it'.

Almost unbelievably, just four days after Samuel's death one of their family's creditors had Susanna arrested for debt and a second threatened the same course of action! At that time the Wesleys' debts totaled over £100, not including a lesser amount owed to a relative. Her sons were able to pay off the importunate creditors and make suitable arrangements with other lenders so that she was kept out of debtors' prison.

SIX

Before long Susanna needed to vacate the Epworth rectory. John and Charles returned to Oxford. Samuel, who arrived at Epworth following his father's death in order to help set the family's affairs in order, took Kezia to live with him in his new home in Tiverton, Devon. He had moved there the previous year to become the headmaster of an endowed school. Susanna, for her part, went to be with Emilia who then lived in Gainsborough, less than ten miles southeast of Epworth.

Three years earlier, in 1732, Emilia, at age forty, had moved to Gainsborough. There, with financial assistance from her brothers, she was able to set up a girls' boarding school. She married a Mr Harper, an apothecary whose business was struggling. He seized whatever profits were generated through her school, eventually leaving her as straitened as she had been at Epworth. Likely Emilia's financial condition had not yet become too desperate during the fifteen or sixteen months Susanna lived with her.

During the summer of 1735, not long after Susanna's relocation to Gainsborough, her daughter Martha, aged twenty-eight, married a man named Westley Hall. He was a member of John and Charles' Holy Club at Oxford and had entered holy orders to serve in the Anglican Church. Some time before Samuel Wesley's death he met and proposed to Martha while she was living in London with her Uncle Matthew. He then visited the Wesley family at Epworth with John and Charles. Curiously, none of the family knew of his existing engagement to Martha. While at Epworth he professed his love to Kezia, but then claimed to have a revelation from heaven that instructed him to return to Martha! After their marriage Westley and Martha moved to the Wiltshire village of Wooton (about thirty miles east of Bristol), where he had been appointed as a curate.

That same year, 1735, Colonel James Oglethorpe, founder of the Georgia Colony in America, recruited John and Charles to accompany him to the colony. John was to serve as a chaplain and a missionary to the Indians while Charles was to be Oglethorpe's personal secretary. Unsure if he should go to America or stay in England to help look after his aging mother, John visited Susanna in Gainsborough and asked her outlook on Charles' and his involvement in the proposed mission. She reportedly responded: 'Had I twenty sons, I should rejoice that they were all so employed, though I should never see them more.' Consequently both her younger sons sailed from England for America in mid-October.

Susanna went to live with her son Samuel in September 1736. Ten months later she took up residence with Westley and Martha at Wooton. When the Halls moved south to Flesherton near Salisbury the following year, Susanna accompanied them. 'Mr Hall ... behaves like a gentleman and a Christian,' she reported, 'and my daughter with as much duty and tenderness as can be expected.' She had no way of knowing that after her death Hall would become involved in several illicit affairs, would desert Martha and would turn from Christianity to deism, then atheism.

During the time Susanna lived with the Halls, first Charles and then John returned from America. They had both experienced deeply trying and discouraging times there. But a seismic shift was about to take place in their personal spiritual lives. Ever since their voyage to Georgia Colony, they had had considerable contact with a group of German Moravian Christians who emphasized justification through faith in Christ alone and having an assurance of one's salvation through the inner witness of God's Spirit. Back in London, first Charles on May 21, 1738, and then John three days later, claimed to have converting experiences in which they laid hold of the doctrine of justification by faith for themselves, and thereby gained a settled assurance that they were truly saved.

When Charles wrote to tell his mother of this, she both rejoiced with him and expressed a degree of uncertainty over exactly what he was claiming:

It is with much pleasure I find your mind is somewhat easier than formerly, and I heartily thank God for it. … Blessed be God, who showed you the necessity you were in of a Saviour to deliver you from the power of sin and Satan …, and directed you by faith to lay hold of that stupendous mercy offered us by redeeming love. …

… But blessed be God, [Christ] is an all-sufficient Saviour; and blessed be His holy name, that thou hast found Him a Saviour to thee, my son! …

I would gladly know what your notion is of justifying faith, because you speak of it as a thing you have but lately received.[25]

In response to another letter from Charles in which he sought to clarify his new convictions, she replied:

I think you are fallen into an odd way of thinking. You say that till within a few months you had no spiritual life nor any justifying faith.

Now, this is as if a man should affirm he was not alive in his infancy, because when an infant he did not know he was alive. All, then, that I can gather from your letter is that till a little while ago you were not so well satisfied of your being a Christian as you are now. I heartily rejoice that you have now attained to a strong and lively hope in God's mercy through Christ. Not that I can think you were totally without saving faith before; but it is one thing to have faith, and another thing to be sensible we have it. Faith is the fruit of the Spirit and the gift of God; but to feel or be inwardly sensible that we have true faith, requires a further operation of God's Holy Spirit.[26]

Many others also struggled to comprehend exactly what John and Charles, who for several years had been ordained by the Church of England, meant in claiming

---

25   Clarke, *Susanna Wesley*, p. 191-2.

26   Ibid., p. 192.

that they had only recently been converted. The Wesley brothers, for their part, set about zealously proclaiming these doctrines of justification and assurance that had but of late transformed their lives. Along with fellow Anglican George Whitefield, another fervent evangelist who emphasized justification through faith in Christ alone, they soon found themselves barred from ministering at nearly all the churches of London.

Not to be thwarted, first Whitefield and then the Wesleys took to open air preaching, oftentimes to audiences numbering in the thousands. As the Spirit of God suddenly began to work mightily through their ministries, hundreds or even thousands of people came under deep conviction and were converted. At times the deep spiritual conviction their hearers came under was exhibited through startling outward manifestations such as swoonings, profuse weeping or loud groaning.

Samuel Wesley was alarmed by reports that came to him of his brothers' novel ministry methods and message. When he expressed concerns to his mother in a letter early in 1739, she responded in measured fashion. She did not affirm, as had been reported to Samuel, that John and Charles were teaching people should seek assurance of salvation through dreams or visions. She also wrote very positively of Whitefield and her younger sons:

> You have heard, I suppose, that Mr Whitfield is taking a progress through these parts … He came hither to see me, and we talked about your brothers. I told him I did not like their way of living, wished them in some place of their own, wherein they might regularly preach, &c. He replied, 'I could not conceive the good they did in London; that the greatest part of our clergy were asleep, and that there never was

a greater need of itinerant preachers than now'; upon which a gentleman that came with him said that my son Charles had converted him, and that my sons spent all their time in doing good. I then asked Mr Whitfield if my sons were not for making some innovations in the Church, which I much feared. He assured me they were so far from it that they endeavoured all they could to reconcile Dissenters to our communion; ... and, he believed, would bring over many to our communion. His stay was short, so I could not talk with him so much as I desired. He seems to be a very good man, and one who truly desires the salvation of mankind.[27]

Some time that same year Susanna moved with the Halls to London. When Samuel learned that she had begun attending the preaching meetings John was then holding there, he wrote her a letter of protest:

It was with exceeding concern and grief I heard you had countenanced a spreading delusion, so far as to be one of Jack's congregation. Is it not enough that I am bereft of both my brothers, but must my mother follow too? I earnestly beseech the Almighty to preserve you from joining a schism at the close of your life, as you were unfortunately engaged in one at the beginning of it. It will cost you many a protest, should you retain your integrity, as I hope to God you will.[28]

Those words, coming as they did from her beloved oldest son, must have pained Susanna considerably. It is not known whether she had the opportunity to respond to them, for she was quite ill at the time, and less than a month after penning those sentiments, Samuel died suddenly. For some time he had not been physically well but thought he was on the mend. On November 5 he went

---

27   Ibid., pp. 189-90.

28   Ibid., p. 196.

to bed seemingly as well as usual but became ill in the middle of the night and passed away about dawn the next morning. Of her response to his death, Susanna wrote to Charles, who was then living in Bristol:

> Upon the first hearing of your brother's death, I did immediately acquiesce in the will of God, without the least reluctance. ... Your brother was exceeding dear to me in this life, and perhaps I have erred in loving him too well. I once thought it impossible to bear his loss, but none know what they can bear till they are tried. ... I rejoice in having a comfortable hope of my dear son's salvation. He is now at rest, and would not return to earth to gain the world. Why then should I mourn? ...
>
> I thank you for your care of my temporal affairs. It was natural to think that I should be troubled for my dear son's death on that count, because so considerable a part of my support was cut off. But to say the truth, I have never had one anxious thought of such matters; for it came immediately into my mind that God by my child's loss has called me to a firmer dependence on Himself; that though my son was good, he was not my God; and that now our Heavenly Father seemed to have taken my cause more immediately into His own hand; and, therefore, even against hope, I believed in hope that I should never suffer more.
>
> I cannot write much, being but weak. I have not been down-stairs above ten weeks, though better than I was lately. ...[29]

That same month, John, with the assistance of many supporters, purchased The Foundery, a former canon factory that had been closed for many years following a deadly explosion. It was renovated into a large meetinghouse that could seat over 1,500 people, and included living quarters for John and, potentially, a few family members. To this new

---

29 Ibid., pp. 199-201.

home John brought his mother, and she shared it with him the remainder of her life. Around that same time Susanna's daughter Emilia was widowed. Leaving Gainsborough, she and a loyal servant came to live with her mother and brother in The Foundery.

John's ministries often took him away from London. In his absence, he left Thomas Maxfield, 'a young man of good sense and piety', in charge of the small bands of Christians that John had established in London. These groups, early Methodist societies, met for Bible study, prayer and mutual encouragement in earnestly, methodically pursuing a life of spiritual growth and holiness. Maxfield met with the classes, reading and explaining the Scriptures to them. From there it was only a short step to preaching sermons, which he was soon doing with fervency and eloquence.

John was disturbed when he received reports of this, for Maxfield was not an ordained minister, and he returned home quickly. When Susanna saw that something was bothering her son and asked him about it, he replied curtly, 'Thomas Maxfield has turned preacher, I find.'

'John, you know what my sentiments have been,' she responded. 'You cannot suspect me of readily favouring anything of this kind. But take care what you do with respect to that young man; for he is as surely called of God to preach as you are. Examine what have been the fruits of his preaching, and hear him yourself.'

Arrested by this unexpected word of caution, he followed her advice. After hearing Maxfield preach, John declared: 'It is the Lord, let Him do what seemeth Him good. What am I that I should withstand God?' This turn of events in time led to lay leaders commonly serving as Methodist evangelists and ministers, a practice that helped to greatly advance the Gospel and the spread of Methodism.

Westley Hall, still a professing and practicing Christian at that time, occasionally filled the pulpit for John at The Foundery. A most significant spiritual event transpired in Susanna's life as he led in a Communion service there in January 1740: 'While my son Hall was pronouncing these words in delivering the cup to me, "The blood of our Lord Jesus Christ which was given for thee", these words struck through my heart, and I knew that God for Christ's sake had forgiven me all my sins.'

Hearing of this, Charles was convinced that she had not been truly converted until that moment. He wrote her a zealous and rather blunt letter in which he apparently declared she had all along been trusting in her own good works to save her and, thus, had been in a spiritually lost condition. She, in turn, responded graciously:

> I thank you for your kind letter. I call it so, because I verily believe it was dictated by a sincere desire of my spiritual and eternal good. There is too much truth in many of your accusations; nor do I intend to say one word in my own defence, but rather choose to refer all things to him that knoweth all things. ...
>
> I am not one of those who have never been enlightened, or made partaker of the heavenly gift, or of the Holy Ghost, but have many years since been fully awakened, and am deeply sensible of sin, both original and actual. My case is rather like that of the Church of Ephesus; I have not been faithful to the talents committed to my trust, and have lost my first love. ...
>
> I do not, I will not despair; for ever since my sad defection, when I was almost without hope, when I had forgotten God,[30]

---

30 This likely is a reference to the brief time discussed in chapter 1 when, as a girl, Susanna fell under the influence of Socinianism and doubted her Christian faith.

yet I then found He had not forgotten me. Even then He did by His Spirit apply the merits of the great atonement to my soul, by telling me that Christ died for me. Shall the God of truth, the Almighty Saviour, tell me that I am interested in His blood and righteousness, and shall I not believe Him? God forbid! I do, I will believe; and though I am the greatest of sinners, that does not discourage me; for all my transgressions are the sins of a finite person, but the merits of our Lord's sufferings and righteousness are infinite! ...[31]

A number of statements that Susanna made in her many writings to her children certainly could be taken as evidence that she believed good works played a part in bringing about one's salvation. However, the above testimony makes it clear she had considered herself a true Christian for many years and that the ultimate basis for thinking herself such was her belief in Christ's atoning death for her sin.

A pair of conversations Susanna had with John further suggest that what she experienced in January of 1740 was not conversion but coming to have a deepened assurance of her salvation through faith in Christ's atoning death. Of a discussion he had with her the previous September 3, John wrote in his journal:

I talked largely with my mother, who told me that, till a short time ago, she had scarce heard such a thing mentioned as having forgiveness of sins now, or God's Spirit bearing witness with our spirit: much less did she believe that this was the common privilege of all believers. 'Therefore,' said she, 'I never dared to ask it for myself.'[32]

---

31   Clarke, *Susanna Wesley*, pp. 204-5.

32   McReynolds, *Susanna Wesley*, p. 117.

When Susanna later told John of the assurance that came to her heart as she received the communion cup from her son-in-law:

> I asked whether her father (Dr Annesley) had not the same faith; and whether she had not heard him preach it to others. She answered, he had it himself; and declared a little before his death, that for more than forty years, he had no darkness, no fear, no doubt at all of his being accepted in the Beloved. But that, nevertheless, she did not remember to have heard him preach, no, not once, explicitly upon it; whence she supposed he also looked upon it as the peculiar blessing of a few; not as promised to all the people of God.[33]

On March 9, 1741, Susanna's youngest child, Kezia, died at age thirty-two. She reportedly never recovered from the heartbreak of Westley Hall having falsely professed his love for her before marrying her sister instead. According to John, 'She refused to be comforted and fell into a lingering illness which terminated in her death.'

Sixteen months later, while ministering in Bristol, John received a note from one of his sisters that his mother was near death. Hastening back to London he found her 'on the borders of eternity' but having 'no doubt or fear'. Her sole desire was 'to depart and to be with Christ' (Phil. 1:23). The next day – July 23, 1742 – John and five of his sisters (Emilia, Sukey, Hetty, Anne and Martha) gathered around their mother's bed. John recorded in his journal:

> I sat down on the bedside. She was in her last conflict; unable to speak, but, I believe, quite sensible. Her look was calm and serene, and her eyes fixed upward, while we commended her

---

33 Clarke, *Susanna Wesley*, pp. 195-6.

soul to God. From three to four the silver cord was loosing and the wheel breaking at the cistern [Eccles. 12:6]; and then, without any struggle, or sigh or groan, her soul was set at liberty. We stood around the bed, and fulfilled her last request uttered a little before she lost her speech, 'Children, as soon as I am released, sing a psalm of praise to God.'[34]

Susanna's funeral was held nine days later, on the afternoon of Sunday, August 1. John reported that 'almost an innumerable company of people' gathered for the service. He used Revelation 20:11-12 as his funeral text, and afterward related, 'It was one of the most solemn assemblies I ever saw, or expect to see on this side of eternity.' Her body was buried in the Bunhill Fields Cemetery where such notable Christians as John Bunyan, John Owen and Isaac Watts are also interred.

---

34 Dallimore, *Susanna Wesley*, p. 165.

2

Fanny Crosby

ONE

When John and Mercy Crosby's daughter, Frances Jane, was just six weeks old, she developed an inflammation of the eyes as the result of a cold. The regular doctor of their community of Southeast in Putnam County, New York, was away at the time. Another man, who claimed to be a doctor but apparently was more of a quack, offered to treat the infant's eyes. He put a hot poultice over her eyes, insisting it would draw out the infection. Instead, it all but destroyed the child's sight. When the Crosbys accused the man, whose name has not been preserved, of blinding their baby, he fled Southeast, never to be heard from again.

To the end of her long life, which stretched out for some ninety-five years, Fanny Crosby was able to see only bright light and vivid colors, and those but faintly. Other than that she was totally blind, being unable to see distinct details or even indistinct shapes. But this seeming tragedy led to her developing an overcoming spirit, an incredibly retentive mind and an exceptional poetic gift, all of which played into her becoming the world's foremost hymnwriter of her generation. As a result, she wrote toward the end of her life of the accident that took her sight and the individual who was responsible for it:

> But I have not for a moment, in more than eighty-five years, felt a spark of resentment against him because I have always believed from my youth to this very moment that the good Lord, in His infinite mercy, by this means consecrated me to the work that I am still permitted to do. When I remember His mercy and lovingkindness; when I have been blessed above the common lot of mortals; and when happiness has touched the deep places of my soul, – how can I repine?[1]

Fanny was born on March 24, 1820, in the small town of Southeast, New York, twelve miles west of Danbury, Connecticut. Southeast then had 1,900 inhabitants, most of whom were descendants of the original settlers of the Massachusetts Bay Colony. Eleven households bearing the name of Crosby resided in Southeast and comprised the community's largest clan. These Crosbys were all related and traced their roots back to Simon and Ann Crosby, who arrived from England in 1635 and settled near Boston.

John Crosby, Fanny's father, was considerably older than his wife, Mercy, for by a previous marriage he had a daughter who was only six or seven years younger than her stepmother. After the widowed John married Mercy, they lived with her parents, Sylvanus and Eunice Foster, in the small house where Fanny was later born. John, like his father-in-law, was a farmer. Fanny had no memory of her father, for he became ill and died eight months after her birth.

---

1   Fanny Crosby, *Fanny J. Crosby, An Autobiography* (Grand Rapids: Baker, 1986), p. 24. This volume was originally published in 1906 under the title *Memories of Eighty Years*.

Shortly after her husband's death, in order to help support herself and her infant daughter, Mercy hired herself out as a maidservant for a wealthy family nearby. In the years that followed, Grandmother Eunice took the primary responsibility in caring for Fanny, and the two became extremely close. 'My grandmother was more to me than I can ever express by word or pen,' Fanny later testified. From as early as she could remember, her grandmother would read the Bible to her and explain everything in terms she could understand. Eunice was a firm believer in prayer and taught her granddaughter many important and practical lessons concerning it. She also sought to help Fanny understand the physical world by describing its numerous facets in intricate detail.

Every Sunday the family walked or rode a mile and a half to the Southeast Church, a Presbyterian meeting-house, located on a prominent hilltop. There parishioners were nurtured on the substantive Calvinistic teaching of the Puritans, doctrine to which the Crosbys adhered. Congregational singing, which was carried out a cappella, was almost exclusively from the biblical psalter. A deacon, often the only person in the room with a printed text, would 'line out' a psalm one phrase at a time, and the congregation would repeat each line after him.

A few weeks after Fanny's fifth birthday her mother took her to New York City for an examination with Dr Valentine Mott, of Columbia University School of Medicine, one of America's premier surgeons at the time. Mercy's hope was that something might be done to restore her daughter's sight. After Mott and Dr Delafield, an eye specialist, examined the girl's eyes, Mott asked her,

'Would you like to have me do something for your eyes that will make you see?'

Fearing the doctor might need to do something that would hurt her in order to help her eyesight, Fanny pressed close to her mother and promptly replied, 'No, sir.'

After a long pause the kindly physician placed his hand on her head and said, 'Poor child, I am afraid you will never see again.'

With that declaration, the last ray of hope in Mrs Crosby's heart that her daughter's sight might someday be restored was extinguished. Fanny, who had no conscious recollection of ever having been able to see, was not bothered by the news. At first Mercy was heartbroken. But in time she was able to encourage her daughter that 'sometimes Providence deprived persons of some physical faculty in order that the spiritual insight might more fully awake'.

Around that same time Mercy took a new job as a housekeeper in North Salem, six miles south of Southeast. There she and her daughter lived in her employer's house. As Fanny grew her mother did not try to hold her back due to her handicap but allowed her to play with children her own age from early in the day till late at night. She climbed trees with the agility of a squirrel and rode horses 'as fleet as the wind' while holding on to their manes for dear life.

Normally she was not bothered by her blindness but 'was determined to be as content as circumstances would allow, and to hope for any good fortune that the future might have in store'. At age eight she composed lines that summarized her prevailing outlook at the time:

Oh, what a happy soul I am,
    Although I cannot see,
I am resolved that in this world
    Contented I will be.

How many blessings I enjoy
    That other people don't!
To weep and sigh because I'm blind
    I cannot nor I won't.

During those years Fanny and her mother attended the only church in New Salem, the Society of Friends. The Quaker meetings struck the young girl's fancy. She was intrigued by the speaker's singsong manner of sermon delivery that led him to gasp for breath between phrases. She was also struck by the 'doleful' hymns with their grave subject matter and somber tunes.

When Fanny was eight or nine years old, she again moved with her mother, this time to nearby Ridgefield, Connecticut. They lived in a house on the village green. There Fanny soon joined a dozen other children each evening to play games and sing songs.

Mercy and Fanny's landlady was Mrs Hawley, 'an old Puritan Presbyterian' who was kind and 'loved beautiful things'. While Mercy was away at her housekeeping job, Mrs Hawley cared for Fanny. She invested countless hours in helping her blind charge to memorize vast portions of Scripture, sometimes as many as five chapters per week, teaching it to her one line at a time. She also assisted her in memorizing many popular poems and portions of profitable secular works.

Just how phenomenal Fanny's memory was became clear at that time. She memorized the first four books of both the Old and New Testaments in her first year under

Mrs Hawley's tutelage. By the end of the second year she could recite by rote not only the entire Pentateuch and all four Gospels but also all of Ruth, many psalms, all of Proverbs and the entire Song of Solomon. Not surprisingly, she earned a Bible in a contest held among the children at her church for being the child who learned the most Scripture. The rest of her life she retained those passages and recited them to herself when she desired to 'read' the Bible.

Throughout her childhood Fanny's mother and other relatives spent much time reading to her. By this means she became acquainted with the best poets and the literary works of such individuals as Homer, John Bunyan and William Shakespeare. She also thrilled to hear tales of the adventures of Robin Hood and the exploits of Don Quixote.

Early on she began to manifest her gift of composing poetry: 'Even before I was eight years of age my imagination was occupied with all sorts of material that I was constantly weaving into various forms; and among these were rude snatches of verse ...'. A few years later, a friend, without telling Fanny she was doing so, sent a little ditty she had written to the *Herald of Freedom*, a small weekly paper published by P. T. Barnum at Danbury. Barnum, who later gained fame as one of the world's greatest showmen, desired to print the entire poem, which described a dishonest miller in the area who sometimes mixed his flour with corn meal. Fanny's mother, however, did not want undue attention called to the blind poetess and her potentially provocative piece, so she allowed only the first stanza to be printed:

> There is a miller in our town,
>> How dreadful is his case;
> I fear unless he does repent
>> He'll meet with sad disgrace.

Fanny also loved to sing. 'Singing schools' were popular in New England in that era. Each winter a singing teacher visited Ridgefield twice a week to instruct young people to sing from Lowell Mason's famous *Handel and Haydn Collection*, songs and anthems with a classical European musical style. She also sang in her church choir.

She and her mother attended Ridgefield's First Church, which had both Congregational and Presbyterian affiliations and ministers at various times in its history. Around age twelve Fanny became acquainted with a Methodist tailor, and she occasionally attended his church with him. There she quickly gained a deep appreciation for the rich hymnody of the Methodists.

As the years passed Fanny became increasingly aware that her blindness was a serious and seemingly insurmountable obstacle to her gaining the wealth of knowledge she had come to intensely desire:

> I used to sigh and wonder if I would ever be able to gain very much of the great store of human knowledge … My heart sank within me, however, when I realized that there was no way for me to learn; and thus, not being satisfied, my longing for knowledge became a passion from which there was seldom any rest. A great barrier seemed to rise before me, shutting away from me some of the best things of which I dreamed in my sleeping and waking hours. I was somewhat impatient, still hopeful; but as the years succeeded each other in their usual round, what frequently seemed to me an oasis, sooner or later, faded like a mirage farther and farther into the dim and distant future.[2]

---

2   Ibid., p. 36.

She sometimes went with other children her age to the village school, but the teacher there was too busy to give her the personal help she needed. After a few days she would quit in frustration.

Fanny often returned to Southeast to visit Grandma Eunice who seemed to understand her desires and disappointments. One evening at twilight the grandmother, sitting in her old rocking chair, took the growing girl (then about ten years of age) on her lap to talk about her concerns. Then they knelt by the rocker and committed those matters to the heavenly Father. After the older woman went quietly downstairs, Fanny crept to the window where she could faintly detect the glow of the moonlight. Kneeling there she repeated over and over a simple prayer, 'Dear Lord, please show me how I can learn like other children.' The results were dramatic and abiding:

> At this moment the weight of anxiety that had burdened my heart was changed to the sweet consciousness that my prayer would be answered in due time. If I had been restless and impatient before, from that time forth I was still eager, but confident that God would point a way for me to gain the education which I craved.[3]

Not many months after that memorable evening Eunice Crosby died at age fifty-three. Some four years later, in the autumn of 1834, Mercy moved with Fanny back to North Salem. That November the mother came to her daughter with a circular from the newly formed New York Institution for the Blind (hereafter the New York Institution). As Mercy read the announcement, Fanny

---

3   Ibid., p. 37.

clapped her hands and exclaimed, 'O, thank God, He has answered my prayer, just as I knew He would.'

TWO

On March 3, 1835, less than a month before her fifteenth birthday, Fanny set out for New York with a woman traveling companion whose name has not been preserved. Fanny had never been away from home for more than two weeks at a time and was 'thoroughly unnerved' at the thought of leaving the security and familiarity of her mother's home. Swallowing her sobs and hurrying from the house lest she break down completely while saying good-bye to her mother, she mounted the stagecoach but did not speak a word for the entire first hour of the journey. Seeing how distressed she was, her companion finally said sympathetically, 'Fanny, if you don't want to go to New York, we will get out at the next station, and take the returning stage home. Your mother will be lonesome without you anyway.'

To that point the girl had not been able to cry, but at the suggestion of returning home she burst into tears. Afterwards she felt better and stated resolutely, 'No, I will go on to New York.'

The New York Institution had been in existence just four years and had thirty students when Fanny arrived. It was only the second such school founded in America, a similar Institution having been established in Boston two years before its New York counterpart. The latter institution leased a private mansion on a pleasant country estate shaded by old willow trees on Manhattan's West Side. At that time the city had not yet extended that far into the country.

The school was then under the superintendency of John Denison Russ, a physician and Yale graduate. He developed a phonetic alphabet and perfected the system of raised characters and maps invented several years earlier by Louis Braille in France. The students were taught to read the Bible, *Pilgrim's Progress* and Coleridge's 'Rime of the Ancient Mariner' in Braille.

Subjects studied included English literature and grammar, history, geography, philosophy, mathematics, science, astronomy, political economy and music. The instructors read their lectures and any related reading materials to the pupils two or three times, then asked them detailed questions about the material. The next day the students were expected to paraphrase the previous lesson back to their teachers. Years of this kind of instruction further strengthened Fanny's powers of mental retention and recall.

The Institution's instructors often read to their students the works of famous poets such as Thomas Moore, James Montgomery, Henry Wadsworth Longfellow, Alfred Lord Tennyson, William Cullen Bryant, Charles Wesley and Lord (George Gordon) Byron. They inspired Fanny to 'more determined efforts' in her own poetical compositions. Her budding poetic gift was recognized by teachers and fellow students alike. The superintendent and other instructors began asking her to compose poems to be recited or sung on special occasions at the school.

Eventually, however, the praise and attention Fanny was receiving for her poetic ability led to 'rising vanity'. Around 1840, when she was twenty years old, Dr Silas Jones, who by then had replaced Russ as the school's superintendent, summoned her to his office. She thought he might ask her for another poem or give her a word of commendation, but instead he spoke plainly to her about her growing pride.

Even after that her teachers apparently felt she was still too preoccupied with her poetry because a few weeks later the superintendent again called her to his office and declared, 'You are not to write a line of poetry for three months.' For Fanny that decision 'came as a bolt of lightning out of a clear sky' and she was 'overwhelmed with astonishment'. But for six weeks Jones 'resolutely enforced his command to the very letter'. As a result, she became listless and her academic performance declined.

When Jones once more summoned her to inquire if she was ill, she responded honestly, 'I find it impossible to keep my mind on my lessons for poetry occupies my thoughts in spite of all efforts to think of other things. I cannot help it.'

'Well,' the superintendent finally relented, 'write as much as you like, but pay a little more attention to the morning lectures.'

Fanny also continued to develop her musical abilities at the Institution. In addition to the guitar, which she had learned to play as a young girl, she became proficient at playing the piano, organ and harp. She sang solos at special functions and in the school's choir.

In 1836 Fanny's mother, Mercy, moved to Bridgeport, Connecticut, to live with her brother Joseph and his family. There she met Thomas Morris, a widower, and they were married in February 1838. Fifteen months later Mercy, at age forty, gave birth to a daughter, Wilhelmina. Fanny was delighted with her new half-sister when she vacationed at her mother's home that summer. But shortly after her return to the institution, the sad news came that the infant had died. About a year later, in August of 1840, Mercy bore another daughter, Julia.

Throughout the 1840s Fanny came to gain considerable notoriety as the New York Institution's premiere student-success story. During those years numerous prominent politicians and other celebrities visited the Institution, and special receptions were held in their honor. Fanny was habitually asked to write and recite a poem (tailor-made for the specific guest), and sometimes also to sing a solo, for those special occasions.

Early in April 1841, William Harrison died suddenly after only one month in office as President of the United States. One afternoon two months later the Institution's new superintendent, Peter Vroom, hastened to Fanny and announced that President John Tyler (Harrison's successor), the mayor of New York City, and the entire city council had unexpectedly arrived for an impromptu visit. 'Give me ten or fifteen minutes,' she stated, 'and I shall have the best welcome that I can prepare in so short a time.' Moments later she stood before the esteemed guests to present that poem of welcome, sing a song, and recite another piece she had written for the previous Independence Day, a composition that included a reference to Tyler.

During the summers of 1842 and 1843 some members of the Institution's Board of Managers took about twenty of its students on a tour through the central part of the state. The purpose of the tour was to show the public to what extent the blind could be educated and to recruit new students for the school. The group traveled along the Erie Canal on a charter boat, tying up at various towns along the route, all the way to Niagara Falls.

At each stop they presented an evening exhibition in the town hall. Usually a clergyman or some other prominent citizen would welcome their group. Different students would then demonstrate their ability to read Braille and their knowledge of such subjects as literature, geography, history and arithmetic. They sang songs, and Fanny always capped off the evening by reciting one of her original poetic compositions.

William Cullen Bryant visited the Institution one day in 1843. For about twenty-five years he had been considered America's foremost living poet. After the special program that the students had for their honored guest, Fanny had the opportunity to meet Bryant. She was astonished when he warmly grasped her hand, said a few words in commendation of her poetry and urged her 'to press bravely on' in her work as a teacher and writer. 'He never knew,' she later testified, 'how much good he did by those few words.'

Beginning in the fall of that same year Fanny became one of the Institution's regular instructors, teaching rhetoric, grammar and Roman and American history. During that same period of time she often stayed up till the wee hours of the morning working on pieces for a book of poetry she had been encouraged by the Institution's managers to compile. The strain proved too much for her, and her health declined noticeably.

The Institution's doctor, J. W. G. Clements, recommended Fanny discontinue her teaching responsibilities and forego participating in an upcoming trip to Washington, D.C., where she was to recite poetry before members of Congress. The managers wished to influence Congress to enact legislation to create institutions for the blind and to provide free education for unsighted children in each state. Fanny's public presentations as part of that effort were considered crucial, and she dearly desired to carry out her important role. Clements concluded she would fret herself into a fever if she was not allowed to go, so he gave his permission on the condition that she would not overly exert herself.

On January 24, 1844, seventeen students from the New York Institution presented a program in the Capitol's Assembly Hall. A number of congressmen as well as private citizens attended. After academic and musical presentations by various students, Fanny recited her 'poetical address', a long poem of thirteen stanzas. The audience gave her a thunderous ovation (which actually frightened her) and called for an encore. While the congressmen were impressed and even deeply touched by the New York Institution's program that evening, they never passed legislation to establish more schools for the blind.

Three months later Fanny's first volume of poetry, entitled *The Blind Girl and Other Poems*, was ready for publication. 160 pages in length, the book contained such poems as 'The Blind Girl', 'The Rise and Progress of the New York Institution for the Blind' and 'To the Heroes of Bunker Hill', as well as some of the poetic addresses she had presented publicly over the past few years.

Her health remained so poor throughout the spring of 1844 that some of Fanny's associates at the Institution, including Dr Clements, began to fear she might never recover. That summer she was sent home to her mother's home in Bridgeport with strict orders to get plenty of rest and drink lots of milk. Standing only four feet, nine inches tall and never weighing more than 100 pounds throughout her life, Clements likely thought she needed some fattening up.

Mercy had borne a third daughter, Caroline, to her husband the previous Christmas Day. But during the spring of 1844, Thomas deserted her and their two daughters after falling under the influence of members of the Church of Jesus Christ of Latter-Day Saints (Mormons). Mercy refused to join Thomas in moving to Nauvoo, Illinois, where Joseph Smith, Mormonism's founder, had his new settlement. Thomas's son by his previous marriage, William, also refused to accompany his father, choosing instead to remain with his stepmother, Mercy. After Smith was assassinated in Nauvoo, Thomas followed Smith's successor, Brigham Young, to Utah. He never returned to Bridgeport, and Mercy and her children never saw him again.

Fanny continued to meet a number of prominent politicians. That same fall, former President Martin Van Buren hosted her out for dinner. The following year she met James Polk, the newly inaugurated President, when he and his staff visited the Institution. By that time the school had grown to over 100 students.

Delegations from the institutions for the blind in New York, Boston and Philadelphia made a collective visit to the nation's capitol in April of 1846 to renew their appeal to Congress for funding to establish schools for the blind throughout the States. President Polk invited those delegations to the White House and during the course of the conversation said, 'Well, Miss Crosby, have you made any poetry since I saw you last year?'

'Yes, sir,' came her ready reply, 'I have composed a song and dedicated it to you.' The President appeared to be pleased. He asked her to take his arm and proceeded to the music room where, according to Fanny, 'we held an impromptu recital'.

During that same visit Fanny met former President John Quincy Adams. She thrilled to hear the aged statesman, then serving as a respected member of the House of Representatives, deliver one of his final public speeches. It was an appeal to accept the bequest that British scientist James Smithson had left to the United States of America for 'an establishment, under the name of the "Smithsonian Institution", for the increase and diffusion of knowledge among men'. While the Smithsonian Bill was passed by both the House and the Senate a short while later, the legislation to fund further schools for the blind ended up buried in committee and was never again considered.

One day in the summer of 1848, President Polk came to the New York Institution unannounced and unattended, stating that he had come to the beautiful retreat to escape the turmoil of the busy city. After dinner Fanny asked him if he would not enjoy a stroll around the grounds. Presently, along the way, she heard the voice of an old servant of the Institution. The servant no longer worked there but had returned for a visit of just a few minutes' duration. Somewhat impulsively, Fanny turned to Polk and asked, 'Will you please excuse me a minute?'

'Certainly,' he replied. When she returned, realizing she had just deserted 'the chief man of the nation' in order to greet a servant, she apologized profusely and tried to explain the circumstance as best she could. But to her surprise 'the great and good man' said, 'You have done well, and I commend you for it. Kindness, even to those in the humblest capacity of life, should be our rule of conduct; and by this act you have won not only my respect but also my esteem.'

In the fall of that same year, 1848, cholera swept over Europe, leaving scores of thousands dead in its wake. It broke out in New York in May of the following year. James Chamberlain, the Institution's superintendent since 1846, gave the students an early dismissal to summer vacation that month, thinking they would be safer away from the city. But a number of students were unable to return home. So Fanny and some other members of the faculty decided to remain, 'being convinced that God would take care of us and that we could be of some help'.

News came in June that President Polk, who had completed his term of office just three months earlier, had succumbed to cholera in Nashville, Tennessee. By mid-July over 2,200 New Yorkers had perished from the dread illness. In the end, twenty members of the New York Institution contracted cholera and ten died from it.

Fanny assisted the Institution's physician, Dr Clements, in making pills to try to fight the sickness. A school just one block from the New York Institution was turned into a cholera hospital. The Institution's sick were taken there, and both Clements and Fanny served there. Frequently as she sat by a patient's bedside at night the stillness was shattered by the harsh cry of a city official outside the door of some bereaved home nearby, 'Bring out your dead.' Sometimes she was startled to bump against a casket as she moved around the hospital ward.

After several nights of almost no sleep near the end of July Fanny felt like she might be coming down with the sickness. After a generous dosage of medication and a long night of sleep she felt fully restored. But hearing of the close call, Chamberlain sent her home to Bridgeport for the remainder of the summer. The students still at the Institution were taken to another town that had not been visited by the deadly sickness. After the first hard frosts of fall it was deemed safe for people to return to the city, and the Institution reopened in early November.

THREE

Fanny's experiences in the cholera epidemic certainly would have brought her face to face with her own mortality and likely played a part in life-changing spiritual developments that took place in the months to follow. Dating back to her first years at the Institution, she had attended the class meetings at the Eighteenth Street Methodist Church. In those early days she was timid and never spoke in public if she could at all avoid doing so. She would attend the meetings and play for them on the condition that she would not be called on to speak. By her own admission she had grown somewhat indifferent toward spiritual matters.

In the autumn of 1850 revival meetings were held at the Methodist Broadway Tabernacle on Thirtieth Street. Fanny and some others from the Institution attended the meetings each night. Twice when the invitation was given at the close of the service, she went forward, seeking peace from her inner spiritual struggles, but found none. Finally on November 20, it seemed to her 'that the light must indeed come then or never'. That evening she went to the altar alone. As she prayed the congregation began to sing Isaac Watts' grand old hymn, 'Alas! and Did My Savior Bleed?' When they reached the great words of consecration contained in the last verse – 'Here, Lord, I give myself away' – Fanny expressed that commitment as the desire of her heart, yielding her life to Christ. Immediately her 'very soul was flooded with a celestial light' and she sprang to her feet, literally shouting, 'Hallelujah!'

The following Thursday evening she gave a public testimony at the class meeting. Afterward she felt Satan suggested to her mind, 'Well, Fanny, you made a good speech, didn't you?' She instantly realized that her old spirit of pride was returning. This left her greatly depressed for a few days until a good friend suggested she needed to make a complete surrender of her will to God. She did by promising to do her duty whenever the Lord should make it clear to her. A few weeks later she was asked to close one of the meetings with a brief prayer. Her first thought was, 'I can't.' To which her conscience responded, 'But your promise.' Some sixty years later, she testified, 'and from that hour, I believe I have never refused to pray or speak in a public service, with the result that I have been richly blessed.'

In 1851, Fanny published a second collection of her poems entitled 'Monterey'. That same year she began collaborating with George F. Root, who had served as the New York Institution's music instructor since 1845, in providing lyrics for his musical compositions. He was already 'well known as the composer of many sweet hymns and various secular pieces that were exceedingly popular'. Over the course of the next three years Root and Fanny produced fifty or sixty songs together, several of which gained immense popularity. She also wrote the words for two cantatas he composed at that time.

But Fanny did not share in the considerable promi-nence and financial benefits that Root gained through the publication of those songs. He paid her a dollar or two for each of her poems, the standard fee with which publishing companies normally compensated their poets. But he published the songs solely under his own name. He considered himself under no further financial obligation to Fanny, though some of the songs brought in enormous profit. The royalty on the most popular song she wrote at that time ('Rosalie, the Prairie Flower'), for instance, amounted to $3,000.[4] Many other songs, as well, netted Root (but not his lyricist) considerable wealth. Fanny seems never to have resented this arrangement or to have thought of it as anything other than normal music publication procedure.

By the fall of 1853 some significant personnel changes had taken place at the Institution. Fanny, then aged thirty-three, had become the 'Preceptress' (Dean of Students) and was recognized as the school's best-loved teacher. The Institution was under the direction of a despotic new superintendent, T. Colden Cooper. A young man named William Cleveland was appointed head of the school's literary department. His sixteen-year-old brother, Grover, who would later become the President of the United States, was hired to teach younger children and to serve as Superintendent Cooper's personal secretary.

Grover came to the Institution shortly after his father's death. One morning William stopped by Fanny's classroom with a request: 'I have a favor to ask of you. … The death of our father grieves my brother very much. When you are at leisure I wish you would speak to him and try to divert his mind from sad thoughts. You can comfort him better than I can.'

---

4   Bernard Ruffin, *Fanny Crosby* (United Church Press, 1976), p. 78.

She promised to do her best and that afternoon paid a visit to 'Grove' (as she would come to call him) at the Superintendent's office. A fast friendship sprang up between them. The young Cleveland volunteered to serve as her amanuensis by recording her poems as she dictated them to him.

Thirteen years earlier, when Fanny was twenty years of age, a nine-year-old boy named Alexander Van Alstyne[5] came as a student to the New York Institution. He had lost his sight early in childhood as a result of illness. But he was endowed with exceptional musical ability, and before his graduation from the Institution he was said to be one of the most accomplished students the school had ever had. He became the first pupil from the Institution to attend a regular college when, in 1848, he enrolled in Union College at Schenectady, New York. There he studied not only music but also Greek, Latin, philosophy and theology.

He returned to the New York Institution in 1855 as a musical instructor. A platonic relationship based on their shared love of music and poetry eventually developed into romantic attraction. Fanny divulged of herself: 'Some people seem to forget that blind girls have just as great a faculty for loving and *do* love just as much and just as truly as those who have their sight. I had a heart that was hungry for love.' She also revealed: 'After hearing several of my poems he became deeply interested in my work; and I after listening to his sweet strains of music became

---

5   'Van Alstyne' is how Fanny always spelled his surname. His name was variously spelled 'Van Alstine' (at his birth and in records of the New York Institution) and 'Van Alsteine' (on his death certificate and burial record). See Ruffin, *Fanny Crosby*, pp. 79-80.

interested in him. Thus we soon grew to be very much concerned for each other.'

Van Alstyne left the Institution in the fall of 1857 to begin giving private music lessons in Maspeth, Long Island, in what is now the borough of Queens. His departure and Fanny's considerable dissatisfaction with deteriorated conditions at the Institution under T. Colden Cooper's superintendency led her to tender her resignation on March 2, 1858. Under Cooper, whom Fanny called a 'cruel incompetent', the Institution had become overcrowded. Teachers were underpaid and the children were treated more like inmates than students. Severe punishments were administered for even minor misconduct. The building was unconscionably cold in the wintertime and the quality of meals declined noticeably.

Fanny had been at the Institution for nearly twenty-three years (eight of those as a student and fifteen as a teacher), and, until recent years, had enjoyed a positive, happy history there. So she could not help but be deeply saddened when she left the school under such unfortunate conditions. She was thrilled, however, to join Van Alstyne in Maspeth where they were married in a private ceremony on March 5. She was nearly thirty-eight years old and he was twenty-seven.

'Van', as Fanny called her husband, was slender and, not surprisingly, much taller than she was. Fanny's beauty came from her bright and engaging personality rather than from her physical appearance. Van Alstyne, by contrast, was a noticeably handsome man. He often did not wear the dark spectacles that Fanny and other blind people of that era habitually wore. Jovial and easygoing, he was well liked by all his acquaintances.

Van Alstyne was an accomplished organist who, in future years, served as the paid organist in two New York City churches. He was also proficient in playing the piano, cornet and other instruments. He taught private classes in both vocal and instrumental music and provided music lessons at low cost to poor children.

The summer after they were married, Fanny compiled a third book of poems, *A Wreath of Columbia's Flowers*. Van Alstyne insisted she continue using her maiden name in her literary work since she was well known to the public by that name. Throughout her career Fanny normally referred to herself as 'Miss Crosby', 'Mrs Crosby' or 'Madam Crosby'. Only on legal documents did she use Van Alstyne as her last name.

Some time the following year, 1859, she gave birth to 'a tender babe' but it lived only a short while. It is not known whether the infant was a boy or a girl, nor the precise cause of its death. Throughout the remainder of her life Fanny hardly ever spoke of this to anyone, and only her closest friends even knew that she had ever had a child.

About a year after this loss, the couple returned to Manhattan. In the years that followed they lived at a number of different addresses, sometimes in old tenement houses in rather poor neighborhoods. Whether they lived in those locations out of financial necessity or in order to minister to the less fortunate of society is unclear.

Always somewhat eclectic in her church attendance, Fanny participated in a number of churches in the ensuing years. She attended the John Street Methodist Church and became active in its sewing society, knitting garments for the poor. She also frequented the Plymouth

Congregational Church to hear her favorite preacher, Henry Ward Beecher. In addition she sometimes attended services at a pair of Presbyterian churches as well as at Trinity Episcopal Church.

Another church she was involved with was the Dutch Reformed Church at 23rd Street. The pastor of that congregation, Peter Stryker, asked Fanny to write a poem that could be used as a hymn at the church's New Year's Eve service at the close of 1863. So impressed was he with her composition that he came to her early the next year with a suggestion: 'Why don't you see Mr Bradbury? He has told me more than once that he was looking for someone who could write hymns. I think you are the person for whom he has been looking, and I will give you a letter of introduction.'

Consequently, on February 2, 1864, Fanny presented herself at the office of William B. Bradbury. He was the most prominent and prolific hymn writer of that period, having composed such popular hymns as 'Just As I Am', 'He Leadeth Me', 'Savior, Like a Shepherd Lead Us' and 'On Christ, the Solid Rock, I Stand'. To her surprise, he said, 'Fanny, I thank God that we have at last met, for I think you can write hymns, and I have wished for a long time to have a talk with you.'

Three days later she returned with some verses about heaven. They were soon set to music and afterward published as her first hymn, 'Our Bright Home Above'. Commented Fanny of this significant development, 'It now seemed to me that the great work of my life had really begun.'

The following week Bradbury sent for her 'in great haste' and announced that he needed a patriotic song immediately. He intended the piece to be entitled 'A Sound among the Mulberry Trees' but she timidly suggested that 'Forest Trees' would sound more euphonious. He at once accepted that recommendation then played for her the melody he had composed. The melody was 'somewhat difficult' but after she heard it two or three times she was able to count the measure to which she would adapt her words. The very next morning she returned to the office with a set of proposed lyrics. As Bradbury was not there, one of his associates played through the song on the piano to see how well her words matched the music. He then exclaimed, 'How in the world did you manage to write that hymn? Nobody ever supposed that you or any other mortal could adapt words to that melody!'

Just then Bradbury entered the office. After looking over the song very carefully he turned to her and stated, 'Fanny, I am surprised beyond measure. And now let me say that as long as I have a publishing house, you will always have work.' So it proved, for she went on to write lyrics for Bradbury and his successors for nearly fifty years. After Bradbury's death, his partners, Sylvester Main and Lucius Biglow, formed the Biglow and Main Company. (Sylvester had actually been a childhood playmate of Fanny's in Ridgefield, Connecticut.) Hubert Main, Sylvester's son, oversaw the company following his father's death in 1873 and worked closely with Fanny for decades.

She wrote many other patriotic poems, several of which were set to music, during the Civil War years. 'A Sound among the Forest Trees' immediately gained great popularity. After the war, she composed a missionary hymn, 'There's a Cry from Macedonia', to go with that same melody, and it proved successful for many years.

From the beginning of her association with Bradbury's firm, as well as when working with subsequent Christian music publishers, Fanny composed lyrics for many songs to be included in children's Sunday School hymnals. Those compositions emphasized numerous themes including Christ's redemptive death, responding to the Gospel call, fulfilling one's Christian duty, manifesting various positive character traits, heaven, temperance and citizenship.[6]

During the summer of 1864 Bradbury introduced her to Philip Phillips, a singing evangelist from Cincinnati, while he was visiting in New York. As Bradbury and Phillips prepared to leave the office for a short while, the latter laughingly said, 'Fanny, I wish you would write me a hymn, and have it ready when we return.' So she composed a hymn of three or four stanzas while they were out. Phillips liked it so well he thereafter often had her supply songs for use in his evangelistic meetings.

In 1866 he published a collection of hymns entitled *The Singing Pilgrim, or Pilgrim's Progress, Illustrated in Song for the Sabbath School and Family*. In preparing that work, Phillips sent Fanny seventy-five quotations of a few lines each from Bunyan's *Pilgrim's Progress*. From those she selected forty that each became the basis for a separate hymn. After composing all forty songs in her mind, she dictated all of them on a single occasion to a secretary at Bradbury's office, to be forwarded to Phillips. Her forty hymns comprised the bulk of Phillips' hymnal that went on to gain a wide circulation.

---

6   Edith L. Blumhofer, *Her Heart Can See, The Life and Hymns of Fanny J. Crosby* (Grand Rapids: Eerdmans, 2005), provides extensive analysis of the themes of Fanny's hymns for children (pp. 185-95) and adults (pp. 251-80).

William Bradbury had battled tuberculosis for several years. He passed away early in January, 1868, at age fifty-one. Fanny related: 'To me the sad occasion was the more memorable because the first hymn that we wrote together ['Our Bright Home Above'] was sung during the service; but the lines of my own production brought comfort to my aching heart ...'.

During the course of her prolific career, Fanny would compose the lyrics for some nine thousand songs, the vast majority of those being hymns. Nearly two-thirds of those songs were written for Biglow and Main. Of the 5,959 poems she submitted to the New York firm, only about two thousand were actually published. Often when the publisher requested works on a certain subject, she would submit three or four possible pieces on that theme. Normally only one of that grouping would be selected for publication.

For two decades Fanny composed between one-third and one-half of the selections included in the various hymnals published by Biglow and Main. She contributed large numbers of hymns for the works produced by other publishers as well. Most of her poems appeared under the name of 'Miss Fanny J. Crosby'. But to make the massive volume of her contributions less obvious, she also employed an extensive array of pen names, initials and even symbols. The use of pseudonyms was a common practice by hymn writers in that day. But no other hymnist came anywhere near the whopping total of 204 different self-designations that Fanny employed.[7]

---

7 Ruffin, *Fanny Crosby*, p. 105. Blumhofer, *Her Heart Can See*, pp. 358-360 lists many of these.

FOUR

Some months before William Bradbury's death, Fanny first met William Howard Doane, another hymn writer from Cincinnati. The wealthy president and general manager of a highly successful manufacturing plant in Cincinnati, Doane was also a devout Christian and a talented musician. Ever since a heart attack nearly ended his life at age thirty in 1862, he had devoted more serious time and effort to writing and publishing collections of sacred hymns.

While in New York in 1867, he visited his friend Dr W. C. Van Meter, director of the Five Points Mission. Van Meter asked Doane to produce a hymn that could be used at the mission's upcoming sixth anniversary celebration. Various sets of lyrics were proposed to Doane but he did not think them well-suited to the occasion. Shortly thereafter he received a letter from Fanny. She had heard of his presence in New York and, at the urging of a friend, had sent him one of her recent poems. Her letter read: 'Mr Doane: I have never met you, but I feel impelled to send you this hymn. May God bless it. Fanny Crosby.' The poem, which began with the words 'More like Jesus would I be, Let my Saviour dwell with me', seemed a perfect fit for the mission's anniversary celebration.

Doane immediately composed music to accompany the poem and the next day played and sang the hymn for Van Meter at a neighboring church. The latter agreed to operate the manual pump that supplied air for the organ's bellows. But as Doane played and sang, Van Meter was so touched by the song that he burst into tears and stopped pumping. The hymn was 'a perfect success' at the anniversary service.

Due to a recent change of residence for Fanny, Doane had to conduct an all-day search before he succeeded in finding her at her new apartment. At the close of their visit he stated, 'I must pay you for the hymn that you sent and which I was more than glad to receive.' He placed what he supposed to be a two dollar bill in her hand. She was struck with the thought that she ought to ask him how much he had given her 'that there might be no mistake about it'. When it was discovered he had actually given her a twenty dollar bill she immediately declined to accept that amount. But he insisted she keep it by asserting, 'The Lord clearly sent that hymn, and this must mean that you are to have the twenty dollars for it.'

Over the course of the next forty-seven years Doane set more than one thousand of Fanny's hymns to music, including some of her most popular and influential songs: 'Jesus, Keep Me Near the Cross'; 'Rescue the Perishing'; 'To the Work! To the Work!'; 'Safe in the Arms of Jesus'; 'Pass Me Not, O Gentle Saviour'; 'Saviour, More Than Life to Me'; 'I Am Thine, O Lord'; 'Only a Step to Jesus'; 'Now Just a Word for Jesus'; 'When Jesus Comes to Reward His Servants'; 'Tis the Blessed Hour of Prayer'.[8]

Among Fanny's other best-known hymns, set to music by various other composers, were: 'All the Way My Saviour Leads Me'; 'Blessed Assurance'; 'Close to Thee'; 'Every Day and Hour'; 'Praise Him! Praise Him!'; 'To God Be the Glory'. (Interestingly, the latter song did not gain widespread popularity until it was commonly used in Billy Graham crusades in the mid-twentieth century.) Virtually all the songs destined to become her most

---

8   Blumhofer, *Her Heart Can See*, p. 219.

prominent works were composed in the first decade of her hymn writing career. Scores of others gained varying degrees of popularity for a time but not in the same abiding fashion.[9]

Not long after Doane first met Fanny he returned with a request that she write a poem using the words 'Pass me not, O gentle Savior'. She agreed to do so, but was not inspired with a particular idea or set of lyrics for several weeks. Then early in the spring of 1868, while speaking at a prison in Manhattan, she heard an inmate cry out piteously during the service, 'Good Lord! Do not pass me by!' Before retiring that evening she penned a poem with these opening stanzas:

> Pass me not, O gentle Saviour,
> Hear my humble cry,
> While on others Thou art smiling,
> Do not pass me by.
>
> Saviour, Saviour,
> Hear my humble cry,
> While on others Thou art calling,
> Do not pass me by.

The composition was sent to Doane who soon set it to music. A few days later the hymn was sung at the same prison where Fanny had returned to minister. The song made a deep impression on the prisoners, reportedly leading to the conversion of several of them.

A few weeks later Doane again stopped by her apartment with the declaration: 'I have exactly forty minutes before my train leaves for Cincinnati. Here is a melody. Can you write words for it?'

---

9   Ruffin, *Fanny Crosby*, pp. 114, 129.

'I will see what I can do,' Fanny replied. She later related: 'Then followed a space of twenty minutes during which I was wholly unconscious of all else except the work I was doing.' At the end of that time she recited the words to 'Safe in the Arms of Jesus' to Doane who quickly copied them down before dashing off to catch his train.

Probably more real life 'incidents' came to be known involving that hymn than any other song Fanny ever wrote. One of the most touching involved a pastor, Dr John Hall, who went to see the ailing daughter of one of his parishioners. When the girl's father came downstairs in tears the clergyman asked, 'My dear friend, what is the trouble? Has the little girl gone home?'

'No,' the father answered, 'but she has asked me to do something that I cannot do. Anything that wealth might buy she may have. But I cannot sing "Safe in the Arms of Jesus" for I never sang a note in my life.'

'Oh, I will go up and sing it for her,' the minister responded reassuringly. He did, and the child slipped into eternity just as he sang the hymn's last two lines:

Wait till I see the morning
Break on the golden shore.

In the summer of the following year, 1869, Doane gave Fanny the title 'Rescue the Perishing' as a suggested hymn subject. Not long thereafter she had the opportunity to address a large group of working men. As she did so the thought kept pressing on her mind that some mother's boy must be rescued that very night or perhaps not at all. So she invited any boy present who had wandered from his mother's teaching to meet her at the platform following the service.

Afterward a young man of eighteen approached her with a question and a confession: 'Did you mean me? I have promised my mother to meet her in heaven. But as I am now living, that will be impossible.' Fanny pointed him to the Savior, and they prayed together. When he arose, he declared with certainty, 'Now I can meet Mother in heaven for I have found her God.' Later that evening she wrote the words to the well-known hymn that begins:

> Rescue the perishing
> Care for the dying,
> Snatch them in pity from sin and the grave;
> Weep o'er the erring one,
> Lift up the fallen,
> Tell them of Jesus the mighty to save.

Doane published that hymn the next year. Many years later, in November 1903, while speaking at a Young Men's Christian Association (YMCA) gathering in Lynn, Massachusetts, Fanny related the incident that led her to write 'Rescue the Perishing'. Among the large number of men who shook hands with her after the meeting was one who seemed to be deeply moved. She was astonished when he said, 'Miss Crosby, I was the boy who told you more than thirty-five years ago that I had wandered from my mother's God. The evening that you spoke at the mission I sought and found peace, and I have tried to live a consistent Christian life ever since. If we never meet again on earth, we will meet up yonder.' He lifted her hand to his lips then, before she could recover from her surprise, slipped away into the crowd without even telling her his name.

The same year Fanny wrote 'Rescue the Perishing', she also contributed more than twenty hymns to a work entitled *Notes of Joy*, which was compiled by Phoebe Palmer Knapp. Fanny and Phoebe had met four or five years earlier. Phoebe was a wealthy woman who devoted much time, effort and money to assisting the poor and promoting social reform. Her husband was Joseph Fairchild Knapp, who later founded the Metropolitan Life Insurance Company. The Knapp Mansion was among the grandest in Brooklyn, and its music room contained one of the finest collections of musical instruments in the country. Fanny was a frequent guest in Phoebe's home and there met a number of prominent and influential individuals. Through four decades Phoebe proved to be a generous, devoted friend to Fanny. Fanny provided Phoebe with many poems which the latter set to music and published. The most famous hymn they collaborated in composing was 'Blessed Assurance', written in 1873.

By the early 1870s Fanny's hymns were beginning to gain popularity in the British Isles. At the same time the works of a prominent English hymnist, Frances Ridley Havergal, were starting to become well known in America. Miss Havergal came to greatly appreciate and admire Fanny's hymns but knew nothing about her other than her name. So in the spring of 1872 Frances wrote to William Sherwin, an American composer with whom she regularly corresponded. Sherwin had written the music for a number of Fanny's hymns.

Knowing that Fanny disliked being called 'the blind hymn writer', Sherwin described her to Frances by stating, 'She is a blind lady, whose heart can see splendidly in the sunshine of God's love.' Taken by this description, Miss Havergal employed it in a poem which she composed in Fanny's honor and sent to her. The poem began:

Sweet blind singer over the sea,
Tuneful and jubilant, how can it be,
That the songs of gladness, which float so far,
As if they fell from an evening star,
Are the notes of one who may never see
'Visible music' of flower and tree.

How can she sing in the dark like this?
What is her fountain of light and bliss?

Her heart can see, her heart can see![10]
Well may she sing so joyously!
For the King himself, in his tender grace,
Hath shown her the brightness of his face;

Dear blind sister over the sea!
An English heart goes forth to thee.
We are linked by a cable of faith and song,
Flashing bright sympathy swift along;
One in the East and one in the West,
Singing for him whom our souls love best,

Sister! What will our meeting be,
When our hearts shall sing and our eyes shall see?[11]

Fanny always considered this the greatest tribute ever paid her. Though the two poets never met in person, they corresponded regularly for the next seven years until Frances Havergal's untimely death from peritonitis at age forty-two.

Fanny was introduced to the world-famous evangelistic team, Dwight L. Moody and Ira D. Sankey, while they were in New York in 1876 for their second evangelistic campaign there. They had already used a number of

---

10   Edith Blumhofer used this descriptive line as the title for her biography *Her Heart Can See, The Life and Hymns of Fanny J. Crosby.*

11   Crosby, *An Autobiography*, p. 222.

Fanny's hymns, most notably 'Pass Me Not, O Gentle Saviour', with great effect in their crusades in both Britain and America. From that year on Sankey began to include many of her compositions in his subsequent editions of *Gospel Hymns and Sacred Songs*, which were published by Biglow and Main.

The summer of the following year Fanny attended the Methodist Episcopal Church camp meeting at Ocean Grove, New Jersey. There she met John Sweney, the song leader at Ocean Grove, and his good friend and colleague William Kirkpatrick. Sweney, a Presbyterian, and Kirkpatrick, a Methodist, both lived in Philadelphia where they were involved in various music ministries and collaborated in composing and publishing books of hymns. In succeeding decades Fanny would supply Sweney and Kirkpatrick with nearly a thousand poems for their hymnals.

She wrote so many hymns in her lifetime, in fact, that more than once Fanny forgot that she was the author of a song that she heard and was blessed by. Once, many years after first meeting Sankey, she attended a Bible conference where he led the congregation in singing 'Hide Me, O My Saviour, Hide Me'. She afterward revealed, 'I did not recognize this hymn as my own production, and therefore I may be pardoned for saying that I was much pleased with it.'

'Where did you get that piece?' she asked the song leader. Supposing she was merely joking, he did not respond to her question. In the afternoon service, however, the song was again used, so she was determined to find out who had written it. 'Mr Sankey,' she insisted, 'now you must tell me who is the author of "Hide Me, O My Saviour".'

'Really,' he replied good-naturedly, 'don't you recall who wrote that hymn? You ought to remember, for you are the guilty one.'

FIVE

The John Street Methodist Church, which Fanny attended regularly, was located near Manhattan's degraded Bowery district, notorious for its innumerable taverns, dance halls, burlesque shows, pornography shops and prostitutes. A handful of Christian missions sought to minister to alcoholics and other morally debauched individuals in that desperate setting. In 1881, at age sixty-one, Fanny became involved with the Bowery Mission. She frequently attended the evening meetings and often was asked to speak. One night, as part of her address, she said, 'If there is a man present who has gone just as far as he can go, he is the person with whom I want to shake hands.'

'The man for whom you are looking sits directly in front of the platform,' the mission superintendent whispered to her after she had concluded her remarks. Following the services she was introduced to that man.

'Do you not wish to come out and live a Christian life?' she asked him.

'Oh, what difference? I have no friends; nobody cares for me.'

'You are mistaken, for the Lord Jesus cares for you; and others care for you too. Unless I had a deep interest in your soul's welfare I certainly would not be here talking with you on this subject.' She continued to share several Scripture passages with him.

Finally he asked, 'If I come here to the meeting tomorrow evening and sign the pledge [of sobriety], will you come with me?'

'Yes, I will be here again; and although I do not discourage you from signing the pledge, it seems to me that the best pledge you can give is to yield yourself to God. Will you do it?'

The man returned for the service the next night. Fanny later related of him: 'before the close of the meeting we saw the new light in his eyes and felt the change in his voice'.

She once explained her guiding principle in seeking to influence this type of individual:

'I could give more than one instance where men have been reclaimed, after a long struggle and many attempts at reformation, because someone spoke a kind word to them even at what appeared to be the last moment. ... Never to chide the erring has always been my policy, for I firmly believe that harsh words only serve to harden hearts that might otherwise be softened into repentance.'

> Speak not harshly when reproving
> >   Those from duty's path who stray;
> If you would reclaim the erring,
> >   Kindness must each action sway.
> Speak not harshly to the wayward;
> >   Win their confidence, their love,
> They will feel how pure the motive
> >   That has led them to reprove.[12]

Fanny encouraged the ministry of other missions as well. Jeremiah ('Jerry') McAuley was likely Manhattan's best-known and most-colorful 'trophy of grace', having been dramatically converted from the depths of thievery, violence, drunkenness and destitution. He established

---

12   Ibid., p. 165.

the Water Street Mission and the Cremorne Mission, at both of which Fanny ministered. She was also involved in Sidney and Emma Whittemore's Door of Hope ministry to prostitutes and 'unprotected girls'.

Around the same time Fanny commenced mission work, she also became involved in ministry to railroad employees. One day while entering a trolley car she accidently stepped on the conductor's foot. Immediately she cried out, 'Oh, Conductor, I know that I have hurt you, but I did not intend to. Will you please forgive me?'

Appreciative of her considerateness, he replied, 'You didn't hurt me at all. And if you had, you made up for it by speaking a kind word.'

This simple incident drew Fanny's attention to these types of workers and their spiritual needs. Less than a month later she was invited to the home of her friend William Rock, President of the New York Surface Car Line. Rock was concerned about the spiritual welfare of his employees, and it was decided to start a one-hour Sunday morning service for the benefit of the conductors and drivers. He asked her to assist in conducting the services, a ministry opportunity she readily accepted.

The following year, she was invited by members of the Railroad Branch of the YMCA to visit their newly-established ministry center in Hoboken, New Jersey, just across the Hudson River from Manhattan. From the 1870s to the 1890s the YMCA started up more than one hundred such centers to minister to the spiritual needs of railroad workers while also providing them with food, lodging, recreation and first aid.[13]

---

13 Blumhofer, *Her Heart Can See*, p. 297.

Beginning in 1882, and continuing for more than thirty years, Fanny regularly ministered at YMCA railroad centers throughout the eastern United States. In her heart she adopted five or six hundred rail workers as 'my boys', and they, in turn, gave her 'a warm place in their affections'.

In 1883 or 1884 Fanny moved from lower Manhattan to its upper east side. There she started attending and, for the first time in her life, officially joined the membership of a church, the Cornell Memorial Methodist Episcopal Church. The church was named in honor of William Cornell, the benefactor of the congregation and of the university that also bears his name. Having been in existence less than twenty years when Fanny joined it in 1887, the vibrant church boasted a sanctuary seating 1,500 and a Sunday School with some 1,250 students.[14]

Modern biographers speculate that this may have been the general time period when Fanny and her husband, Alexander Van Alstyne, stopped living together. Exactly when and why they established separate residences is not known with certainty, but the available evidence indicates they lived apart from each other for a number of years before his death in 1902. However, they never sought a legal separation or divorce. They visited each other occasionally, and apparently maintained an amicable relationship.

Very little is known about the precise nature of their marriage relationship. They shared a strong interest in music and, for a number of years, collaborated in writing not a few hymns together. Various suggestions have been

---

14 Blumhofer, *Her Heart Can See*, p. 115.

made as to why they eventually separated: interpersonal conflicts; a lessening of physical passion with advancing age; drifting apart due to differing interests and circles of friends. All of these and other factors are possible explanations but no hard evidence exists to verify any of them with certainty. While the fact that they eventually chose to lead separate lives certainly indicates a breakdown in their relationship, the exact causes are simply not known. The matter remains an impenetrable, veiled mystery.

Fanny recorded of Van Alstyne and her relationship with him:

> Our tastes were congenial and he composed the music to several of my hymns besides constantly aiding me with kind criticism and advice. ... He was a firm, trustful Christian and a man whose kindly deeds and cheering words will not be forgotten by his many friends. We were happy together many years.[15]

She also once revealed, 'He had his faults – and so have I mine, but notwithstanding these, we loved each other to the last.'[16]

Fanny's mother, Mercy, died on September 2, 1890, at the age of ninety-one. All three of Mercy's daughters were with her at her passing. Fanny, who for many years had written a poem for her mother on her birthday, composed a memorial piece to honor her esteemed departed loved one.

Early the next year Fanny wrote what would become one of her best known hymns, 'My Saviour First of All'. More than a decade later words from that song were

---

15 *Fanny J. Crosby, An Autobiography* (Grand Rapids: Baker, 1995), p. 130.

16 Blumhofer, *Her Heart Can See*, p. 314.

mightily used of the Lord to safeguard a number of people from spiritual deception. A man suddenly appeared in London, claiming to be the Messiah. Charismatic and persuasive, he drew large crowds for many weeks. But one night as he was speaking in a public square, a small Salvation Army band passed by singing 'My Saviour First of All' with its closing lines, 'I shall know Him, I shall know Him, By the print of the nails in His hand'.

The sizeable crowd joined in singing that chorus. Presently someone pointed at the self-proclaimed Messiah and challenged, 'Look at his hands and see if the print of the nails is there.' When no such marks were revealed, the man promptly lost his following.

About a year after producing that song, Fanny wrote what would prove to be her last widely-known hymn, 'Saved by Grace'. She submitted the poem to Biglow and Main, and for over two years it lay, seemingly forgotten, in the firm's vault. Then during the summer of 1894, as she had for several consecutive years, she attended the summer Bible conference that was held at Dwight Moody's hometown of Northfield, Massachusetts. Moody was ministering in England that summer so the Northfield meetings were under the capable direction of prominent Baptist pastor Dr Adoniram Jordan Gordon.

One evening Ira Sankey approached Fanny and asked, 'Will you say something? There is a request from the audience that you speak.'

'Oh, Mr Sankey,' she demurred, 'I cannot speak before such an array of talent.'

Another evangelical luminary, Dr A. T. Pierson, sought to reassure her by stating, 'Yes, you can. There is no one here of whom you need be afraid.'

She relented and, as part of her remarks that evening, recited for the first time publicly the words to 'Saved by Grace':

Some day my earthly house will fall,
I cannot tell how soon 'twill be,
But this I know, my All in All
Has now a place in heaven for me.

Some day the silver cord will break
And I no more as now shall sing,
But, oh, the joy when I awake
Within the Palace of the King.

Some day, when sets the golden sun
Beneath the rosy-tinted west,
My blessed Lord shall say, 'Well done!'
And I shall enter into rest.

Some day – till then I'll watch and wait,
My lamp well-trimmed and burning bright,
That when my Saviour ope's the gate
My soul to Him may speed its flight.[17]

Sankey, along with many in the audience, were deeply moved by the recitation. 'Where have you kept that piece?' he inquired after she returned to her seat.

'I've kept it stored away for an emergency,' she replied.

A reporter at the meeting that night had copied down the poem as she recited it. A few weeks later it appeared in a British religious paper. Sankey then asked a mutual friend of Fanny and his, George C. Stebbins, to compose the music for the hymn which subsequently gained worldwide fame.

---

17 At that time the poem was entitled simply 'Some Day'. Fanny later added a chorus with the words that gave the hymn its well-known title: 'And I shall see Him face to face, And tell the story – Saved by Grace.'

In 1896, at age seventy-six, Fanny moved to Brooklyn where she rented a lodging room in a rather poor part of town. Both the Sankeys and the Stebbinses lived in nicer neighborhoods not far away and regularly checked in on her. Around that time several of her acquaintances began to manifest their concern for her financial welfare. One of her longtime musical collaborators, Dr Robert Lowry (who had written the music for her famous hymn 'All the Way My Savior Leads Me'), encouraged the publication of a fourth collection of her poems. The volume, entitled *Bells at Evening*, included a biographical sketch of her life written by Lowry, select poems from her three earlier volumes, later secular poems and what she considered to be her best hymns. The publisher, Biglow and Main, sold the work at fifty cents per copy and saw to it that all the profit went to her. The volume sold well, and several editions were printed.

Phoebe Knapp approached Will Carleton, author of numerous works of popular sentimental poetry and editor of the magazine *Every Where*, about publishing the story of Fanny's life in serial form in his periodical. Both Carleton and Fanny agreed to the proposal, and a series of articles resulted. She was paid ten dollars for each article.

These well-intentioned friends may have failed to realize fully that Fanny's rather impoverished financial condition was due in large part to her own generosity and outlook on money. She never expected to be paid more than the minimal going rate for the many hymns she produced for various publishers. She frequently refused honorariums for her numerous speaking engagements. Often she gave all the money in her possession to help some needy individual, then asked the Lord to provide what she needed for her own food, rent and other basic necessities of life. She repeatedly cited Proverbs 3:9-10 as the guiding principles for her financial decisions and lifestyle.

One day someone said to her, 'If I had wealth I would be able to do just what I wish to do; and I would be able to make an appearance in the world.'

'Take the world but give me Jesus,' she instantly replied. That remark led her to write one of her most famous hymns which bore those words as its title.

SIX

In the spring of 1900, not long after her eightieth birthday, Fanny fell gravely ill with bronchial pneumonia. As she recovered, at the insistence of her widowed half-sisters, Julia (Jule) Athington and Caroline (Carrie) Rider, Fanny finally agreed to leave Brooklyn to live in Bridgeport. Ira Sankey paid the rent each month for Fanny and Carrie to live in a spacious, five-room apartment in a fine brick home in a nice section of town. In addition he sent Carrie a monthly sum to help provide for Fanny's other living expenses.

Carrie selflessly served as Fanny's personal secretary. She read Fanny her often-voluminous daily mail and sent back her dictated replies. Each morning she also wrote down any poem or hymn that 'Sister Fan' had mentally composed during the night. Eventually the services of a professional secretary, Eva Cleaveland, were procured to assist with those considerable responsibilities.

When in Bridgeport, Fanny normally worshiped with Jule at First Methodist Church. She officially transferred her membership to that congregation in 1904. Shortly after her move to Bridgeport she became involved in the King's Daughters, a charity affiliated with the Methodist Church that helped run a hospital and provided food, clothing and coal for the poor. She also became active in Bridgeport's Christian Union, the town's rescue mission, where she was a regular speaker.

Fanny continued to travel a great deal and to carry out an extensive public speaking ministry for several years after settling in Bridgeport. Numerous times per year she ventured to various states where she addressed highly-appreciative audiences at Bible conferences, churches, Sunday Schools, missions, YMCAs, Christian Endeavor youth conventions, Chautauqua gatherings, patriotic rallies and other types of meetings. She regularly spoke to audiences numbering in the hundreds or even thousands.

By that time she had become a national celebrity in Christian circles and was commonly known as 'Aunt Fanny'. People were drawn and responded warmly to her contagious cheerfulness, her concern for others and her encouraging messages. Everywhere she went people were amazed at her youthful vitality. Her face and bent form betrayed her advanced age; she commonly dressed in styles that were decades out of date. But her voice, mind and movements were all so vigorous that many reported she seemed twenty years younger than she actually was.

Once during that time, while ministering in Buffalo, New York, a baritone soloist named Jacobs was singing Fanny's hymn 'Saved by Grace' before she was to speak. Sitting behind him on the platform, she suddenly rose and began to sing with him. He immediately lowered his powerful voice so the audience could better hear hers. Her voice at first seemed 'quavering and faltering' but by the time they reached the chorus her soprano tones rang out clear and strong. The audience sat spellbound at the impromptu duet and wept at its pathos and beauty.

After battling cancer for over a year, Alexander Van Alstyne died on July 18, 1902. When Fanny received the news she at first considered having his body interred in Bridgeport so she could eventually be buried beside him. In the end, however, she had him buried in Olivet Cemetery in Maspeth, Queens, near where they had first lived together as newlyweds. When she was taken to his gravesite the following spring, she reportedly fell, weeping, on the grave. She repeatedly declared that she was 'constantly lamenting his temporary loss'.

In honor of Fanny's eighty-fifth birthday in March of 1905, friends and admirers encouraged churches to honor her by designating Sunday, March 26 (two days after her birthday), as Fanny Crosby Day. The widely read *Christian Herald* went so far as to urge pastors and priests of all denominations to use only her hymns in their services that day and to highlight her life as a commendable example of Christian witness. In addition, love offerings to be given in her support were promoted.

Many churches – not only in America and Britain but also in such unlikely countries as Tasmania and India – participated in the special day. Letters of congratulation were received from many locations and individuals, including a special tribute from former President Grover Cleveland, her one-time amanuensis at the New York Institution for the Blind. The love offerings that poured in from the participating churches amounted to several thousand dollars. Fanny was overwhelmed and pleased with all this. She considered it a crowning blessing on her long, full life. She also wanted to make certain that God rather than she received the glory.

That same year Fanny finished compiling her autobiography, *Memories of Eighty Years*. Having been encouraged by friends to produce such a volume, she had initially given attention to the project two years earlier. But upon hearing of her intention, Will Carleton informed her of his desire to reproduce in book form the magazine articles he had earlier written about her. He offered her the twenty-five percent royalty that he normally received from his publisher for his own works of poetry. She agreed, and he subsequently published the articles in a volume entitled *Fanny Crosby's Life Story*.

At the urging of Phoebe Knapp, Carleton included a 'publisher's advertisement' in the book stating that the work was being sold so that Fanny might 'be enabled to have a house of her own, in which to pass the remainder of her days'. Fanny, who had no idea that such an appeal would be included in the book, was displeased by it. When Carleton ended up reducing the royalty he paid her to ten percent, others loyal to Fanny accused him of seeking to profit himself at her expense. Fanny, ever willing to think well of her friends, did not harbor any hard feelings toward Carleton or Mrs Knapp over how this affair unfolded, but assumed they had only tried to act in her best interest.

She and others did think that Carleton's book was very incomplete as it focused mainly on the early years of her life and gave little attention to her career as a hymn writer. Consequently, she continued to work on her autobiographical *Memories of Eighty Years*, which was published in 1906.

In June of the following year, Carrie died of intestinal cancer at age sixty-three. During Carrie's illness the two sisters had moved into the nearby home of their niece, Florence Booth, the married daughter of Fanny's stepbrother William Morris. By then Fanny's output of hymns had decreased from two hundred per year to one a week. But she still traveled and spoke quite extensively, carried on a sizeable correspondence and received numerous guests when home in Bridgeport. In the spring of 1908, while carrying out other ministry engagements, she visited Phoebe Knapp in New York, Ira Sankey in Brooklyn, and Grover Cleveland in Princeton. Before the summer ended, all three of those cherished, longtime friends had died.

Fanny celebrated her ninetieth birthday in Hackettstown, New Jersey, with the congregation of Samuel Trevena Jackson, a young clergyman who took a particular interest in her during the closing years of her life. He recorded many of her personal recollections and perspectives on various events and topics. These were published shortly after her death in a small volume entitled *Fanny Crosby's Story of Ninety-four Years, Retold by S. Trevena Jackson.*

In the spring of 1911 she traveled to New York City to be one of the featured speakers at the 'Tent, Open-Air, and Shop Campaign' of the Methodist Episcopal Church's Evangelistic Campaign. Some five thousand people gathered at Carnegie Hall. Led by a large choir, the congregation sang a number of her hymns. As she was led on to the platform, the choir sang one of her more recent popular songs, 'We're Traveling On'.

She returned to New York one final time that October. On that occasion Fanny visited with Helen Keller, whom she had first met a decade earlier, and ministered once more at the Bowery Mission. Shortly after that trip she contracted pneumonia and was brought very low. Everyone, herself included, thought her life on earth was about to end, but to the amazement of all she recovered fully.

Curiously, and for no apparent reason, during the final years of her life Fanny seldom attended church except when asked to speak. Her ninety-third birthday fell on Easter. That evening, for the first time in several months, she attended Bridgeport's First Methodist Church and addressed the congregation. The Sunday before her next birthday she spoke for the final time at that same church. She addressed a packed auditorium on the topic of the efficacy of prayer. A newspaper reporter described her as 'feeble in body, yet strong in mind ... buoyant in spirit, with a trust and faith in God as firm as the everlasting hills'.

In August of that year, 1914, Fanny suffered a mild heart attack. She realized her earthly life would not likely continue many months longer, and she joyously welcomed her approaching departure. On February 11, 1915, about six weeks before her ninety-fifth birthday, she uncharacteristically chose to stay in her bed and not to eat throughout the day. At nine o'clock that evening she dictated a letter to a neighbor family that had recently lost a young child, assuring them that 'your precious Ruth is "Safe in the Arms of Jesus"'. She then had her personal secretary, Eva Cleaveland, record what proved to be her final poem:

In the morn of Zion's glory,
When the clouds have rolled away,
And my hope has dropped its anchor

In the vale of perfect day,
When with all the pure and holy
I shall strike my harp anew,
With a power no arm can sever,
Love will hold me fast and true.

About three thirty the next morning, February 12, Florence heard Fanny walking down the hall and got out of bed to assist her. The elderly woman fainted into her arms and had to be carried back to her bed. Two doctors were immediately summoned. But before they arrived Fanny smiled, turned her face heavenward and peacefully slipped into eternity. Florence afterward commented, 'What a meeting she must have had with all gone before when – as she said so many times – the first her eyes would behold would be her Jesus.'

Fanny's funeral, held four days later at the First Methodist Church, was reportedly the largest ever held in Bridgeport, surpassing even P. T. Barnum's. People lined up for blocks to pass by the bier. Quite habitually during her life Fanny had carried a small silk American flag, and one now rested in her right hand. Violets, her favorite flower, filled the auditorium. Her favorite hymn – Frederick Faber's 'Faith of Our Fathers' – was sung along with two of her own signature hymns, 'Safe in the Arms of Jesus' and 'Saved by Grace'. Poetic tributes were read. In presenting the eulogy, the church's pastor, Dr George Brown, stated, 'You have come to pay tribute and to crown a friend. There must have been a royal welcome when this queen of sacred song burst the bonds of death and passed into the glories of heaven.'

Her body was buried in the Morris family plot at Bridgeport's Mountain Grove Cemetery. As she wished, only a small, simple gravestone marked her resting place. Employing an allusion to the woman in Mark 14:8 who devoted her precious perfume to honor Christ Jesus, the stone read: 'Aunt Fanny, "She hath done what she could"'.

3

Catherine Booth

ONE

Nine-year-old Catherine Mumford skipped along happily, pushing her hoop with a stick down one of the streets of Boston, Lincolnshire, England. Rounding a corner, she was confronted with a raucous crowd coming toward her. The crowd shouted and jeered at a young man, obviously drunk, who was being dragged along by a policeman.

Catherine had often heard her father, a zealous proponent of total abstinence, speak publicly on the evils of drunkenness. A tenderhearted child, she instinctively felt pity for this individual obviously under the destructive influence of alcohol. Though normally shy, she now boldly stepped forward, took the drunkard's hand and smiled up at him. That simple act of compassion and support had a calming effect on the man. Ignoring the continued ridicule of the crowd, Catherine bravely walked alongside the drunk, helping to steady him as he was led off to the town jail.

This was an early manifestation of the compassion and courage that Catherine would exhibit throughout her life in coming to the aid of hurting, needy people. Those commendable qualities would play a significant role in the ministry to down-and-out individuals that she and her future husband, William Booth, would come to have in the formation of the Salvation Army.

Catherine was born to John and Sarah (Milward) Mumford on January 17, 1829. The Mumfords lived at that time in Ashbourne, Derbyshire, in central England. John was a carriage builder by trade as well as an itinerant Methodist lay preacher. Sarah had been raised in the Church of England but, as a young woman, came to personal faith in Christ through the ministry of the local Methodist Church, a congregation she then joined.

In addition to their daughter Catherine, whom they normally called Kate, the Mumfords had four sons. But only one of their sons, John, survived past infancy. Little is known of him except that he emigrated to America at age sixteen.

The Mumfords followed a strict code of conduct, common to Methodists of that day, which was intended to separate them from activities and fashions that were considered worldly. Card playing, dancing and attending the theatre were eschewed while plainness of dress and hairstyle were adhered to. Sarah was a strong-willed woman with definite convictions on many subjects. Catherine came to share in her mother's strong personality and convictions.

Mrs Mumford educated her children at home, fearing they might be contaminated through associations with 'badly brought up children' or by deceptive teachings in the public school setting. Various religious books were read but the primary reading text was the Bible. Before she was twelve years old Catherine had read through the entire Bible eight times. The reading of novels and, interestingly, the study of French were strictly avoided for fear of the corrupting influence they might have on the children.

In 1834 the Mumfords moved to Boston, near The Wash, a prominent estuary on England's east coast. By that time Catherine's father, a melancholy man, had begun to manifest a degree of diffidence toward spiritual matters. He no longer served as a lay preacher but was still a strong supporter of the temperance movement.

The Mumfords attended the Wesleyan chapel in Boston. An acquaintance there persuaded Sarah that the teachers at a particular school shared her convictions about educating children in a religious environment where serious study and strict discipline were promoted. Consequently, from 1841 to 1843 Catherine was permitted to attend that school. There she studied history, geography, English composition and mathematics.

Unfortunately, that opportunity abruptly ended when she developed a spinal problem and was bedridden for a few months. Catherine was always considered a child of delicate constitution. She and her mother were constantly concerned about various aspects of her health. That seemingly excessive preoccupation with health problems characterized Catherine the rest of her life.

Her somewhat isolated childhood could not help but be rather lonely. She developed a special attachment to the family dog, a retriever named Waterford. According to her they were 'inseparable companions'. One day she visited her father at his place of business, leaving Waterford outside. As she entered the building she stumbled and cried out. The protective dog, seeking to come to her aid, crashed through the large plate glass window. John Mumford was so outraged at the damage the dog had caused that he immediately had the creature destroyed. Catherine was heartbroken and inconsolable.

Throughout her life she had a special sensitivity about the treatment of animals. She suffered physically and emotionally when she saw animals being mistreated and often intervened personally to prevent a horse, donkey or dog from being beaten or otherwise treated harshly. Her awareness of animal slaughter practices later led her and her husband, as well as their children, to become strict vegetarians.

When Catherine was fifteen, the Mumfords moved to London and settled in the neighborhood of Brixton. Initially only her mother joined Brixton's Wesleyan Methodist Church though Catherine habitually attended worship services there. She also participated in the weekly Methodist class meeting designed to nurture the spiritual growth and commitment of individuals through small group edification and accountability.

Catherine herself was going through 'a great controversy of soul' at that time. While she lived an outwardly blameless life and was zealous for the Gospel, she still struggled with sins, including an angry temper occasionally. She was full of self-doubts and had no assurance that she was definitely a child of God. 'It seemed to me,' she afterward reflected, 'unreasonable to suppose that I could be saved and yet not know it.'

That season of struggle continued past Catherine's sixteenth birthday. Then one morning her eyes fell on words from a Charles Wesley hymn with which she was very familiar: 'My God, I am Thine, What a comfort

Divine, What a blessing to know that my Jesus is mine!'
She later testified of the immediate and ongoing impact
of those lines:

> Scores of times I had read and sung these words, but now they
> came home to my inmost soul with a force and illumination
> they had never before possessed. It was as impossible for me
> to doubt as it had been before for me to exercize faith. ...
> I no longer hoped that I was saved, I was certain of it. The
> assurances of my salvation seemed to flood and fill my soul.
> I jumped out of bed, and without waiting to dress, ran into my
> mother's room and told her what had happened. ... For the
> next six months I was so happy that I felt as if I was walking
> on air. I used to tremble, and even long to die, lest I should
> backslide, or lose the consciousness of God's smile or favor.[1]

Shortly after that spiritual breakthrough Catherine joined
the Wesleyan Church in Brixton. A few months later, in
the fall of 1846, she developed symptoms of tuberculosis.
For half a year she was confined to her bedroom but
gradually recovered.

Her father had proven unstable in his commitments
and habits throughout her childhood years. He often was
out of work and penniless. In time he forsook his total
abstinence conviction and eventually became an alcoholic.
He also renounced religion outright. Catherine revealed
the remarkable depth of her loving concern for him in
a diary entry she recorded when eighteen years of age:

> I sometimes get into an agony of feeling while praying for my
> dear father. O my Lord, answer prayer and bring him back
> to Thyself! Never let that tongue, which once delighted in
> praising Thee and in showing others Thy willingness to save,

---

1   Roger J. Green, *Catherine Booth, A Biography of the Cofounder of The
    Salvation Army* (Grand Rapids: Baker, 1996), p. 31.

be engaged in uttering the lamentations of the lost. O awful thought! Lord have mercy! Save, oh save him in any way Thou seest best, though it be ever so painful. If by removing me Thou canst do this, cut short Thy work and take me home.[2]

Great tensions were swirling in England's Wesleyan Methodist denomination around that same time. Reform-minded individuals desired to see the denomination become more democratic in its approach to governance, as had already occurred among American Methodists. The reformers were also open to the use of new and controversial methods to promote revival which were being employed and popularized by American evangelists Charles Grandison Finney and James Caughey.

Catherine found herself in sympathy with the Methodist reformers and attended several of their meetings. She did that despite being warned by her local church not to show open support for the reformers. As a result, her membership in the local class meeting eventually was not renewed when it came up for the usual quarterly approval. By that means she was practically expelled from the Wesleyan Methodist Church.

Subsequently, Catherine and her mother both joined the reformers who held services in a hall near their home. From 1852 to 1855 she taught a Sunday school class of fifteen girls who ranged in age from twelve to nineteen. She was deeply concerned about the spiritual well-being of each of her pupils and structured the class along the lines of the Methodist class meeting. It was during this period that she met the man with whom her life and ministry endeavors were to become permanently joined.

---

2   Ibid., p. 21.

TWO

William Booth was born in Nottingham on April 10, 1829. His parents, Samuel and Mary (Moss) Booth, were Anglicans, so William grew up attending Nottingham's St Mary's Church until he was a teen. His mother was a saintly woman while his father was a nominal Christian. Samuel Booth's ventures as a nail manufacturer and in the building trade proved unsuccessful, and throughout William's boyhood the family was desperately poor. At age thirteen, just a few months before his father's death, he was apprenticed as a pawnbroker's assistant.

An elderly neighbor couple had earlier taken William to the Broad Street Wesleyan Methodist Chapel, and following his father's passing he started attending that church regularly. There, at age fifteen, he came to personal faith in Christ as his Savior. Two years later he joined a zealous group of Methodist street preachers in Nottingham and quickly became their leader.

In 1849 he moved to London where he took a job in a pawnbroker's shop in order to continue supporting his mother and sisters back home. But proclaiming the Gospel continued to be his primary interest, and he apparently began preaching at various Wesleyan chapels in London. When he spoke at the Walworth Road Wesleyan Chapel he greatly impressed a wealthy boot and shoe manufacturer named Edward Rabbits. The successful businessman, a friend of Catherine Mumford's family, was himself a lay preacher with sympathies for the reformers. He was impressed with Booth's fervent evangelistic preaching and in June of 1851 persuaded him to work among the reformers.

Consequently, one of the reformers' chapels where Booth spoke a few months later was Binfield House, located on Binfield Road, Clapham. This was the church to which Catherine belonged and where she taught a girls' Sunday School class. She heard Booth preach that day, was favorably impressed with his sermon and indicated so to Rabbits. Two weeks later she and Booth were introduced to each other at an afternoon tea that Rabbits hosted in his home for some of the area reformers. In the months that followed their paths occasionally crossed at various gatherings.

Booth's twenty-third birthday the next April fell on Good Friday and proved memorable for a pair of reasons. Rabbits had encouraged him to pursue his dream of becoming a full-time minister and pledged to support him financially for the first three months of his ministry. He was thus enabled to leave the pawnbroker shop for good on his birthday.

According to Booth that was also the day 'I fell over head and ears in love with the precious woman who afterward became my wife'. That evening, following a 'chance' encounter with and invitation from Rabbits, he attended a reformers' meeting in a schoolroom on Cowper Street. Catherine was also there, though in somewhat poor health. The young preacher offered to drive her to her home. She was impressed with his concern for her and with how much they had in common:

> I had been introduced to him as being in delicate health, and he took the situation in at a glance. His thought for me, although such a stranger, appeared most remarkable. The conveyance shook me; he regretted it. The talking exhausted me; he saw and forbade it. And then we struck in at once in

such wonderful harmony of view and aim and feeling on varied matters that passed rapidly before us. It seemed as though we had intimately known and loved each other for years, and suddenly, after some temporary absence, had been brought together again, and before we reached my home we both suspected, nay, we felt as though we had been made for each other, and that henceforth the current of our lives must flow together.[3]

The couple remained so sure of this that a little over a month later they became engaged.

They were perplexed, however, over exactly where their future path of service was to take them. Due to autocratic tendencies, jealousies and divisiveness Booth was seeing among Methodist reformers, he was disinclined to continue ministering among them. Around that time, Catherine, for reasons that are not clear, began attending a Congregational church in Stockwell. They considered training and ministering among Congregational churches but, for theological reasons, decided against that. However, Catherine continued to attend the Stockwell New Chapel until her marriage to Booth three years later.

That November 1852, Booth accepted the call to be the minister of the rural Spalding circuit in Lincolnshire. Spalding was a market town located about twelve miles southwest of The Wash on England's east coast. Wesleyan reformers were in the majority at Spalding but apparently Booth believed he could still have a fruitful ministry in that more isolated setting. He was warmly received there and for the next fourteen months ministered effectively in Spalding and other small towns in the district.

3   Ibid., p. 44.

Catherine and William exchanged many letters during that time. As would be the case throughout their years of courtship and marriage, she readily gave him her very definite advice, often unsolicited, on all variety of subjects. During Booth's Spalding ministry she advised him on what to study and read as well as how to preach and conduct his meetings. She gave particular emphasis to her concerns that he avoid carnal ambition in his ministry endeavors, that he cultivate sufficient time for study and that he maintain clear teaching on the temperance issue.

'As quite a young girl', according to Catherine, she had made up a list of four qualifications which she considered 'indispensable' for the man she would marry. First, he must be a sincere, truly-converted Christian (as opposed to a nominal one, a mere church member) whose religious views coincided with hers. Secondly, he must possess basic common sense rather than being a fool. 'The third essential consisted of oneness of views and tastes, any idea of lordship or ownership being lost in love.' Finally, she was resolved never to marry a man 'who was not a total abstainer, and this from conviction, and not merely to gratify me'.

Later in life Catherine also disclosed four other rules she considered essential for maintaining a happy, healthy married relationship. She determined never to keep any secrets from her husband 'in anything that affected our mutual relationship or the interests of the family'. She also never kept a separate, secret purse apart from her husband's finances. Her third and fourth principles had to do with how differences of opinion were handled:

In matters where there was any difference of opinion, I would show my husband my views and the reasons on which they were based, and try to convince in favour of my way of looking at the subject. This generally resulted either in his being converted to my views or in my being converted to his, either result securing unity of thought and action. My fourth rule was, in cases of difference of opinion, never to argue in the presence of the children. I thought it better even to submit at the time to what I might consider to be mistaken judgment, than to have a controversy before them. But of course when such occasion arose I took the first opportunity for arguing the matter out. My subsequent experience has abundantly proved to me the wisdom of this course.[4]

William Booth's continued dissatisfaction with the Reform Methodists led him early in 1854 to affiliate instead with New Connexion Methodism. That branch of Methodism offered Wesleyan theology, a pronounced emphasis on evangelism and a governing structure that included representation from laity and clergymen alike. In February he returned to London and immediately began preaching at the Brunswick Street Chapel, where he was used of God to lead many to Christ.

That same year Catherine wrote an article for the *Methodist New Connexion Magazine* on 'the best means for retaining new converts'. It was the first of hundreds of articles and several books she would write during her lifetime. This particular article ended with a strong appeal for both men and women to be actively used in the service of Christ's kingdom. That would prove to be a primary point of emphasis for Catherine throughout her ministry career.

---

4   Ibid., p. 58.

She had very definite views about the complete equality of women with men. She believed that as common prejudices against women were removed and as they were given equal opportunities to men, their equality would become readily apparent and be fully realized. Because of that equality she thought women should be allowed and encouraged to minister in the same ways that men did, including in public preaching and teaching. However, at this point in her life she had not yet come to the point where she felt led of the Lord to engage in such public teaching ministries herself.

In April 1855, Catherine shared her perspectives on these matters in a letter to William. As she was obviously very eager for him to agree with her, his reply doubtless came as quite a disappointment to her. While he agreed that women were equal to men in many ways, and even their superiors in some regards, he did not think woman 'capable of becoming man's equal in intellectual attainments or prowess'. In that regard he very much reflected the common perspective of his era and society. He indicated mixed perspectives with regard to women preaching:

> I would not stop a woman preaching on any account. I would not encourage one to begin. You should preach if you felt moved thereto: felt equal to the task. I would not stay *you* if I had power to do so. Altho', *I should not like it.* ... I am for the world's *salvation*; I will quarrel with no means that promises help.[5]

Booth afterward called this the 'first little lovers' quarrel, and the only serious lovers' quarrel we ever had'. In time

---

he came to share Catherine's perspectives concerning the equality of men and women. He would also become an enthusiastic supporter and proponent of lady preachers, among whom his future wife became chief in his own generation.

Booth's obvious evangelistic gifts continued to manifest themselves, and he received invitations to preach and conduct revival meetings in Bristol, Guernsey, Longton and Hanley. He often preached to large congregations, some numbering upwards to two thousand, and saw many people won to Christ. At the Annual Conference of New Connexion Methodism held in May 1855, he was appointed as a traveling evangelist for the denomination, allowing him to devote himself entirely to the ministry for which he was particularly gifted.

On June 16 of that year William and Catherine were married in a small, private wedding ceremony at Stockwell's Congregational New Chapel, her home church for the past three years. Following a one-week honeymoon at Ryde on the Isle of Wight, they sailed directly to Guernsey where William had earlier ministered and now did so again. Thus they began thirty-five years of shared ministry as husband and wife.

THREE

Following revival meetings at Guernsey and Jersey, islands in the English Channel off the coast of Normandy, the Booths returned to London where they stayed with Catherine's parents. Due to her chronically precarious health she was not always able to travel with William, though she sought to do so whenever she was well enough.

She became pregnant immediately after their marriage and likely was feeling the early effects of that. Throughout the years that followed she devoted a great deal of attention to seeking to remedy her own ailments and those of her husband and children using homeopathy, hydropathy and vegetarianism.

After William ministered alone in York, Catherine joined him for campaigns in Hull, Sheffield, Dewsbury and Leeds. Over eight hundred conversions were recorded in the latter location. February and March of 1856 found them in Halifax where more than six hundred professed faith in Christ. Their first child, William Bramwell, was born there on March 8.

The Booths then ministered in Macclesfield, Yarmouth and Sheffield. In Sheffield twelve hundred people attended a farewell tea in their honor, and the evangelist was presented with a portrait of himself as a token of the townspeople's appreciation. During the next campaign in Birmingham, evangelistic street meetings were successfully employed. Booth had personal misgivings about how well his ministry would be received when he ventured to Nottingham, his birthplace, the following month. While those meetings were considered a success, they were spoiled somewhat by P. J. Wright, the superintending minister of Nottingham. Though he had consented to the invitation that was extended to Booth, he opposed the evangelist and his revival work.

Catherine returned with her son to the Mumfords in London while her husband continued on to Chester. She rejoined him for campaigns in Bristol and a pair of towns in Cornwall, a bastion of Methodism from the time of the eighteenth century Wesleyan revivals. Even in that Methodist stronghold, dramatic results attended Booth's ministry efforts. Large numbers of people made public commitments, either of initial conversion or of subsequent rededication of their lives to the Lord. The Booths found they needed to be the voice of moderation in that setting by encouraging people not to be carried away with excessive emotionalism or to put too much stock in purported supernatural dreams and visions.

Inevitably, jealousies began to surface over Booth's success and popularity in the Methodist New Connexion. At its 1857 Annual Conference, by a vote of forty-four to forty, the delegates removed Booth from his position as an evangelist and directed him to serve as the resident minister of single preaching circuit. P. J. Wright of Nottingham took the lead in calling for this change. Booth was given three reasons for the decision: some thought the travel expenses of an itinerant evangelist excessive; others believed he, as a young man (he was then twenty-eight years old), was having too much influence in the denomination; still others thought his fitness for ministerial ordination in the Connexion could only be evaluated by his ability to supervise a circuit as a regular circuit preacher.

Booth peacefully submitted to their decision as the Lord's will. Catherine bristled at the jealousies she perceived were motivating some ministers and at the injustices she felt were being carried out against her husband. He was appointed to the Halifax circuit, with their living quarters being in Brighouse, about twenty-five miles northeast of Manchester. Brighouse was reputed to be 'one of the most obscure and least successful circuits'. There Catherine gave birth to her second son, Ballington, on July 28.

The Brighouse work proved unexceptional and held many disappointments for the capable, young ministry couple. One significant ministry development that came about during that otherwise discouraging year, however, was that Catherine had some initial public teaching opportunities. In addition to teaching a girls' Sunday School class, she started leading a class meeting for female members of the chapel. She also delivered a pair of temperance addresses to the Brighouse Chapel's Junior Band of Hope. Of these latter two opportunities, she revealed in letters to her parents:

> If I get on well and find that I really possess any ability for public speaking, I don't intend to finish with juveniles. … When we were in Cornwall I went to hear a very popular female lecturer, and felt very much *encouraged* to try my hand. If I could do so, I should be able to fit in with William's efforts on his evangelistic tours nicely. I only wish I had begun years ago.

> I addressed the band of hope on Monday evening and got on far better than I expected. I felt quite at home on the *Platform* – far more so than I do in the *Kitchen!*[6]

At the Annual Conference the following year, 1858, William Booth was ordained into the ministry of the Methodist New Connexion. Many circuits petitioned to have him serve them. In the end the conference assigned him to minister at Gateshead, a city of fifty thousand located just across the Tyne from Newcastle in northern England. The Bethesda Chapel at Gateshead held 1,250 people.

Shortly after their arrival at Gateshead, Catherine agreed to lead another class meeting so long as she could

---

6   Ibid., p. 134.

do so in her home. The chapel was over half a mile from their home, and she was then carrying her third child. That baby, a daughter who was named Catherine, was born on September 18.

Revival services were held at Bethesda a few weeks later. Notices of the special meetings were distributed from house to house all over town with Catherine herself contacting one hundred and fifty homes. Of a special service held at the conclusion of the meetings, she reported to her mother:

> I ventured to chapel on Tuesday night to the public recognition service. The persons brought to God since we have been here were admitted by ticket into the body of the chapel, while the old members and the public occupied the gallery. It would have done your soul good to have seen the bottom of the large chapel almost full of new converts, most of them people in middle life, and a great proportion men.[7]

One Sunday evening while making her way to Bethesda, Catherine passed down a densely populated street. She began to notice the way individuals, especially the women, were loitering around the doorways of houses or leaning out of windows, as though they had no direction or purpose in life. Overcoming her natural timidity and fear of speaking with strangers, she stopped to invite some of them to meetings at the chapel. She spoke to people on the street and even knocked on the doors of some homes. People listened politely to her and seemed relieved that someone was paying attention to them.

One woman sitting on a doorstep declared she could not attend church because of her shoddy appearance and

---

7   Ibid., p. 90.

because her husband, a mean drunkard, would never allow it. Catherine asked to meet the man and was led into the house. Though drunk, he received her civilly. She was deeply moved by the deplorable conditions in which the family was living in the two-room flat. In the long conversation that followed she shared the Gospel, prayed with the couple and obtained the husband's promise that he would sign a total abstinence pledge. He did so when she returned the very next day with pledge in hand.

That encouraged Catherine to seek out and minister to other alcoholics. Within a few weeks she succeeded in getting 'ten drunkards to abandon their soul-destroying habits' and to meet with her once a week for Scripture reading and prayer.

She began devoting two evenings per week to carrying out 'a systematic course of house-to-house visitation'. She met with people and conducted cottage prayer meetings in not a few hovels that had no furniture and no ventilation. Of one particularly pitiful home visit Catherine wrote:

> [I found] a poor woman lying on a heap of rags. She had just given birth to twins, and there was nobody of any sort to wait upon her. I can never forget the desolation of that room. By her side was a crust of bread, and a small lump of lard. ... I was soon busy trying to make her a little more comfortable. The babies I washed in a broken pie-dish, the nearest approach to a tub that I could find. And the gratitude of those large eyes, that gazed upon me from that wan and shrunken face, can never fade from my memory.[8]

Catherine gave birth to her fourth child and second daughter, Emma, on January 8, 1860. In May all four of

---

8   Ibid., p. 93.

her children came down with whooping cough, which she treated with homeopathic remedies.

Around that same time, she took a decisive step – to begin a public preaching ministry – which dramatically changed the remainder of her life. William had been encouraging her in that direction for quite some time but she had hesitated due to a natural timidity and bashfulness she had concerning public ministry. But on Whitsunday (Pentecost) 1860, Catherine publicly dedicated herself to that ministry. At the conclusion of her husband's morning message, she rose from her pew and walked to the front of the chapel. About 1,000 people were in attendance, including a number of preachers and other outside guests. Thinking something must be wrong, Booth stepped down from the platform to ask, 'What is the matter, my dear?'

'I want to say a word.'

He was so surprised he practically parroted her by announcing, 'My dear wife wants to say a word', then sat down.

Facing the congregation, Catherine said:

> I dare say many of you have been looking upon me as a very devoted woman, and one who has been living faithfully to God, but I have come to know that I have been living in disobedience, and to that extent I have brought darkness and leanness into my soul, but I promised the Lord three or four months ago, and I dare not disobey. I have come to tell you this, and to promise the Lord that I will be obedient to the heavenly vision.

That evening Catherine began to fulfill that commitment by returning to the chapel and preaching her first public sermon on the theme of 'Be Filled with the Spirit'.

The following summer Booth's health broke down, and Catherine began fulfilling many of his preaching and administrative responsibilities at Gateshead and in other parts of the circuit. He spent that fall undergoing hydropathic treatments in Matlock, Derbyshire, about 130 miles south of Gateshead. People greatly appreciated her speaking ministry, and she found she relished it. She normally preached for an hour or longer. Booth returned with restored health to Gateshead just before Christmas, and on New Year's Day Catherine wrote her parents: 'At a society meeting held last week they passed a resolution that some blanks be left on the next "plan" for Sunday nights at Bethesda, and that I be requested to supply them.' She soon had more invitations to speak at various churches than she could fulfill.

FOUR

In March of 1861 Booth penned a lengthy letter to the retiring president of the Methodist New Connexion. In it he carefully and respectfully stated his conviction that the time was right for him to be reassigned to evangelistic work in the denomination. Though he had not been an itinerant evangelist for four years, he still firmly believed that was the ministry to which God had called him and for which he was best suited.

The New Connexion Annual Conference took place in Liverpool that May. When the question of Booth's appointment came up for discussion, his old nemesis, P. J. Wright, opposed the proposal. A misguided compromise was put forth by a well-meaning Booth supporter and approved by the delegates: Booth would again be assigned as the minister of a circuit but could conduct revival services elsewhere after fulfilling his normal pastoral responsibilities. Such an arrangement had already proved largely unworkable at Gateshead.

Catherine was seated in the gallery during the proceedings. A popular legend, very likely greatly exaggerated, has developed that when this decision was reached, Catherine, full of indignation, leapt to her feet. Leaning over the balcony railing and locking her eyes on her husband, she declared to him with a voice that rang throughout the auditorium, 'Never!' Booth supposedly then sprang to his feet, waved his hat in the direction of the door and, amidst cries of 'Order! Order!', hastened to the foot of the gallery stairs where he met and embraced his wife. Turning their backs on the conference, they exited the meeting, determined to trust their future to God, come what may, and to follow their convictions regarding the work they believed He would have them to do.

Less-theatrical accounts report that Catherine and others in the balcony stood because the conference chairman requested visitors in the gallery to withdraw so the discussion could continue behind closed doors. She may have mouthed 'Never!' to Booth from the balcony. But she likely did not do so in a resounding fashion because some eye-witnesses of the incident had no recollection of her saying anything to him. The couple apparently did embrace at the base of the gallery stairs and then left the meeting together.[9]

The conference assigned William to be superintendent of the Newcastle circuit, which was considered to be

---

9   Ibid., pp. 110-13.

one of the most important in the New Connexion. An assistant minister was appointed to substitute for him during his absences. The Booths moved to Newcastle immediately. In the ensuing weeks Booth held a series of revival meetings outside the Newcastle circuit at Alnwick. He also traveled to London where he twice preached in the open air with an independent group dedicated to promoting evangelistic revivalism.

In mid-July the New Connexion's supervising annual committee sent Booth a letter of reprimand for not yet fulfilling his ministerial duties to the Newcastle circuit. Both he and Catherine took that as an indication the committee was not truly supportive of his carrying out both pastoral and evangelistic ministries. With Catherine's hearty support, Booth promptly tendered his resignation from the Methodist New Connexion.

Many churches were closed to the Booths both because of William's evangelistic methods and because they could not endorse a woman preacher. In August, however, the New Connexion pastor in Hayle, Cornwall, invited both of them to minister to his congregation. Invitations followed from other Methodist chapels, both New Connexion and Wesleyan, and a ministry that was initially expected to last about seven weeks in Cornwall stretched out to eighteen months.

From Hayle the Booths moved on to St Ives. Over 1,000 converts were recorded during their ministry of three and a half months there. It was during that time, through Catherine's influence, that her own father was brought back to the Lord. At their next set of meetings in St Just, she began holding some meetings exclusively for women, a feature that would be common in her subsequent revival work. In those services she addressed such issues as fashion, women in public ministry, child rearing and adoption. At one of those meetings she remarked, 'It will be a happy day for England when Christian ladies transfer their sympathies from poodles and terriers to destitute and starving children.'

While ministering next in Penzance, Catherine gave birth on August 26, 1862, to her fifth child, a son named Herbert. Just one month later they were invited to hold evangelistic meetings at the Free Methodist Chapel in Redruth. Their final Cornish ministry took place at Camborne where reportedly thousands professed conversion.

Continuing on to Cardiff, in Wales, they rented a spacious circus tent at which to hold their meetings rather than using churches. In time the use of large 'public and unsectarian' buildings became commonplace in their work. This allowed them to reach larger numbers of people and provided a neutral location where Christians of various persuasions could unite and where non-churchgoers were willing to attend.

After one of the meetings in Cardiff, Catherine approached seven-year-old Bramwell as he sat in the audience. It was obvious he was under deep conviction. 'You are very unhappy,' she stated tenderly, then asked, 'You know the reason?' He indicated he did. But when she asked if he was ready to make a public decision for Christ, he immediately and emphatically responded, 'No!' Years later he reported: 'She put her hands suddenly to her face and I can never forget my feelings on seeing the tears fall through them on to the sawdust beneath our feet. ... But I still said "No!"'

Returning to England, Catherine was prevented by influenza from participating in evangelistic meetings in Newport. But she soon rejoined William in future revival endeavors. Another feature that became common in their meetings at that time was the incorporation of testimonies from converted drunkards and gamblers as well as former 'pugilists, horse-racers and poachers'. When Booth seriously injured his leg at Walsall, Catherine preached in all the meetings for two weeks.

Following one Walsall meeting conducted specifically for children, she was delighted to find Bramwell kneeling among the group of penitents at the close of the service. The tenderhearted lad wept aloud over his sins. When his mother knelt and prayed with him, he experienced God's forgiveness and knew he had been saved.

In March of 1864 the Booths secured a house in Leeds. Their sixth child and third daughter, Marian, was born there on May 4, 1864. Soon after birth she started having seizures. Her health was delicate, she apparently had a significant learning disability, and in later years she was unable to 'take part in public life'.

Just five weeks after Marian's birth, Catherine resumed her preaching. From that point on, however, she conducted her own evangelistic meetings, as the Booths had concluded they could increase their effectiveness by holding separate campaigns. That proved to be a difficult period for the Booths due to the strain of separation, the care of the children being made difficult by inept or dishonest governesses, and the fact that Catherine's spine was bothering her.

In the opening months of 1865, while Booth ministered in Lincolnshire and Yorkshire, Catherine conducted evangelistic meetings at a pair of Free Church Methodist chapels in the southern portion of London. Having decided to make their permanent home in London, the Booths moved their children from Leeds and settled in Hammersmith on London's west side. Around that same time Catherine was invited to minister at a meeting of the Midnight Movement for Fallen Women. Two or three hundred prostitutes were at the meeting, and she spoke to them 'as one sinful woman to another'. So fervent was her appeal, that some of them responded to her plea to reform their lives.

Booth, meanwhile, completed his ministry in Yorkshire and joined his family in London. He was invited to lead a six-week mission in London's East End. That section of the city was infamous for its extreme poverty, degradation and despair. Unemployment, drunkenness, prostitution and all variety of crime abounded. Diseases were rampant and premature death was commonplace. Throughout July and August Booth preached in a large tent in an unused Quaker cemetery. But that arrangement proved unsuccessful because during inclement weather, as he colorfully reported, 'the dribblings from the leaky tent washed the unsaved away'. He next rented a dancing academy in which to hold his three Sunday services.

The East London Christian Revival Union was formed to help raise prayer and financial support for the fledgling ministry. In addition, in Catherine's expanding ministry to well-to-do audiences in London's West End she was able to acquaint them with and raise support for the East End mission.

Booth soon sensed the Lord's leading to discontinue itinerant evangelistic ministry in order to devote himself to this new mission. As he saw the overwhelming needs of the 'masses of poor people', their eagerness to hear his messages and their ready response to his salvation invitations, his 'whole heart went out to them'. Without consulting his wife, one night, after walking from the East End to their home in the West End, he announced to her:

> O Kate, I have found my destiny! These are the people for whose salvation I have been longing all these years. As I passed by the doors of the flaming gin-palaces tonight I seemed to hear a voice sounding in my ears, 'Where can you go and find such heathen as these, and where is there so great a need for your labours?' And there and then in my soul I offered myself and you and the children up to this great work. Those people shall be our people, and they shall have our God for their God.

Catherine later recorded her initial responses to that declaration:

> I remember the emotion that this produced in my soul. I sat gazing into the fire, and the Devil whispered to me, "This means another departure, another start in life!" The question of our support constituted a serious difficulty. Hitherto we had been able to meet our expenses out of the collections which we had made from our more respectable audiences. But it was impossible to suppose that we could do so among the poverty-stricken East Enders – we were afraid even to ask for a collection in such a locality.

> Nevertheless, I did not answer discouragingly. After a momentary pause for thought and prayer, I replied, "Well, if you feel you ought to stay, stay. We have trusted the Lord *once* for our support, and we can trust Him *again*!"[10]

---

10 Ibid., p. 157.

FIVE

In order to be closer to the East End, the Booths moved to the Hackney borough of London. Catherine gave birth to their seventh child, Evelyne, on Christmas Day, 1865. She was normally referred to as Eva and in adulthood changed her name to Evangeline.

Though William and Catherine were heavily involved with their public ministries, they were also devoted to the upbringing of their children.[11] Family Bible reading and prayer was an everyday occurrence. In keeping with their conservative convictions, drinking, smoking, dancing, playing cards, going to theatres and dressing in worldly fashions that called attention to oneself were strictly forbidden. While the Sabbath was carefully observed, Catherine believed Sunday should be a happy day. When the children were younger, she held Sunday meetings for them at home. Those services included singing, praying and a lesson she always sought to make interesting for her children. The children began attending public services after they were old enough to take an interest in them.

Catherine was a great believer in fresh air and encouraged her children to play outdoors a great deal. They especially enjoyed tennis, soccer and cricket. Catherine insisted on having a good degree of peace and quiet in her home, but she did not want to thwart her children's energetic

---

11 Helpful summaries of the Booths' rearing of their children are found in: P. W. Wilson, *General Evangeline Booth of The Salvation Army* (New York: Scribner's, 1948), pp. 31-9; Richard Collier, *The General Next to God, The Story of Wiliam Booth and The Salvation Army* (Glasgow: Fontana/ Collins, 1985), pp. 48-50; Trevor Yaxley with Carolyn Vanderwal, *William & Catherine: A New Biography, The Life and Legacy of the Booths, Founders of The Salvation Army* (Minneapolis: Bethany, 2003), pp. 160-7.

play. So the Booths had a double floor (packed with sawdust between as a sound barrier) installed between the children's upstairs playroom and the ceiling of the house's main story. The children could thus romp upstairs without disturbing the tranquility of the rest of the house. Occasionally William Booth would join his children for a lively game of Fox and Goose in which he always led the chase and provoked the squeals of excitement. Many of the games the children played reflected their Christian upbringing, as when they reenacted Bible stories or held pretend revival meetings.

The children were encouraged to keep a variety of pets both as a way of enjoying some of God's creatures and as a means of learning to care responsibly for others. Dogs, rabbits, mice, guinea pigs (the latter numbering nearly a hundred at one time) and other creatures made up the family's revolving menagerie. Some time after the Booths had established The Salvation Army, young Evelyne had a mischievous pet marmoset named little Jeannie. A hired servant who worked in the kitchen made a miniature Salvation Army uniform for the recalcitrant creature. When Catherine spotted the uniformed monkey she said nothing but immediately began to unclothe it. 'But, Eva,' came the mother's quiet reply when the daughter began to protest, 'she doesn't live the life.' The concept of 'living the life' stayed with Evangeline throughout her long career of Christian service.

Most of the educating of the children was done at home under their mother's watchful eye and with the help of a governess. Catherine considered it of greatest importance not only to impart knowledge but also to shape character and train the heart. Over the home's five-foot bookcase she exercised a vigilant though broadminded censorship aimed at reserving the children's attention for literature that was really worth their time.

Her reservations about public education were reinforced by an unfortunate experience Bramwell, then aged ten, had while attending a preparatory school the year after Eva was born. The other boys nicknamed him 'Holy Willie' and taunted him mercilessly. One day some bullies repeatedly bashed him against a tree in an effort to 'bang religion out of him'. The traumatized youngster staggered home, bruised and spitting blood.

William and Catherine diligently taught their children that their lives were not their own to do with as they pleased. Rather, they rightly belonged to God who had redeemed them, and their lives were to be devoted to serving Him and the needy world around them. From the time they were teens the Booth children were given significant responsibilities in their parents' mission work. Each of them except the more limited Marian eventually served as officers in The Salvation Army, some at the highest levels.

Catherine's reputation as a powerful preacher continued to grow. Early in 1867, following a successful three-month campaign in St. John's Wood, in northwest London, a delegation of gentlemen offered to build her a church larger than Charles Spurgeon's Metropolitan Tabernacle! She declined, believing she could best invest her time and energy visiting 'the various important centers' from which she was receiving an increasing number of invitations to speak. At the suggestion of others, she spent that summer ministering at the seaside resort of Margate on the eastern coast of Kent, England. There she was accompanied by her children, much to their delight.

William Booth's ministry, now called The East London Christian Mission, continued to grow. Preaching services were held in such unique venues as a stable, a skittle alley and a pigeon shop. Often the missioners would hold a street meeting before marching to a designated building for a further service. Not uncommonly the street meetings and processions were interrupted by jeers, taunts and physical blows. All variety of objects were thrown at the brave Christian witnesses, including rotten vegetables and even dead cats and rats.

Through the help of generous supporters the mission was able to rent the spacious Effingham Theater for its Sunday services and to purchase a beer house, The Eastern Star, as its first headquarters. By early 1868 the Mission had thirteen preaching stations with a total seating capacity of 8,000. While the evangelistic meetings were the primary focus at those stations, other beneficial ministries included a Drunkards' Rescue Society, a soup kitchen, a savings bank, visitation of the sick and poor, as well as classes in reading, writing and arithmetic.

The Booth's eighth child and fifth daughter, Lucy, was born on April 28, 1868. That October the Mission began its own magazine, *The East London Evangelist*. William and Catherine were its first editors. She wrote many articles for the periodical, some of which were later reproduced and circulated more widely in her books. In December the Booths moved to a larger home in Hackney, taking in boarders to offset the additional expense. As would be the case throughout the remainder of Catherine's life, their home became a second headquarters for carrying out the business of their mission organization. When the Mission's work expanded beyond East London the following year, its name was changed to The Christian Mission and its periodical was renamed *The Christian Mission Magazine*.

That same year, 1869, Catherine's mother battled cancer. Catherine persuaded her to move from Brixton to settle next door to their home in Hackney so she could help care for her during the final months of her life. As the time of Mrs Mumford's death drew near, she lapsed into unconsciousness for several hours. As Catherine knelt by her mother's bedside holding her hand, she quite suddenly regained consciousness. Opening her eyes wide she exclaimed, with radiant face, 'Kate! – Jesus!', then stepped into eternity.

The first official conference of The Christian Mission was convened in 1870. A constitution was adopted along Methodist lines, although it included three distinctive provisions: much authority was given to William Booth as the Mission's general superintendent; the equality of women in ministry was clearly delineated; Christian Mission officeholders needed to be total abstainers. Catherine's influence in these distinctives is readily apparent.

The years 1870 through 1872 proved difficult for the Booths with William's health incapacitating him for periods at a time and Catherine needing to fulfill many of his responsibilities despite her own health limitations. They were heartened by the arrival of George Scott Railton, a zealous, capable ministry associate, in 1872. He lived with the Booths for eleven years, serving as secretary of The Christian Mission and later as first commissioner of The Salvation Army.

After Booth was able to resume his full administrative oversight of the Mission, Catherine was freed to resume her public speaking ministry outside the confines of the Mission stations. During a campaign in Portsmouth on the southern coast of England in March of 1873, the meetings had to be moved to a 3,000-seat music hall after the original venue with its 1,000-person capacity proved inadequate to accommodate her audiences. That ministry stretched out for seventeen weeks. When the journey to and from London proved too difficult, she rented an apartment in Portsmouth and brought six of her eight children to be with her there.

During her next major campaign in Chatham, east of London, she suffered a heart attack. She was just forty-four years old at the time. William took over her speaking responsibilities until she was able to resume them a few weeks later.

Bramwell was then seventeen years old and frequently visited the sick on 'a little street of workmen's houses' nearby his own family's home. One of those visits was in the home of a factory foreman who was part of The Christian Mission's work in Bethnal Green. He had a large number of children, and his wife, who had recently given birth to yet another child, was gravely ill. When it became apparent she was dying, her last request to Bramwell was that he would take charge of her baby. Bramwell later commented:

> Perhaps not altogether realizing what I was undertaking, I promised that I would. Naturally I turned to my mother for assistance, and after a certain amount of negotiation the little boy – Harry, we called him – was brought into our home and placed under the care of my sister Emma … who was at the time in delicate health, and who found in the training of this baby delightful occupation. The child grew and prospered and

gave early evidence of being a child of God. While still in his
teens he developed a singular gift for caring for the sick.[12]

This adopted son, who also went by the nickname 'Georgie
Booth', grew up in their home as one of their own. At
age fifteen he went with Emma to India and subsequently
became the first Salvation Army doctor there.

At the end of that year Catherine went with her
children, most of whom had been suffering from
whooping cough, to Hastings on England's southeast
coast. Though supposedly there to recoup her health and
that of the children, she could not resist the temptation to
engage in public ministry as well. She thus held a series of
meetings at the Royal Circus with its 2,500-seat capacity.

The Christian Mission had thirty-one preaching
stations by 1874. Catherine's public ministry had played
a significant role in the establishment of several of those.
That year she carried out a round of ministry visitation
at nine of them. She also ministered in various locations
where the mission did not yet have a presence, including
two months of meetings at Ryde on the Isle of Wight.
While the younger children accompanied her during
that campaign, daughter Catherine ('Katie') and sons
Bramwell and Ballington, all older teens, remained in
London to carry out administrative duties, song leading
and street preaching for the Mission.

Both William and Catherine were laid aside again
for a time the next summer, 1875, he with a sprained leg
and she with a second heart attack. Some of their older
children helped pick up the slack by fulfilling speaking
engagements at various mission stations.

---

12 Yaxley, *William & Catherine*, p. 143.

SIX

As time passed William became increasingly disillusioned with the democratic structure that had been given to The Christian Mission at its founding just a few years earlier. He came to believe the whole system of local class meetings, elders' meetings, quarterly circuit meetings, conference committees, and the Annual Conference was too cumbersome to permit the rapid advances he longed the Mission to experience. He concluded the Mission should be patterned after the military, with himself as the general superintendent being in charge. Just as the commander-in-chief of an army gathers around himself his principal officers, receiving from them information and advice upon which to base his military operations, so the Mission would be run in the future.

That sweeping change was approved at the June 1877 Annual Conference of The Christian Mission. At that time thirty-six evangelists were employed full-time by the Mission, and all of them supported the change. Another measure approved at that conference, this one mirroring Catherine's increasing influence, was that total abstinence would now be required not only of mission leaders but of all its members.

George Scott Railton recounted how the Mission's name came to be changed to The Salvation Army:

The adoption of the new name for this organization was almost accidental. We were drawing up a brief description of the Mission, and, wishing to express what it was in one phrase, I wrote, 'The Christian Mission is a volunteer army of converted working people.' 'No,' said Mr Booth, 'we are not volunteers, for we feel we must do what we do, and we are always on duty.' He crossed out the word and wrote 'Salvation'. The phrase immediately struck us all, and we very soon found that it would be far more widely effective than the old name.[13]

Considerable military terminology and symbolism soon came to be used. Lay members of the mission were now soldiers and mission stations were called corps. Evangelists were captains and lieutenants while elders and class leaders were sergeants and sergeant majors. Booth as the mission's general superintendent was referred to as the General. Catherine never held a rank in The Salvation Army, but she did eventually assume the honorary title of the Army mother.

The Salvation Army's Annual Conference became known as a War Congress and its magazine was dubbed *The War Cry*. The Army flag was created, its red, yellow and blue colors signifying salvation through Christ's blood, the baptism of the Holy Spirit and holiness. The motto inscribed on the flag, 'Blood and Fire', represented the blood of Christ and the fire of the Holy Spirit.

Uniforms were adopted as well. Catherine was influential in the design chosen for the uniform that the women would wear. She desired uniforms that would be plain, yet distinctive and attractive. They needed to meet her requirements for both simplicity and modesty in order to serve as a sign of separation from a society she perceived to be sinfully fashion-conscious.

Much of the attention, both positive and negative, that the Army received during its early years centered on the public ministries of its Hallelujah Lasses in their plain black uniforms and bonnets. The sight of women

---

13   Green, *Catherine Booth*, p. 189.

parading behind brass bands, preaching in the streets or speaking publicly in churches or theatres was astonishing to some and scandalous to others. Often sizeable crowds gathered primarily to witness that novel sight. Despite public disapproval and often ridicule, many women – largely from Nonconformist backgrounds and the working classes but also including a number from the middle class – were attracted to the ministry opportunities afforded them in the Army. Female officers were soon supervising fully one-third of the corps.

During 1878 and 1879 Catherine was kept constantly on the go, speaking at war councils in various cities and towns, presenting the colors to new corps, and explaining as well as defending the Army's mission and methods to supporters and critics alike. Such ministries took her to fifty-nine towns in 1879. The Army was then experiencing explosive growth. In just one year's time it more than doubled in size, growing from fifty corps and eighty-eight officers in 1878 to 130 corps and 195 officers in 1879.

Beginning in 1880, The Salvation Army's ministry mushroomed beyond England and Wales to other parts of the world. By the fall of that year twelve corps had been established in the United States. A dozen corps sprang up in Australia over the course of the following twelve months. Within a year and a half of the first Salvation Army street meeting in Canada, a whopping 200 corps under the direction of 400 officers had been established.

Two training homes were opened in 1880 for the purpose of preparing future Army officers. Ballington Booth, age twenty-three, supervised the home for young men while Emma Booth, but twenty years of age, was in charge of the home for young women. Salvation

Army cadets were often commissioned as officers while still in their mid- to late-teens. Their initial residential training lasted between four and six months. The primary training was in evangelism and the winning of souls. But educational instruction was also provided, as needed, in reading, writing, arithmetic, history and geography. The training involved a large variety of active, hands-on ministry experiences, including 'open-air marches, meetings, house-to-house visitation, *War Cry* selling, slum, attic and garret work, the hunting up of drunkards, the Little Soldiers' work, and, in short, … any and every kind of active warfare'.[14]

Catherine continued to find it necessary to defend The Salvation Army against its numerous detractors. Anglican clergy denounced the Army as having no part in historic orthodox Christianity. When the Army began its work in Carlisle, the local bishop condemned it in a sermon he delivered at the cathedral. Catherine, in turn, rented an old theatre in Carlisle in order to have a platform from which to make a public response. Her address was published in three successive issues of *The War Cry* during October 1880.

Upper class individuals and members of the Established Church were especially critical of some of the Army's novel methods: marching in the streets; preaching the Gospel in theatres and circuses; adapting secular tunes to many of the spiritual songs employed in their services; showcasing in public meetings trophy converts rescued from notorious pasts. To one critic of such measures Catherine earnestly responded:

14   Ibid., p. 212.

Oh, my dear sir, if you only knew the indifferent, besotted, semi-heathenish condition of the classes on whom we operate, you would, I am sure, deem any *lawful means* expedient if only they succeeded in bringing such people under the sound of the Gospel. It is a standing mystery to me that thoughtful Christian men can contemplate the existing state of the world without perceiving the desperate need of some more effective and aggressive agency on the side of God and righteousness.[15]

The Salvation Army also experienced persecution from the 'Skeleton Army'. Mobs, often incited by individuals with vested interests in the alcohol industry, used intimidation and physical violence in an effort to silence Nonconformist groups that dared to challenge traditional social customs and religious beliefs. Quakers, Methodists, Baptists, Congregationalists and The Salvation Army were all targets of such mob violence. Police and local magistrates often turned a blind eye to the brutal attacks.

Early in 1881, the Booths' oldest daughter, Katie, now in her early twenties and a captain in the Army, was commissioned to 'open fire' in France by establishing a beachhead for the ministry in Paris. Katie was accompanied in the endeavor by Florence Soper, the daughter of a Welsh physician, and Adelaide Cox, whose father was an Anglican vicar. While Catherine approved of her daughter's involvement in leading that mission, her mother's heart 'felt unutterable things' as she contemplated the hardships it would almost certainly entail for Katie. To a friend she wrote, 'The papers I read on the state of society in Paris make me shudder, and I see all the dangers to which our darling will be exposed!'

---

15   Ibid., p. 218.

In what would prove to be her only journey to a country outside Great Britain, Catherine visited Paris in April 1882. There she preached under worse conditions than she had ever experienced in England. Utterly desperate people attended the meetings. A general uproar, including vile shouting and blasphemous screaming, erupted between the singing and attempts at preaching. Following Catherine's first meeting, Colonel Arthur Clibborn (who would marry Katie a few years later) and some of the Army's soldiers were kicked and beaten by members of the departing crowd.

The most brutal assault on The Salvation Army in England had taken place just three months earlier in Sheffield. A large contingent of Salvationists gathered there for meetings at Albert Hall. During an advertised march through the city's streets, the soldiers were attacked by the Sheffield 'Blades', a local gang of thugs who were well-known for their intense animosity toward religion. They were especially enraged to see one of their local heroes, a champion Northumberland wrestler, riding his horse in the march. Lieutenant Emmerson Davison was one of the Army's recent converts. Many of the Salvationists were beaten during the march and Davison had to be taken to the hospital. William and Catherine, riding in a carriage, were unharmed. During the riot, the Army's indomitable General stood in the carriage and directed his troops. When he greeted his bleeding comrades after the march, he suggested that would be an appropriate time to have their photographs taken.

In that year (1882) alone, sixty buildings used for Salvation Army purposes were attacked, and sometimes all but destroyed, by rioting crowds. Sixty hundred and sixty-nine Salvationists were assaulted, including 251 women and twenty-three young people under the age of fifteen. Two female Salvationists died as the result of injuries sustained in an attack at Guildford. A group of Salvation Army lasses in Whitechapel, East London, were tied together with rope and pelted with live coals.[16]

Such harrowing incidents drew considerable attention to the unjust treatment The Salvation Army was experiencing in various parts of Britain. Public sympathy began turning in its favor. The right of the Army to conduct street marches was defended in both the House of Commons and the House of Lords.

That same year, The Salvation Army established its international headquarters on Queen Victoria Street, within sight of St. Paul's Cathedral. The Army also initiated the purchase of the Eagle Tavern with its attached Grecian Theatre and Dancing Grounds for the sizeable sum of £16,750. By year's end The Salvation Army had also extended its ministry into India, South Africa, New Zealand and Sweden.

Bramwell Booth married Florence Soper (who had assisted his sister in establishing the Army's presence in France) in 1882. The wedding was held at a former London orphanage the Army had acquired, renovated and renamed Congress Hall. Five thousand people filled the hall to capacity. The couple was married beneath The Salvation Army flag and, as part of the ceremony, pledged their allegiance not only to each other but also to the Army. Both William and Catherine spoke at the wedding, with the latter testifying, 'the highest happiness I can wish to

---

16 Yaxley, *William & Catherine*, pp. 182-3.

my beloved children is that they may realize as thorough a union of heart and mind, and as much blessing in their married life, as the Lord has vouchsafed to us in ours'.

Katie Booth led a contingent of officers in establishing The Salvation Army's work in Switzerland the following year. Early opposition to their ministry resulted in their being imprisoned. The Booths sought help from 'Parliamentary friends' and even Britain's Prime Minister, William Gladstone, but received little assistance. Finally, after several months, the matter came to trial, at which time Katie defended the Army, explaining its aim, message and methods. It was determined the officers had not acted with culpable intention so they were released. Katie returned to London where a large thanksgiving meeting was held in Exeter Hall.

A number of addresses Catherine delivered during 1883 and 1884 were soon published as three separate books. In *The Salvation Army in Relation to Church and State* she sought to show how invaluable the Army's ministry was to both. The second work, *Life and Death*, delineated 'some more direct and pointed truth on the subject of personal Salvation'. The third volume, *Popular Christianity*, dealt forthrightly with such 'burning topics' as false christs, mock salvation and cowardly service.

SEVEN

One of the moral blights on Victorian England was prostitution. Girls as young as twelve years of age were lured to cities with the promise of domestic work only to be, instead, enslaved in brothels. Some were even sold into prostitution by unscrupulous parents desperate for money. The age of sexual consent had been set at just thirteen by British parliament in 1875. Three times during the decade that followed the House of Lords passed bills recommending that age be raised, but all three recommendations failed in the House of Commons. Many insisted that child prostitution and enforced prostitution occurred on the Continent but not in England. The Salvation Army, which had ministered to prostitutes for years, knew the case to be otherwise.

In 1884 the Army rented a house on Hanbury Street in London's Whitechapel borough for the purpose of providing for the spiritual and physical needs of such 'fallen women'. Florence Soper Booth, though of a retiring nature and then only twenty-two years of age, was put in charge of the home and ministry. She was assisted by Adelaide Cox who had served with Katie Booth and her in founding the Army's ministry in Paris three years earlier. During Florence's subsequent thirty years of oversight of the Women's Social Services, its ministry grew from the initial rescue home to 117 homes for women in Britain and around the world. Catherine immediately took a marked interest in the home on Hanbury Street and helped to furnish it.

Catherine and Bramwell became convinced that public attention needed to be drawn to these festering evils in England, especially as they related to girls as young as twelve and thirteen years of age. In launching what became known as the Purity Crusade and the Maiden Tribute Campaign, they enlisted the help of W. T. Stead, editor of London's *Pall Mall Gazette*. Stead determined to expose 'the white slave trade' in his newspaper, thus forcing a change in the age of consent law through the tide of public opinion.

A secret commission of the *Gazette* devised a plan which Stead proposed to Bramwell. The journalist also informed the Archbishop of Canterbury, the Bishop of London and Cardinal Manning, head of the Roman Catholic Church in Britain, of his plan and its desired outcome. His plans and objectives met with their approval.

Stead contacted Rebecca Jarrett, a former prostitute and brothel keeper who had been converted to Christ through the Army's influence. With Catherine's assistance, Rebecca had found refuge in a ministry to women in Winchester, away from the evil influences of her former acquaintances in London. With understandable reluctance she agreed to assist Stead in an undercover capacity. Through some unsavory contacts from her past life, she was able to purchase a thirteen-year-old girl, Eliza Armstrong, from her mother. Though it was made clear the girl was being procured for immoral purposes, Mrs Armstrong sold her daughter for a single English pound (then equaling approximately five American dollars).

Accompanied by one of Stead's associates, Sampson Jacques, Rebecca took Eliza to Madame Mourez, a midwife and professional procuress, who certified that the girl was a virgin. From there Rebecca and Sampson brought their young charge to a brothel where Stead had rented a pair of rooms. After spending some time with Eliza, Rebecca encouraged her to sleep and left her alone in one of the rooms. Some time later, presuming the girl would by then be asleep, Stead entered her room. Eliza bolted up and cried out, 'There's a man in the room! Take me home; oh, take me home.' Stead slipped silently from the room and Rebecca came to reassure the girl.

Rebecca then took Eliza to a surgeon's house in Nottingham Place where they spent the night. There it was also verified that no harm whatsoever had befallen the girl. The next day, accompanied by another Salvationist, Madame Elizabeth Combe, Rebecca and Eliza journeyed by train from London, England, to Paris, France. There Eliza remained under their care and that of other Salvationists.

Both W. T. Stead and Bramwell Booth believed they had built a strong case. They had demonstrated that 'although this particular girl had received no whit of harm, it was shown to be possible for a procuress to buy a child for money, to certificate her, bring her to a house of ill fame, leave her with a man she had never seen before, and send her off to the Continent so that nothing further need be known of her'.[17]

Stead, who had been extensively researching the scourge of child prostitution in England for weeks, published his exposé in the *Pall Mall Gazette* in a series of ten articles entitled 'The Maiden Tribute of Modern Babylon'. The articles made their way to both the Continent and America, and circulation of the *Gazette* skyrocketed from twelve thousand to over a million. When some bookstalls refused to sell the *Gazette*, thinking the articles indecent, William Booth offered the Army's International Headquarters as a distribution center, and cadets from the officers' training homes distributed the newspapers on the streets.

Throughout the latter half of 1884 and the first several months of 1885, Catherine threw her weight behind the cause. She spoke out forcefully on the issue at a number

---

17   Green, *Catherine Booth*, p. 253.

of mass meetings that were held in an effort to increase the pressure of public attention on this cancerous malady. She also wrote Prime Minister Gladstone and Queen Victoria, urging them to advance legislation that would raise the age of consent to sixteen.

The Booths wrote a petition to the House of Commons that in just seventeen days was signed by 393,000 people. Its first two provisions were 'The age of responsibility for young girls must be raised to eighteen' and 'The procuration of young people for seduction or immoral purposes must be made a criminal offence, having attached to it a severe penalty.' The signature pages of the petition stretched out nearly two miles in length and were bound up into a gigantic roll. Eight cadets carried the petition on their shoulders into the House of Commons where they laid it on the floor because there was not adequate room for it on the customary Commons table.

The desired legislation was adopted on August 14, 1885, raising the legal age of consent to sixteen. A massive thanksgiving rally was held in Exeter Hall, and thousands of Salvationists and other citizens across England rejoiced over the great moral victory. Additionally, the Army was prepared with homes to care for the young girls who found themselves out on the streets as a result of the new law.

Eliza's mother, Mrs Armstrong, likely motivated by greed and reporters from a rival newspaper to the *Gazette*, insisted on having her daughter returned to her. Eliza was brought back from Paris and reunited with her mother. Further troubles arose when on September 8, less than one month after the breakthrough legislation had been adopted, criminal charges were brought against W. T. Stead, Bramwell Booth, Rebecca Jarrett, Elizabeth

Combe, Sampson Jacques, and Madame Mourez, the midwife and professional procuress.

When Rebecca arranged for the purchase of Eliza, she dealt only with the girl's mother and never spoke to her father. Rebecca and everyone else involved in the charade assumed Eliza's father had consented to the sale of her as well. It was now asserted, however, by a man claiming to be Eliza's father, that the mother had acted on her own in the matter and that he had never given his consent. (A decade later it would be discovered that this man, Charles Armstrong, was not actually Eliza's father so had no rightful parental authority over her. But at this time he was thought to be her paternal guardian.) As a result, Stead, Bramwell, Rebecca and the others were charged with having abducted Eliza from the care of her father and with aiding and abetting an indecent assault on the girl.

When the case came to trial six weeks later the presiding judge ruled that any evidence as to the motives which governed Stead's and Rebecca's actions was inadmissible. In the end, Bramwell Booth and Elizabeth Combe were acquitted. Stead received a three-month prison sentence and his assistant, Sampson Jacques, a one-month jail term. Rebecca was sentenced to six months in prison without hard labor – a sentence she needed to fulfill herself despite the fact that a female Army captain volunteered to take her place. Madame Mourez, who was convicted for having assaulted Eliza, was sentenced to six months with hard labor, and died in prison. Catherine wrote once more to Queen Victoria and three times to England's Home Secretary, appealing unsuccessfully for a remission of the prison sentences handed down to Stead and Rebecca.[18]

---

18 For fuller accounts of the Purity Crusade see: Collier, *The General Next to God*, pp. 107-29; Green, *Catherine Booth*, pp. 247-67.

Despite the considerable attention devoted to these matters, and perhaps partially due to the significant publicity The Salvation Army gained through them, the Army's work continued to experience marked expansion in 1885. In that one year the number of corps in Great Britain increased from 637 to 802 while foreign corps rose from 273 to 520, an addition of 412 corps. By the end of that year the Army had 1,322 corps and 3,076 officers stationed around the world.

EIGHT

The Purity Crusade and the subsequent trials took a toll on Catherine's health, and for several months afterward she stayed at home to convalesce. When she resumed her public speaking ministry the following year, 1886, her pronounced emphasis was once again on the saving of souls rather than the moral reformation of society through legislative processes.

She and William shared that priority ministry emphasis. In the closing years of her life, she was one of the key individuals who assisted her husband in working out an extensive plan to minister to the pressing economic needs of England's 'submerged tenth', the percentage of the nation without the basics of food, shelter and work. Shortly after her death that plan was published in William's major work, *In Darkest England and the Way Out*. That same year The Salvation Army launched a greatly expanded program for addressing those needs. But even then such social work was clearly seen as secondary to the primary spiritual ministry of leading people to Christ. In the Booths' minds, social work was appropriate and necessary for alleviating human suffering and for gaining a hearing for the Gospel. But lasting economic and moral reform in individual lives and in society could only come about as people were led to saving faith in Christ and had their lives transformed by His Spirit. As Booth expressed in the preface to *In Darkest England*:

> My only hope for the permanent deliverance of mankind from misery, either in this world or the next, is the regeneration or remaking of the individual by the power of the Holy Ghost through Jesus Christ. But in providing relief of temporal misery I reckon that I am only making it easy where it is now difficult, and possible where it is now all but impossible, for men and women to find their way to the Cross of Our Lord Jesus Christ.[19]

Catherine had the joy of seeing three of her children married in a period of just over a year and a half, beginning with Ballington's marriage to Maud Charlesworth on September 17, 1886. Maud had served as Katie's lieutenant during her ministry in Switzerland. Katie herself was wed to Colonel Arthur Clibborn on February 8, 1887. A former Quaker, Clibborn had served with the Army in France and Switzerland. Emma married Frederick Tucker on April 10, 1888, William's fifty-ninth birthday. Tucker had opened the Army's ministry in India in 1882, and after their wedding he and Emma returned there to continue the work.

Just two months before Emma's wedding Catherine received fearful news when she was diagnosed as having a small cancerous tumor in one of her breasts. An immediate operation to remove it was advised, and family

---

19   Green, *Catherine Booth*, p. 270.

members strongly encouraged her to follow that course of action. But being ever suspicious of medications and surgical advances, she steadfastly refused, knowing she would likely have fewer than three years to live. William Booth later provided a poignant description of the initial impact of these developments on Catherine and himself:

> After hearing the verdict of the doctors she drove home alone. … She afterwards told me how as she looked upon the various scenes through the cab window it seemed that the sentence of death had been passed upon everything; how she had knelt upon the cab floor and wrestled in prayer with God; of the unutterable yearnings over me and the children that filled her heart; how the realisation of our grief swept over her, and the uncertainties of the near future, when she would be no longer with us.
>
> I shall never forget … that meeting. I had been watching for the cab and had run out to meet and help her up the steps. She tried to smile upon me through her tears, but drawing me into the room she unfolded gradually to me the result of the interviews. I sat down speechless. She rose from her seat and came and knelt beside me, saying, 'Do you know what was my first thought? That I should not be there to nurse you at your last hour.'
>
> I was stunned. I felt as if the whole world were coming to a standstill. … She talked like a heroine, like an angel to me: she talked as she had never talked before. I could say little or nothing. It seemed as though a hand were laid upon my very heart-strings. I could only kneel with her and try to pray.[20]

Catherine was able to speak at Emma's wedding. In her remarks she shared two perspectives that encapsulated her primary purposes and priorities for all of life and ministry:

---

20   Ibid., pp. 279-80.

Before I was fifteen years of age, God had, in an especial manner, taught me what I consider the first and fundamental and all-comprehensive principle of Christ's salvation – of real Christianity – that every act of our lives, every relationship into which we enter, every object at which we aim, every purpose that inspires our souls, should be centered and bounded by God and His glory, and that, whether we eat or drink, or whatsoever we do – whether we marry or are given in marriage, do business, or become Salvation Army officers or whatever we do – we should do all to the glory of God.

There are plenty of other people about all other kinds of work, and I am always glad to hear of anybody doing anything good and kind and true and helpful to humanity; whether it is feeding little boys and girls or the poor, or enlightening the ignorant, or building hospitals, or anything else whatever so long as they are doing more good than harm, I say 'Amen, God bless you!' But that is not the particular work Jesus Christ has set His people to do. There are plenty of people to do all that kind of work, but there are few for the peculiar work which Christ has set His people to do. The great characteristic of His people in the world was that they were to be saviours of men – Salvationists. Their work was to be to enlighten men with respect to God's claims upon them, and enlighten them with respect to what God is willing to do for them, and enlighten them with respect to what God wants to do by them in the salvation of others; therefore, I ask you to help us. ... Help us save the world. Amen.[21]

Catherine's final public address (except for brief remarks shared at a subsequent special Salvation Army gathering) was delivered on Thursday, June 21, 1888, at the invitation of Dr Joseph Parker in his Congregational church, the City Temple of London. For the better part of an hour she spoke to a large audience that filled the main auditorium

---

21   Ibid., pp. 270, 275-6.

and most of the gallery on the missionary task of the church in seeking to win the whole world to Jesus Christ. Afterwards she sat exhausted for nearly an equal amount of time before being helped to her cab and taken home. Thus ended her formal preaching ministry of twenty-eight years.

She spent a few weeks that fall in Clacton-on-Sea, Essex, on England's east coast, then returned to London. As the cancer progressed, the attendant hemorrhaging and nausea continued to weaken her. She was able to attend her husband's sixtieth birthday celebration at Clapton Congress Hall on April 10, 1889, and to briefly greet the Salvationists and other guests assembled on that occasion.

As she left London to go again to Clacton the following August, Catherine expressed the conviction that she would never return to the metropolis. The home where she stayed in Clacton became something of a secondary headquarters for The Salvation Army. Some rooms were converted into offices while others were used as living quarters for members of the Booth family, a nurse, secretaries and visitors. Catherine was able to carry on an extensive correspondence ministry, now dictating rather than writing those letters herself. She also met with the many officers, soldiers and other friends who came to visit her one final time. In addition, she and William spent considerable time discussing and refining the plan he was preparing for publication as *In Darkest England*.

In December Catherine sank so low it seemed her passing was imminent. She sent a message, which she believed to be her last, to Salvationists on December 19: '1:18 p.m. – The waters are rising, but so am I. I am not going under, but over. Don't be concerned about your dying; only go on living well, and the dying will be all right.' To everyone's amazement, including her own, Catherine rallied. On Easter Monday, April 6, 1890, she again nearly died before once again rallying.

At times Catherine's suffering was all but unbearable. The cancerous tumor developed into a gaping wound that frequently produced scorching jolts of pain which she described as scorpions in her breast. While her faith remained strong, Booth felt his own faith wavering in the face of his wife's protracted agonies. As many do in the face of excruciating trials, he asked, 'Why does God allow this? How can it be? How can it be?' Only gradually did the realization come to him that such difficulties remind people of their need for God and drive them on to Him for His help and support.

Though unable to attend the Army's twenty-fifth anniversary celebration at London's Crystal Palace that summer, Catherine wished to communicate a greeting to the assembled audience. Her message was written in large letters on a long sheet of calico that was scrolled across the platform. In this way the greeting could be easily read by all, even those in the farthest corners of the enormous auditorium:

My Dear Children and Friends,

My place is empty, but my heart is with you. You are my joy and crown. Your battles, sufferings, and victories have been the chief interest of my life these past twenty-five years. They are so still. Go forward! Live holy lives. Be true to the Army. God is your strength. Love and seek the lost; bring them to the Blood. Make the people good; inspire them with the Spirit of Jesus Christ. Love one another; help your comrades in dark hours. I am dying under the Army Flag; it is yours to live and fight under. God is my Salvation and Refuge in the storm. I send you my love and blessing – Catherine Booth.[22]

W. T. Stead greatly assisted William Booth in the composition of *In Darkest England*. When the extensive volume was finally completed on a Sunday morning that September, the journalist stated to those gathered around Catherine's bed, 'That work will echo around the world. Its influence for good, its effects upon others far beyond the ranks of the Army, will be quite incalculable. I rejoice with an exceeding great joy.'

Summoning her strength, Catherine replied earnestly in a whisper, 'And I most of all. Thank God. Yes, thank God, we may rejoice that something on an adequate scale is to be done at last. Through all these years I have labored and prayed that this matter might be done; but, thank God! Thank God!'

William and a number of family members were with Catherine in Clacton throughout the final four days of her life as she sank ever closer to death. Sometimes she was racked with pain while at other times she slept. Those attending her sought to comfort her with their prayers and words of love as well as by singing some of her favorite songs. Her husband and family were by her side when she was released from her prolonged suffering and stepped into eternity on Saturday afternoon, October 4, 1890. She was sixty-one years old.

Catherine's body was placed in a plain oak coffin with a glass cover and transported to Congress Hall in London for the viewing. An estimated 50,000 people filed

---

22 Ibid., pp. 282-3.

past the casket during the course of the five-day viewing. Her funeral service was held on Monday, October 13 in the Olympia, a cavernous exhibition center with seating to accommodate 36,000 people. It was filled to capacity for the funeral, and thousands had to be turned away. The next day 3,000 Salvation Army officers joined the Booth family in making up the official procession that accompanied her coffin as it was transported the four miles from the Army's International Headquarters on Queen Victoria Street to the Abney Park Cemetery at Stoke Newington. Thousands of other officers and soldiers as well as countless individuals not belonging to The Salvation Army came out to observe the procession and pay their final respects.

William Booth bravely soldiered on twenty-two more years following Catherine's death. After persevering through additional years of sometimes intense opposition and criticism, he and the Salvation Army eventually came to be appreciated and highly regarded in Britain and numerous other countries where they served. Booth chose never to remarry. He was promoted to glory at age eighty-three on August 21, 1912.

4

Mary Slessor

ONE

Largely owing to the fact that her father was an alcoholic, Mary Slessor grew up in grinding poverty and had to expend her teen and early adult years in exhausting factory labor as a primary provider for her family. Thanks to her devout mother, she was raised with a spiritually sensitive heart, a lively awareness of worldwide missionary endeavor and an earnest desire to serve Christ by ministering to the needs of her fellow man. Both the negative and positive facets of her girlhood were used of God to forge within her the selfless, indomitable spirit that would be needed to fulfill the career of daunting, heroic service He had for her.

Mary was born on December 2, 1848, in Gilcomston, a suburb of Aberdeen, Scotland. She was the second of her parents' eventual seven children. Her father, Robert, was a shoemaker whose challenge to support his growing family was exacerbated by his drinking problem. Her mother had been brought up as the only child in a home characterized by refinement and piety. She was patient, gentle, retiring and of a 'deeply religious disposition'.

Mrs Slessor was a member of the Belmont Street United Presbyterian Church. She had an active interest in the foreign missionary enterprises her denomination was carrying out in India, China, Japan, Kaffraria (part of the southeastern cape of present-day South Africa) and Calabar (the southeastern coastal region of modern Nigeria). Mary later testified, 'I had my missionary enthusiasm for Calabar in particular from her – she knew from its inception all that was to be known of its history.'

Mary's older brother, Robert, used to announce his intention to be a missionary when he became a man. Young Mary was crestfallen because a missionary career was not then open to girls. But Robert consoled her by promising that when he was a missionary he would take her into the pulpit with him. Whenever she played teacher with her dolls she imagined they were dark-skinned children from Calabar.

Increasingly difficult circumstances overtook the Slessors. Robert, the eldest son, died of illness, and Mr Slessor lost his job due to his intemperance. In 1859 he moved with his wife and five remaining children to Dundee. The money the Slessors had gained from the sale of their furnishings in Aberdeen quickly evaporated, so their new home was bare and comfortless. Father Robert eventually went to work in one of the city's mills. The youngest child, Janie, was born in Dundee. Two other Slessor children became ill and died, leaving Mary with three younger siblings – Susan, John and Janie.

In Dundee Mrs Slessor joined the Wishart Church, named in memory of George Wishart, the renowned sixteenth century Scottish reformer and martyr. She took her children, 'with a drop of perfume on their handkerchief and gloves and a peppermint in their pockets for sermon-time', to the regular church services and also had them attend the Sunday School.

Despite such influences, Mary later described herself as 'a wild lassie' during that period. But that changed quite suddenly through the influence of an old widow who used to watch the neighborhood children playing outdoors. Concerned for their souls, she would gather some of the girls together and talk to them about spiritual matters. One winter afternoon she invited a group to warm themselves by the fireplace in her home. Seizing it as an opportunity to portray the dangers that awaited those who neglected salvation, she exclaimed, 'Do ye see that fire? If ye were to put your hand into the lowes [flames] it would be gey sair [very painful]. It would burn ye. But if ye dinna [don't] repent and believe on the Lord Jesus Christ your soul will burn in the lowin' bleezin' [flaming, blazing] fire for ever and ever!'

The words lodged like arrows in Mary's heart. She could not get the vision of eternal torment they produced out of her mind, so much so that she was unable to sleep. As a result she soon 'repented and believed', having been driven, as she would afterward say, by the threat of hell-fire into Christ's kingdom. Interestingly, however, throughout her long, subsequent ministry career, she never sought to lead people to the Savior by using the tactic that played such a significant role in her own conversion.

Not many months after the move to Dundee, Mrs Slessor had to enter one of the factories to help support her family. Mary was left to care for her siblings and undertake many of the household responsibilities. Less than a year later, when Mary was just eleven years old, she too was put to work in a factory to help supply needed income for the family. At first she was a 'half-timer' in a textile factory, working half the day and attending a school connected with the factory the other half. By the time she was fourteen she had become a skilled weaver and went to work fulltime while continuing her education at the school by night. She worked at the factory from 6 a.m. to 6 p.m. with an hour break for both breakfast and lunch. She arose at five o'clock each morning to help with household chores and had to carry out similar duties after returning home at night.

She learned elementary reading, writing and arithmetic at the factory school. She borrowed and read books from the library of her Sunday School. She often read late into the night as well as while walking to and from the mill. Like David Livingstone had done at Blantyre before her, she laid an open book on her factory loom and read from it in any free moments.

As her father descended deeper into alcoholism, conditions grew increasingly desperate for the family. Any money he could lay his hands on was spent on drink, and his wife was often left with nothing to feed and clothe the children. As a result, not infrequently Mary was sent on a mission that she always found loathsome and shameful – to sell a parcel of household goods at the nearest pawnbroker's shop in order to cover the most pressing expenses of the week.

Saturday nights were tense, fearful occasions for Mary and her mother. Having received his weekly pay in cash, Robert Slessor would stay out late drinking and then stumble home thoroughly inebriated. When his wife and eldest daughter offered him the supper they had denied themselves in order to provide for him, he often threw it into the fire. Sometimes when he became violent Mary was forced to flee into the streets where she wandered, alone and sobbing, in the dark.

These tensions ended when her father died. But the pressures on her remained enormous as she had become the primary wage earner for the family. Her life at that time was said to be 'one long act of self-denial'.

Her only source of interest outside of work and helping to care for the family was her church and its ministries. In addition to attending a Bible class for teens and adults, she participated in the weeknight prayer meetings and taught a class of 'lovable lassies' in the Sabbath School. Despite her wearisome work hours and the long walk to and from the church, she never missed any of its services or meetings.

Wishart Church was located in the slums, among tall tenements out of which poured hordes of rough, unruly children. The church began a mission to reach these needy young people, and Mary was given charge of classes for boys and girls both on Sundays and weeknights. When she and a few others attempted to carry out open-air evangelistic ministry, roughs opposed them, pelting them with mud.

One night a gang that seemed determined to break up the mission surrounded her on the street. The leader swung a lead weight fastened to the end of a cord closer and closer to her head. She courageously stood her ground and did not flinch even when the weight grazed her forehead. Amazed and impressed, the leader allowed his weapon of intimidation to fall to the ground and exclaimed, 'She's game, boys!' Out of admiration, the entire gang attended her meeting that night, and some of its members continued to do so in the future. The youth who had swung the lead weight was converted and transformed, and he afterward pointed to that occasion as the turning point in his life.

In time Mary worked with the Sunday morning youth mission service that was started by a new congregation, the Victoria Street United Presbyterian Church. Before the services she would dart through the tenements, knocking on doors, rousing children from sleep and urging them to attend the meeting. She also visited those families in their homes, sharing tea with them at the table or assisting an overtaxed mother by nursing her baby beside the fire.

Like most of the members of the United Presbyterian Church, Mary and her mother eagerly read reports of the denomination's foreign missionary activities in its monthly publication, *Missionary Record*. Whenever those revered missionaries returned on furlough, people thronged to their meetings; Mary and her mother were always present at such gatherings.

Once after hearing a veteran missionary present the spiritual needs of Calabar, Mrs Slessor was so moved she longed to dedicate her son John to that work. He was apprenticed to a blacksmith, but his health began to decline and a change of climate was considered imperative. He emigrated to New Zealand but died only one week after arriving there.

That grievous loss of both a brother and a cherished family hope started Mary wondering: Would it ever be possible for her to become a missionary? Could she take her brother's place? Only gradually did those thoughts, which she expressed outwardly to no one, begin to form into a definite desire and determination.

The news of David Livingstone's death early in 1874 created a new wave of missionary enthusiasm and played a part in leading many, Mary Slessor included, to offer themselves for service on the Dark Continent. When she broached the subject with her mother, she received her happy consent. Most of Mary's trusted spiritual confidantes also encouraged her in pursuing the possibility. She offered her services to the Foreign Mission Board in May of 1875 and was accepted as a teacher for Calabar.

The Mission Board brought her to Edinburgh for three months of specialized training during the spring of the following year. She attended the Normal School in Canongate and served in various missions in the city. Her influence led two of her companions during those months to offer themselves to the Foreign Mission Board, and both were accepted for service in China.

TWO

Her preparation completed, Mary sailed aboard the steamship *Ethiopia* from Liverpool on August 5, 1876. Five weeks later the ship steamed into the estuary, twelve miles wide at its mouth, where the Cross and Calabar Rivers empty into the Atlantic Ocean at the southeastern coast of Nigeria.

The land known as Calabar to which Mary came was considered one of the deadliest and most degraded in all of Africa at that time. For centuries its inhabitants had been carried off as slaves in large numbers by African and Arab nations to the north and east as well as by European slave traders supplying the markets of the West Indies and America. While the European slave trade had been largely abolished decades earlier, Calabar's population continued to be ravaged by intertribal warfare, disease and various pagan practices. Britain considered Calabar as being within its sphere of influence but had little control over its people.

Though trading vessels had carried slaves, spices, gold dust, ivory, and palm oil from the coast of Calabar for hundreds of years, very little was known of conditions more than just a few miles inland. The coastal peoples jealously guarded their prerogative to act as middlemen for the lucrative trade that took place between trading vessels and inland tribes. Even the missionaries who had ministered there for three decades had made little progress in moving inland. Their main accomplishment had been in establishing a strong base of ministry near the coast.

About thirty-five miles from the coast the steamer that was transporting Mary left the Cross River and traveled a few miles northeast up the Calabar River. There it came to a pair of settlements, Duke Town and Old Town, located just a couple of miles from each other. Atop a hill in the former were the mission buildings of the United Presbyterian Church. In addition to those two towns, the Mission had established ministries in Creek Town, Ikunetu and Ikorofiong, located between ten and thirty miles away, to the northwest, along the Cross River and another of its numerous tributaries. Ministry was carried on at several outstations as well.

Mary's initial responsibilities included teaching in the school on Mission Hill and visiting local people at their homes. She made a tour of the stations and outstations, being accompanied by three African boys in the exhausting treks through the bush and across innumerable streams.

The sight of a white woman was so rare in some of the districts that many young children ran away from her, screaming with fright. The women, on the other hand, crowded around her, excitedly talking, gesturing and touching her until the chiefs dispersed them with a whip.

Mary soon learned that the basic social unit in the bush villages consisted of a House, over which a master or chief had autocratic and absolute authority. A cluster of mud huts, in which lived related families, comprised the village compound or yard. Each chief had several wives and slaves, the latter of which could be sold or killed at the master's will. Everyone who belonged to a House was under its protection.

Outside the villages people were protected by no laws and were at the mercy of Egbo, a strange secret society that alternately terrorized and protected individuals in the wilderness. The representatives of that society, known as Egbo runners, supposedly represented a supernatural being in the bush. They would suddenly appear, wearing fierce masks and some fantastic garb, and would fall on people with their long whips. At the first sign of them, women fled deep into the bush, for if the Egbo runners caught them they flogged them and stripped off their clothes. Oddly enough, Egbo was often appealed to as an aid in upholding law and order.

Efik was the language of Calabar as well as the trade language understood to one degree or another over a wide region of the surrounding country. Mary picked it up quickly by ear from the people rather than from a book, and soon was able to take a larger part in the Mission's various ministries.

Through her visits to local dwellings she had many opportunities to minister to spiritually needy individuals. One Sunday morning in Duke Town she saw a man sitting at the door of his hut and asked, 'Why are you not going to God's House?'

Rocking himself, he replied, 'If your heart was vexed would you go any place? Would you not rather sit at home and nurse your sorrow?'

Inquiring further, she learned that his only child had died and been buried in the house. As was customary at the loss of a loved one, the family was sitting in squalor and drunkenness. He took her into a room where the mother sat with her head bowed over the grave. Mary read from John 11 and shared with them the Christian certainty of eternal life through faith in Christ. 'Do you not find comfort in these words?' she asked the bereaved mother gently.

'No. Why should I find comfort when my child is gone?'

Still wishing to help the woman, Mary told her of her own mother's loss of several of her children to death, and how she had found comfort in the thought of being reunited with them in heaven someday. At the thought of such a prospect the African woman wept.

In the poorest section of town she came upon a group of men selling rum. They quickly put the liquor away and begged her to stay. The men quietly listened to what she had to say until she denounced the sale of alcohol. 'What for white man bring them rum suppose them rum no be good?' one man inquired in broken English. 'He be god-man [who] bring the rum – then what for god-man talk so?'

Mary was fully aware that civilized countries were deluging Calabar with trade liquor. She felt bitterness toward the unscrupulous individuals who profited at the expense of the moral, social and financial degradation of others. But knowing that even British rum-dealers were viewed by the Africans as Christians, she was frustrated that she could not provide a convincing answer to the man's objection.

At times Mary found Calabar's climate with its extremes of dry and rainy seasons to be difficult to bear. The dry season, which lasted from December to March, was especially trying to her. Its excessive heat and 'smokes', a haze of fine dust that blew in from Africa's north-central desert regions, seemed to sap all her energy. She was frequently laid low by fever and once in her first term of service was thought to be at the point of death. Mary also experienced serious bouts of loneliness and homesickness. In June, 1879, after three years in Africa, she was delighted to return to Scotland on furlough, where she could enjoy the more temperate climate and the company of family members and friends.

When Mary arrived back in Africa in October, 1880, she learned to her joy that she was to be in charge of the work at Old Town and its small outstations of Qua, Akim and Ikot Ansa. While Old Town was located just two miles upriver from Duke Town, the fact that she was being given the oversight of this portion of the Mission's work indicated the trust she had earned as a missionary.

The first sight that greeted her upon her arrival at Old Town was a human skull hung on a pole at the town entrance. Her home there was built of wattle and mud, had a mat roof and was whitewashed on the interior. She began to subsist wholly on local food, a habit she would follow throughout her long missionary career. Missionary colleagues assumed she did this out of preference; she actually did it to economize in order to send more of her salary home to help support her mother and sisters.

Mary's household at that time consisted of a young woman and several younger boys and girls. She invested much time in their training and they assisted her in various aspects of her work. Regular school sessions were held at Old Town, Qua and Akim, with both children and adults attending as students. She led Sunday morning church services at a couple of the outstations, usually with between eighty and one hundred people in attendance at each. Along the way to and from those services she visited the sick or stopped in to have a friendly visit and prayer with this or that chief and his household. By midday she was back at Old Town to conduct a large Sunday School, and nearly the entire community attended the weekly Sunday evening church service there.

One of the horrifying, superstitious practices that Mary and the other missionaries strove earnestly to overcome was the custom of killing twin babies. Calabarians believed that the father of one of the infants was an evil spirit and that at least one of the twins was a monster. Twin babies were seized, their backs were broken and they were crushed into a calabash or water pot. After being removed from the house – by a hole broken in the back wall rather than through the doorway – they were thrown into the bush to be eaten by wild animals or insects. The mother of the twins was thought to be guilty of a great sin and was banished from the community to live alone in the wild.

In order to rescue these innocent infants, the missionaries sought to gain possession of them as soon as they were born. Twin babies were taken to the Mission compounds where they were protected and cared for. At first it was useless to take the mother of a set of twins with them to a compound because, believing herself accursed, she would try to kill the infants herself before escaping to the bush. But gradually that changed and some of those mothers came to seek refuge at the compounds as well.

Another type of infant the missionaries had to rescue regularly was a baby whose slave mother had died. No slave had time to raise another woman's child, and even if she did, the child, when grown, would be taken from her to become the property of the master. As life was considered of little value, the Africans thought it best to leave a motherless slave baby in the wild to perish.

Mary spoke out against the evils of these forms of infanticide and took a few such rescued children under her care. At first the people viewed this with suspicion, thinking her in league with a devil and expecting to see her suffer ill effects as a result. But in time their superstitious suppositions faded and she became known everywhere as 'the white Ma who loves babies'. (In Calabar and neighboring regions 'Ma' was a term of respect for a woman.)

Over time her influence began to hold sway in Old Town. The heathen god of the town was banished and the community leaders admitted their laws and customs were not in keeping with those of the God of Scripture. Eventually several pagan customs were outlawed, including the murder of twins, the stripping and flogging of women by Egbo runners and the making of human sacrifices. In the latter practice, which, like the other customs, had been carried out in the region for centuries, men and women were bound and left to perish beside rivers to appease the god of shrimps. Unfortunately, in the outlying towns and remote bush regions, such pagan practices continued to be carried out with varying degrees of secrecy and openness.

THREE

Mary began to visit other communities along the river. She had earlier met and formed a friendship with King Eyo Honesty VII, the influential Christian monarch of Creek Town, situated ten miles northwest of Old Town. Now a chief named Okon invited her to visit his town of Ibaka (later James Town), located thirty miles upriver. When King Eyo Honesty VII learned of this, he provided a royal canoe, complete with oarsmen, for the venture. Mary and the four children under her care at that time were transported the ten-hour journey upstream to Ibaka.

There they were taken to the chief's compound where they were to stay in his house. Their room opened out into the women's yard which was shared by Chief Okon's several wives. In keeping with accepted etiquette, all the wives sat as close as possible to their honored guest. As Calabarian chiefs liked their wives to be corpulent (a sign of health and prosperity), each wife sought to be heftier than her rivals. In the evenings, with a number of heavy, perspiring women pressing close to her in the room, which had no ventilation, Mary found the arrangements nearly unbearable. In addition, lizards rustling in the roof matting showered down dust on the room's occupants, and at night rats darted across them as they tried to sleep.

Each day Mary held a morning and evening service in which she taught the local people, some of whom came from great distances. For many of them it was their first time to see a white woman and to hear of Christianity. She also used her supply of medicines and bandages to tend to the physical needs of many.

One morning it was discovered that two of the master's young wives had violated the strictest of cultural taboos by leaving the women's yard and entering a room where a boy was sleeping. The chief and leading men of the district gathered to discuss the offense. They determined that each of the two young wives should receive one hundred lashes with a leather strap. Mary knew that mutilation and even dismemberment were not out of the question.

When she approached Chief Okon with her reservations about the severe punishment, he responded: 'Ma, it be proper big palaver, but if you say we must not flog we must listen to you as our mother and our guest. But they will say that God's Word be no good if it destroy the power of the law to punish evildoers.'

Chief Okon agreed to let her address the offending wives, their judges and the other townspeople at a midday gathering. Speaking first to the wives, she stated: 'You have brought much shame on us by your folly and by abusing your master's confidence while the yard is in our possession. Though God's word teaches men to be merciful, it does not countenance or pass over sin, and I cannot shelter you from punishment. You have knowingly and deliberately brought it on yourselves. Ask God to keep you in the future so that your conduct may not be a reproach to yourselves and the word of God which you know.'

187

Turning to the assembly, she continued: 'Ay, but you are really to blame. It is your system of polygamy which is a disgrace to you and a cruel injustice to these helpless women. Girls like these, sixteen years old, are not beyond the age of fun and frolic. To confine them as you do is a shame and a blot on your manhood. Obedience such as you command is not worth the having.'

Some of the old men responded, 'When the punishment is severe, neither slave nor wife dare disobey. The old fashions are better than the new.' A heated debate ensued. But in the end Mary succeeded in getting the punishment reduced to ten lashes with no additional consequences.

After two weeks at Ibaka, Mary and her four African children were transported back to Old Town. Toward the end of that year, 1882, a tornado seriously damaged her home there and the presbytery had her return to the Mission compound in Duke Town. Her health had been so weakened by various stresses that in April of the following year she was sent back to Scotland. She had to be carried on board, and some considered it doubtful she would even survive the voyage. But Mary apparently thought otherwise, for she took with her a small twin girl whom she had rescued and named Janie after her own sister back home.

In Scotland she spent most of her time with her mother and sisters while recuperating her health and caring for little Janie. By January of 1884 her health was restored and she was eager to return to Calabar. But in the meanwhile Mary had begun addressing the women's missionary societies of various congregations. They found her reports of the work in Africa so compelling that they urged the Foreign Mission Board to retain her in Scotland for a time so she could travel about the country promoting the cause of missions to other women's groups. This was against Mary's natural inclination, for while she was bold and confident in ministering to the people of Calabar, in her homeland she had 'a humbling consciousness' of her social and educational defects and was extremely shy about speaking in public.

Finally, at the end of that year, the Foreign Mission Committee gave its permission for her to return to Calabar. Shortly thereafter, however, the health of her sister Janie collapsed, and it was determined she must be moved to a warmer climate. At the recommendation of an acquaintance Mary took her sister to Devonshire in the south of England. When Janie's health began to improve, a house was rented in Topsham, and Mary brought her mother to live with them there.

Just as they were comfortably settling in, news arrived that Mary's other sister, Susan, had died suddenly back in Scotland. Friends in Topsham assured the missionary that they would look after her mother and sister Janie. So she once again began to make plans to return to Calabar. But a month before she was to set sail, her mother's health suddenly failed. Mary was in turmoil over what she should do until a former factory friend from Dundee agreed to come and care for her mother and sister.

She arrived back in Calabar toward the end of 1885. By March of the following year the heartbreaking news arrived that both her mother and sister Janie had died. For a time she was overwhelmed with a sense of desolation and loneliness. 'I, who all my life have been caring and planning and living for them, am left, as it were, stranded and alone,' she wrote. 'There is no one to write and tell all my stories and troubles and nonsense to.' She also stated her slender consolation: 'Heaven is now nearer to me than Britain, and no one will be anxious about me if I go up-country.'

Mary's third term of service in Calabar began in Creek Town, ten miles upriver from Old Town. In addition to caring for a number of children in her own household, she taught in the Mission's day school, Sunday School and Bible class. She had a regular stream of visitors who came to her for food, medical help and advice with their problems.

In October of 1886, the Calabar Mission Committee granted Mary the longtime desire of her heart by giving her permission to carry out pioneering missionary work in the previously unreached Okoyong region, a densely forested wedge of land between the Cross and Calabar rivers north of Creek Town. Three times over the course of the next year and a half, delegations from the Mission went with her to seek permission from the Okoyong people for her to settle and start a school among them. But the Okoyongese had a long history of complete isolation from any and all outsiders and each of those requests was refused.

The people of Okoyong were taller and more muscular than the coastal residents of Calabar. They were thought to be the westernmost remnant of the Bantu race that had pressed into the area from Central and South Africa some time in the distant past. Morally they were far more degraded than the people to whom Mary had been ministering to date. They readily practiced witchcraft and animal sacrifice. They were a lawless people who indiscriminately plundered property, stole slaves and carried out all variety of theft. Chiefs lived with their extended households in isolated clearings with armed scouts constantly on the lookout along all the trails leading to each community. A chief sought to acquire as many wives and slaves and to have as many children as possible, thus strengthening his household and increasing its likelihood of survival. If a community failed to remain strong it would certainly fall prey to a stronger, neighboring chief.

Their notions of justice and judicial methods were thoroughly pagan and barbaric. Two superstitious trials by ordeal were commonly used to determine a person's guilt or innocence if suspected of a crime. In one, boiling palm oil was poured over a suspect's hands. If the skin became blistered, he was condemned as guilty and punished further. In the other, the poisonous esere bean was pounded into powder, mixed with water and drunk. If the person's body vomited the poison, thus delivering him from death, it was taken as a sign of innocence.

The illness or death of a freeman was invariably considered the result of someone having practiced sorcery against him. The witchdoctor was called in and individuals he named, both slave and free, were chained and tried. The African people found much grim merriment in seeing the victims writhe in agony and in their ultimate decapitation. Appeal could be made to the law of substitution, and sometimes a younger brother or a number of slaves were executed in the place of a man or woman who had been judged guilty of a crime.

A man's position in the afterlife was thought to be determined by his rank and wealth in his earthly life. When a chief died, many individuals were put to death to accompany him into the spirit world. Not long before Mary settled among them, following a fourth exploratory visit, a chief of moderate means died; eight slave men, eight slave women, ten boys, ten girls and four of his free wives were buried with him. Those were in addition to the men and women who had died from the poison ordeal that was carried out in connection with his death. After settling in Okoyong and carefully investigating these practices, Mary concluded that within a twenty mile radius at least 300 people per year perished as a result of such group burials, trials by ordeal and decapitations. Many others died each year in the warfare that constantly raged between various tribes. Infanticide also destroyed much life, with twin murder being carried out 'with an even fiercer zeal' than had been the case in Calabar.

Liquor, guns and chains were practically the only items of commerce that entered Okoyong. Gin or rum was in every home and was drunk by every adult and child, beginning from infancy. Drunkenness and the resulting disputes were commonplace.

To these desperately needy people Mary returned in June of 1888, to see about settling among them. Leaving the canoe that carried her upriver at the landing beach, she made her way alone four miles inland through the jungle to a village of mud huts named Ekenge. The chief, Edem, was sober at the time and received her warmly. The next day she trekked two miles north to the neighboring village of Ifako. At both settlements she gained permission from the chiefs to build a house and live among them, as well as their promise of land for a schoolhouse. They also agreed that the two schools and her two homes would be places of refuge for criminals, those accused of sorcery and those liable to be killed for the purpose of accompanying the dead, until their cases could receive equitable consideration.

FOUR

Mary moved from Creek Town to Ekenge on Saturday, August 8, taking with her the five children (three boys and two girls, ranging in ages from eleven to less than a year) who were then entrusted to her care. She was accompanied by Mr Bishop, the printer for the Mission staff, and several Africans from Creek Town who were sent as oarsmen and carriers. It was already growing dark and a heavy rain was falling when they reached the landing beach for Ekenge. Mary at once set out with the children through the frightening forest with the understanding that Bishop and the carriers would follow shortly with dry clothes, cooking supplies and other goods.

When her colleague arrived he reported that the men claimed to be exhausted and refused to transport any belongings through the forest until morning. As Mary and the children had no food or dry clothing, and as she desired the Sabbath to be fittingly observed the next day, she immediately plunged back into the forest to return to the beach. She was pleased and comforted when one of her adopted African boys came running to keep her company on the difficult trek. Reaching the river, Mary good-naturedly but firmly routed the men out of the canoe where they had fallen asleep. Though shamefaced at first, they were soon offloading the boxes in good humor, and by midnight the essential supplies had been transported to Ekenge.

The room set aside for Mary and her adopted children was one of those in the women's yard of Chief Edem. In addition to many wives, children and slaves, the crowded premises were filled with cows, goats, birds, cats, rats, cockroaches and centipedes. The wives constantly bickered and scolded, and the most strident of them continually vented her ill temper by striking a naked, sickly slave. Wives and other visitors considered it their duty to keep Mary company so she would not become lonely, making it extremely difficult for her to have time for personal prayer and reflection.

She found an ally in Chief Edem's sister, Eme Ete, who was commonly called Ma Eme. She was one of the widows of another important chief in the area and had only recently returned from the superstitious ceremonies carried out after her husband's death. All the chief's widows had come under suspicion of having caused his death by sorcery, and only through a witchdoctor's caprice was Ma Eme judged not guilty and spared from execution. She was a tall, large woman who acted as a mother to all by scolding, encouraging and advising in turn. Ma Eme was an intercessor and peacemaker between her brother the chief and his wives whenever he was drunk or peevish. She looked after Mary's comfort and needs, and, unknown to others, at the risk of her life, secretly made the missionary aware of all the underground activities of the tribe.

Immediately Mary started having daily school sessions at Ekenge and Ifako. About thirty students, mainly young people, attended the afternoon lessons at Ifako. At Ekenge school was held in the outer yard of Chief Edem's house in the evening, when the wives and slaves had some free time. Many men and women, boys and girls, slaves and free crowded into the yard. The sessions included lessons on reading (starting with the learning of the alphabet) and mathematics as well as Bible stories and singing.

Some time after Mary settled in Okoyong, the principal wife of a neighboring harem went to visit her son and daughter at a village near the Cross River, an eight-hour journey from Ekenge. Upon arriving, she discovered that the chief was near death and the whole community was awaiting, with mixed expectancy and terror, the slaughter that was sure to follow his death. The visiting woman encouraged them to send for the white Ma at Ekenge who, with her medicines, had the power to heal and had saved many. Mary was summoned and, against the objections of Chief Edem and Ma Eme (who feared for her life), set out the next morning in a torrential rain. A delegation of free women and armed men from the distant village accompanied her.

As they hastened through the wet, heavy brush, Mary had to take off her cumbersome boots and outer garments. These were placed in the calabashes the African women carried on their heads. After three hours of struggling through the steaming bush they came to a marketplace in a clearing where hundreds of local people had gathered. They stared in amazement at the barefooted white woman whose light dress was drenched and covered with mud. Humiliated at her own appearance, she passed swiftly through their midst, wondering if she had 'lost face' and their respect. Only later did she learn that the self-denial and courage she exhibited in undertaking that trek did more than anything to win their hearts and esteem.

Though she was cold and feverish by the time they reached the ailing chief's village, Mary immediately tended to his precarious condition. Through the Lord's blessing on her care and use of medicine, the chief regained consciousness and recovered his strength. Because of this, not only was a mass killing avoided, but the villagers also expressed their desire to establish peaceful relations with Calabar and to 'learn book'. Ever after this self-sacrificing, successful mission of mercy, Mary found all of Okoyong open to her.

In time a mud hut was built for Mary and her foster children on a separate piece of property designated for that purpose in Ekenge. The small home included two rooms, each eleven feet by six, a shaded verandah and a shed. In neighboring Ifako a larger building was constructed which served as both the church and schoolhouse. Its meeting room was thirty feet by twenty-five, and two smaller rooms were attached at one end where Mary could stay when circumstances prevented her from returning to Ekenge.

The missionary longed to undermine the prevailing and devastating liquor traffic in Okoyong by introducing its people to other forms of legitimate trade. She invited indigenous traders from Calabar to come with cloth, pots, dishes and other useful articles, but they flatly refused, fearing the Okoyong warriors and not trusting her influence over them. Mary eventually convinced all the chiefs in her neighborhood to join her in making a trading expedition to Creek Town. They took bags of palm kernels and a barrel of oil for trading purposes. At Mary's resolute insistence they left behind their guns and swords, but only after protesting vigorously: 'Ma, you make women of us! Did ever a man go to a strange place without his arms?'

This venture proved beneficial in more than one way. Most importantly, productive trade relations were established between the peoples of Calabar and Okoyong, with the latter producing palm kernels and oil to sell to the factories downriver. This left them with less time and inclination for useless drinking, quarreling and fighting. In addition, seeing how Mary had been treated as a superior by esteemed King Eyo Honesty VII and the other African leaders in Creek Town gave the Okoyong chiefs an elevated opinion of her. Immediately after returning to Okoyong they declared that they must treat her in keeping with her rank and station by building a proper house for her to live in, and promptly set out to do so.

The following summer, 1889, a carpenter named Charles Ovens arrived from Scotland to assist in finalizing construction of the home. The house was spacious and elevated. A verandah, six feet above the ground, ran along the entire front of the building. In addition to living quarters, the house included a kitchen and medical dispensary.

Just as progress was moving along smoothly on the mission home, a tragedy occurred involving Chief Edem's oldest son, Etim. He was soon to be married and was in the process of building a house of his own. While handling a log to be used in the home, it slipped and struck the back of his neck, paralyzing him. Knowing his death would cause great trouble, Mary attentively cared for him for two weeks, vainly seeking to preserve his life.

When Etim died, Edem shouted, 'Sorcerers have killed him, and they must die! Bring the witchdoctor!' The medicine man fixed the blame for the tragedy on a certain village. Ekenge warriors immediately went to the settlement, sacked all the houses and captured more than a dozen men and women who had not been able to escape into the forest. These prisoners were brought back in chains and fastened to posts in Chief Edem's yard.

What Mary did next seems weird, even shocking, to civilized sensibilities, but it was done in an effort to allay the destruction of much life that otherwise was certain to take place:

> Anxious to pacify the rage of the chiefs, father and uncle, Mary undertook to do honour to the dead lad by dressing him in the style befitting his rank. Fine silk cloth was wound round his body, shirts and vests were put on, over these went a suit of clothes which she had made for his father, the head [hair] was shaved into patterns and painted yellow, and round it was wound a silk turban, all being crowned with a tall black and scarlet hat with plumes of brilliant feathers. Thus attired the body was carried out into a booth in the women's yard, where it was fastened, seated in an arm-chair, under a large umbrella. To the hands were tied the whip and silver-headed stick that denoted his position, while a mirror was arranged in front of him, in order that he might enjoy the reflection of his grandeur. Beside him was a table, upon which were set out all the treasures of the house, including the skulls taken in war, and a few candles begged from Mary.[1]

The Ekenge villagers were 'frenzied with delight' when they saw the high honor paid to the chief's deceased son. But rather than calming them, it set off a course of drinking, dancing and menacing behavior toward the shackled prisoners. For several days one barrel of rum after another was consumed in the chief's yard as the villagers danced around their captives with guns and machetes. Throughout that time, Mary and Ovens were

---

1   W. P. Livingstone, *Mary Slessor of Calabar, Pioneer Missionary* (London: Hodder and Stoughton, 1916), p. 93.

forced to take turns staying in the yard day and night in order to keep watch over the prisoners.

Day after day Mary pleaded with Chief Edem to release the prisoners rather than subject them to the poison bean ordeal. The chief and others were furious with her for interfering with their time-honored traditions. He could not conceive of his firstborn son being buried without the honor of a retinue to accompany him into the spirit world. But, surprisingly, he began to release small groups of prisoners until only three remained. At that point Ma Eme interceded by kneeling at the feet of her brother and suggesting that one of the captives, a heavily manacled woman, be left in her chains but placed in Mary's charge at the mission house. The chief agreed to this and also released the one remaining male prisoner, a freeman. Late that evening, likely with the secret assistance of Ma Eme, the last female prisoner managed to cut through one of the links in her chain and escape to the mission house. That same night the funeral for Edem's son took place, and only a cow was buried with the young man's body.

Just when Mary thought calm was about to be restored, new waves of trouble crashed through the region. Two parties of Africans from neighboring locations chanced to meet in the bush while one was coming to and the other returning from the chaotic events at Ekenge. A past conflict between the two groups quickly reignited. The party returning from Ekenge, thoroughly drunk, killed one of the men from the opposing group and carried his head back to their own village as a trophy. Further fighting ensued between the two factions and many were seriously wounded.

Meanwhile, one afternoon the whole village of Ekenge went wild with terror at the news that the dreaded Egbo were approaching, probably with the intent of restoring order in the area. All the women, children and unarmed men rushed to the Mission house for protection. Mary packed as many women and children into her room as it would hold, then ordered the others to hide in the bush at the back of the Mission premises. Before arriving at Ekenge, the invading Egbo runners set fire to every house at one village and burned alive all the livestock at another. But they remained only a short time in Ekenge and no serious harm was done to its people or property. For over a week, however, Edem's village remained on edge and indiscriminately shot down any man or woman who passed nearby in the forest. Much blood was shed before the various warring bands wearied of the conflict and returned to their respective communities.

This entire incident proved to be the longest and severest strain to which Mary would ever be subjected in dealing with the Africans' passions and pagan customs. It marked the first time in the known history of Okoyong that the death and funeral of one with the rank of a chief took place without the sacrifice of any human life. As a result Mary's reputation spread throughout Okoyong and even beyond into yet unexplored regions. Eventually one evening Edem came alone to Mary, kneeled before her, clasped her feet and thanked her repeatedly for her love and courage, her brave insistence that they should not take people's lives at his son's death, and all the peaceful measures she was promoting. Other free people, one by one and unknown to each other, secretly came to her, thanking her for the increased safety she was bringing about. They encouraged her to keep a brave heart and to continue doing away with the old customs, traditions that invariably produced death.

FIVE

Mary did continue to manifest marked courage in her dealings with the indigenous people. On numerous occasions Charles Ovens saw her take large, drunken men by the neck, pull them away from their alcohol and throw them to the ground! When an intoxicated African carrying a loaded rifle came to see her, she ordered him to stand the weapon in a corner of the verandah. When he refused, she wrenched the gun from him, set it in a corner and defied him to touch it. She once stopped and confiscated a canoe-load of machetes that were being taken upriver for use in war. On another occasion she intervened between two tribes that were on the verge of attacking each other. Though her heart was beating wildly, she stood between them and made them pile their rifles on opposite sides of her. With mounds of weapons heaped up over five feet high on both sides, Mary then negotiated a peaceful settlement to the conflict. That was just one of a number of occasions when she played a key role in preventing tribes from going to war with each other.

The missionary had a favorite and curious device that she used while involved in the lengthy palavers that were required to settle disputes among tribes or to determine a person's innocence or guilt in connection with an alleged crime – the whole time she sat knitting. She thought the activity helped her not to be nervous and kept her from showing fear. The sight of her continuing to knit quietly and steadily, even in the midst of considerable uproar, had a way of helping to calm undue excitement. She claimed it was only during those long disputations that she could get some knitting done. An official who witnessed one such proceeding reported that Mary stayed listening and knitting through an entire day and night, until the opposing parties became hungry and withdrew without a fight.

Throughout Okoyong twin babies and orphaned infants continued to be killed or left to perish in the bush. Mary always showed special attentiveness and tenderness in seeking to rescue and care for such endangered infants. Most of the wee ones brought to her for care were already so sickly and physically broken that they would not ultimately survive. But she always washed them, cared for them with utmost patience and tenderness, and did all she could to comfort them and save their lives. Whenever one died, she dressed it attractively, placed its little body among flowers in a box, held a service over it and buried it in a small cemetery, which in time became full of tiny graves. Four local girls – Janie (also called Jean), Mary, Alice and Annie – who did survive, for several years made up the inner circle of the missionary's family and grew up to become a great comfort to her.

Late in 1890, just before Mary returned to England for a year of furlough, she was secretly engaged to Charles Morrison, a member of the Mission staff serving in Duke Town. Then twenty-five years old (some seventeen years younger than Mary), Morrison was said to be 'a man of fine feeling, with a distinct literary gift'. He had seen Mary on several occasions, was attracted to her, and had been very attentive and kind to her in one of her periods of illness. They became engaged with the understanding that he would come to live and minister with her in Okoyong.

When Mary revealed this to the Mission Board while on furlough the following September, she made it clear she had given her word to the people of Okoyong not to leave them, and not even for personal happiness would she break that promise. Of her submissive outlook on the situation she wrote:

> I lay it all in God's hands, and will take from Him whatever He sees best for His work in Okoyong. My life was laid on His altar for that people long ago, and I would not take one jot or tittle of it back. If it be for His glory and the advantage of His cause there to let another join in it I will be grateful. If not I will still try to be grateful, as He knows best.[2]

The Board's response was a qualified refusal of Mary and Morrison's proposal. Likely the Board had concerns over the couple's significant difference in age, temperament and ministry gifting. The Mission directors underscored the importance of Morrison's ministry at Duke Town and indicated they could not sanction his leaving there until a suitable replacement had been found.

'What the Lord ordains is right,' Mary responded simply to the Board's decision. A short while later Morrison was forced by failing health back to Scotland, where a medical specialist advised against his returning to Calabar. He later went to America where he died shortly after a fire destroyed his cherished collection of literary papers. The loss affected him greatly and was thought to hasten his death.

---

2   Ibid., p. 114. See also Basil Miller, *Mary Slessor, Heroine of Calabar* (Minneapolis: Bethany, n.d.), p. 79.

When Mary returned to Calabar early in 1892 she was enlisted by the British government to carry out a new judicial responsibility in Okoyong. For many years British authorities had exercised only minimal influence over the coastal regions of the country, and tribes further up the Cross River wholly ignored and opposed their directives. In 1889 the British government succeeded in gaining approval from the principal chiefs of the area to establish the Niger Coast Protectorate. Sir Claude MacDonald, who had carried out those negotiations, was appointed Consul-General in 1891.[3] Recognizing Mary Slessor's unique position and influence in Okoyong, he asked her to organize and supervise an indigenous court and empowered her to do all that was necessary to promote the reception of new laws in the region.

Mary presided over the court at various locations throughout Okoyong. Large groups of tribal leaders also came to consult her about adjusting their customs to the new laws. Through these activities justice was promoted for the local people and the rule of law was promoted in the region. Though Mary did not relish that type of service, she sought to carry it out faithfully, believing it to be part of the ministry the Lord had for her to do.

Some time in 1894 a slave in an outlying village was accused of causing his master's death by witchcraft. Rather than submitting to Mary's authority in hearing the case, the village chief ordered the man to be taken to a town outside of Okoyong. There, beyond the reach of the missionary's jurisdiction, the slave could be subjected

---

3   Less than a decade later MacDonald gained considerable acclaim while serving as the British minister in Peking during the Boxer Rebellion. He afterward served as the first British ambassador to Japan.

to the poison bean ordeal. Mary promptly resorted to a measure she had never before employed. She appealed to the British Consulate at Duke Town, seeking government assistance not only in rescuing the accused individual but also in ending use of the poison ordeal throughout all of Okoyong. The British Vice-Consul held a conference with many of the Okoyong chiefs. They promised to abstain from killing at funerals and to allow 'Ma' the opportunity to save and care for infant twins.

While the former practice was curtailed, the destruction of twins continued unabated. Consequently, the following year she again appealed for consular intervention. This time Sir Claude MacDonald himself came to review and renew the agreement with the chiefs. Those leaders, believing that evil spirits were involved in the birth of twins, genuinely feared that misfortune might befall them if such children were allowed to live. Nevertheless, they indicated they would try to stop the killing of twins, though they would not agree to keeping them in their homes. Mary reiterated her willingness to be responsible for the twins' welfare if the people would but notify her of their births. Three years later she was able to report that throughout her years of service in Africa she had rescued fifty-one twins from destruction.

Throughout her years of active and sacrificial service, Mary was strengthened and sustained through constant prayer and the regular study of Scripture. Of the former she once testified:

My life is one long daily, hourly, record of answered prayer. For physical health, for mental overstrain, for guidance given marvelously, for errors and dangers averted, for enmity to the Gospel subdued, for food provided at the exact hour needed, for everything that goes to make up life and my poor service, I can testify with a full and often wonder-stricken awe that I believe God answers prayer. … I have proved during long decades while alone, as far as man's help and presence are concerned, that God answers prayer. … It is the very atmosphere in which I live and breathe and have my being, and it makes life glad and free and a million times worth living. … I am sitting alone here on a log among a company of natives. My children, whose very lives are a testimony that God answers prayer, are working round me. Natives are crowding past on the bush road to attend palavers, and I am at perfect peace, far from my own countrymen and conditions, because I know God answers prayer. Food is scarce just now. We live from hand to mouth. We have not more than will be our breakfast today, but I know we shall be fed, for God answers prayer.[4]

Mary normally did her personal Bible reading first thing in the morning, as soon as there was enough daylight. Numerous times over the years she read carefully and patiently through the Bible. She would not move on to a new chapter until she was satisfied she had thoroughly considered the previous one; sometimes she spent three days in a single chapter before proceeding to the next. As she read she underlined key words and phrases. Mary packed the margins of nearly every page in her Bible with handwritten observations and applications from the text of Scripture: 'God is never behind time'; 'If you play with temptation do not expect God will deliver you'; 'We must see and know Christ before we can teach'; 'The smallest things are as absolutely necessary as the great things'; 'Blessed the man and woman who is able to serve cheerfully in the second rank – a big test'.

The Gospel of John was her favorite Bible book. She also had a special interest in the opening books of Scripture

---

4   Livingstone, *Mary Slessor of Calabar*, p. 293.

because they depicted moral and social conditions similar to what she dealt with in Calabar. Notations such as 'a chapter of Calabar history' or 'this happens in Okoyong every day' were common in those books. Each time she read through God's Word she did so using a different Bible. In this way she found that new thoughts came to her when, as the years passed, she returned repeatedly to previously-considered Scripture passages.

After seven years of ministry in Okoyong, Mary found it difficult to speak with certainty of the number of Africans who had come to genuine saving faith in Christ. A number of women, boys, girls and even a few men professed to have 'placed themselves in God's hands'. One prominent freewoman had clearly committed her life to Christ, despite the definite persecution that commitment brought her. All the children in Mary's area were sent by their parents to her school, and in them she had her greatest hopes that the younger generation of Okoyongese might more fully embrace Christianity.

By 1896 Mary was no longer centrally located among the people to whom she had been ministering. When the soil where they had been living became depleted, the indigenous people gradually moved on to richer land elsewhere. A new market was opened at Akpap, located south of Ekenge, farther inland and closer to the Cross River. Farms and villages sprung up around it, and Mary realized the necessity of following the population there.

At first the Mission was hesitant to approve this plan because the nearest boat landing to Akpap was six miles away, at Ikunetu on the Cross. Eventually the decision was made to build a mission house at Ikunetu. But long before it was constructed, Mary moved to Akpap. There she, along with her several children and their furnishings, were packed into a small two-room shed that had a dirt floor and no windows.

Tragically, a new baby taken into the cramped quarters brought with it an infectious disease, leading to the deaths of four children under Mary's care. Around that same time a small-pox epidemic swept through the region, killing hundreds. For hours each day, she was kept busy vaccinating all who came to her for help.

The epidemic devastated her old village of Ekenge. Returning there, the missionary converted her former house into a hospital. Those with the disease flocked to her. But all who were able had already fled, and she was unable to find anyone to nurse the patients or bury the dead. When Chief Edem contracted the disease she battled day and night to save his life. But ultimately he, too, succumbed. With no one to assist her, Mary built a coffin, placed him in it, dug a grave and buried him. Utterly spent, she managed to trek through the forest back to Akpap where she collapsed into bed.

Another member of the Mission staff went to retrieve some belongings from the mission house in Ekenge two days later. He found the village full of corpses; not a living person was to be seen. Ekenge was never again inhabited and gradually it was engulfed in brush and vanished without a trace.

In 1898 Mary returned to Britain for a year of much-needed furlough. She took with her four girls – Janie, Mary, Alice and Maggie – and there was a great stir of interest in them wherever they went. Eager missions' supporters flocked to see and hear this renowned missionary whose reputation had, by then, taken on near legendary proportions. Mary still disliked and naturally shrank back from such public ministry but sought to fulfill it as her Christian duty.

For three years after she returned to Akpap, Mary ministered in isolation and ill health. Plans had been drafted by the Mission for improved staffing of the station but those fell through, and only occasionally was she visited by one or another of the lady missionaries in Calabar. Throughout that same time Mary also had to struggle through long periods of low-grade fever and insomnia. At one time her health was so poor she was forced to spend three months in bed.

Mary continued to expend tremendous amounts of time and energy, however, in seeing to it that throughout Okoyong people were adhering to the new laws they had agreed to follow. Her ongoing school and Bible class ministries began to bear dividends as well. Six of the most promising boys of free birth and good standing in the district had become Christians and were working as teachers in the surrounding villages.

The missionary's fame had spread to the extent that Africans came from as far away as 100 miles to meet her. As she desired to minister to these people, she began making numerous trips further up the Cross River to visit various townships along the banks. In those journeys she traveled by canoe or in the Mission's steamer, the *David Williamson*, which Sabbath School children in Scotland had provided with their offerings.

During one of those journeys she thought for the first time that death was at her side when an infuriated hippopotamus savagely attacked the canoe in which she and some of her children were riding. She was 'almost unnerved' by the snapping of the massive jaws, the oarsmen shouting and fiercely thrusting with their paddles and the children crying, 'O God, Father, please save us, Oh!' In the end they were all able to escape the grave danger unharmed.

In August of 1903, on the fifteenth anniversary of Mary first settling in Okoyong (then at Ekenge), a Christian Communion service was observed in the territory for the first time ever. Seven young Christians were baptized and accepted into the membership of the Presbyterian Church the night before receiving communion. Eleven other children, including six Mary had rescued from death, were baptized on the day of the Communion service. A throng of people who had gathered to observe the Communion service and baptisms overflowed the church building and spilled out on to the grounds.

SIX

To the northwest of Okoyong, the serene and scenic waterway of Enyong Creek flowed down into the Cross River. For centuries the creek had been a primary artery for transporting slaves to Itu, the slave-market town at the confluence of the Enyong and Cross. The slave market had operated there until very recent years, while along the upper reaches of Enyong Creek both human sacrifice and cannibalism continued to be practised. Recently, following the death of a chief, sixty slaves had been killed and eaten.

The vast area above the Enyong and between the Cross and Niger Rivers was home to the Ibo tribe, which numbered about four million. Dominant among the Ibo was the Aros clan. The Aros lived in twenty or thirty communities situated closely together in the region surrounding Arochuku. The latter, located approximately twenty miles northwest of Itu, had prominence because of its near proximity to a famed fetish shrine known as the Long Juju. The shrine was located on a small island in the middle of a stream that ran through a secret, well-guarded gorge.

People came from great distances to make sacrifices at the shrine and to consult its priests on all variety of subjects. That individuals did so is astounding, for many who entered the area were either captured and sold into slavery or sacrificed and eaten. Just a few years earlier a group of some 800 people from the Niger River region to the west ventured to Arochuku to visit the Long Juju. Individuals supposedly connected with the shrine led them off in groups of ten or twenty under pretext of taking them to the Long Juju but then sold them into slavery. Only 136 managed to escape the trap and to report the travesty to British officials.

The area south of Enyong Creek was inhabited by another tribe, the Ibibios. They lived in small isolated huts and villages deep in the forest in order to reduce the risk of being captured by their feared Ibo neighbors. Their children went completely naked while the women, who were treated merely as beasts of burden, wore only a small palm-fibre loincloth.

In 1900 Britain established two protectorates, Northern and Southern Nigeria, with Sir Ralph Moor being appointed High Commissioner of the latter. The Ibos, especially the Aros, continued to resist the government's conciliatory efforts to bring an end to cannibalism and slavery in the region. At last a British military expedition was conducted through the area to convince the people by show of force that they must comply with the new governmental regulations. Sir Ralph met with Aros leaders at Arochuku and spelled out the government's demands of disarmament, suppression of the Juju worship and prohibition of slavery. Over 2,500 guns were surrendered and slavery was officially stopped, but human sacrifices secretly persisted in the depths of the forest.

As Mary learned more about Ibo and Ibibio, she came to have a pressing desire and a settled conviction that the Presbyterian Mission should expand its ministry into those needy regions. She viewed Itu, the former slave-market town, and Arochuku, with its proximity to the newly-defunct Long Juju, as strategic bases for such missionary advance. In January, 1903, she took two boys and one girl she had trained at Akpap in Okoyong, and set out for Itu. Mary left them there to teach and hold church services. Their efforts succeeded beyond anything she had dared hope for, and before long she returned to Itu to oversee the construction of a church and school building atop a hill with a magnificent view. By August over 300 'intelligent and well-dressed' people were meeting in the church they had built themselves.

Two months earlier, in June, she was able to visit Arochuku for the first time and found it to be a densely populated region where 30,000 people lived in an area of a few square miles. She returned to the district a short while later with two other trained young people from Akpap. That pair was left to open a school at Amasu, a town near Enyong Creek and a few miles south of Arochuku. Over a hundred children plus women and men, some of them former slave traders, immediately gathered as students.

During that same trip, while traveling back down the Enyong, several miles southeast of Amasu, Mary's canoe was intercepted by an African who informed her, 'I have been waiting for you; my master at Akani Obio sent me to waylay you and bring you to his house.' There she met Onoyom Iya Nya, president of the region's indigenous court and the only chief who had not been disarmed recently by the British government.

Onoyom Iya Nya had been raised in heathenism and had attended the cannibal feasts at Arochuku. After marrying, he experienced the misfortunes of his house burning down and his young child dying. While seeking to determine the individual who had brought these tragedies upon him through witchcraft, he met an African who once had been a teacher for the Mission in Calabar but now was a backslidden, homeless drunkard. 'How do you know,' the drunk asked, 'that it is not the God of the white man that is angry with you? He is all-powerful.'

'Where can I find this God?' the chief inquired.

'I am not worthy to say, but go to the white Ma at Itu, and she will tell you.'

Thus Mary had been sent for. 'And now,' the chief queried after explaining all this, 'will you show me what to do?' She was delighted to share about the Savior with him and his family and to pray with them. Before leaving she promised to return and see what could be done about establishing a station there.

Nearly five years had passed since her last furlough, but Mary did not have 'the slightest intention' of returning to Britain. Instead, she sought the Mission Council's permission to be relieved of her responsibilities at Akpap in Okoyong for six months in order to 'in a very easy way, try to keep up an informal system of itinerating between Okoyong and Amasu'. In time the Council approved that plan, indicated it would send two young lady missionaries to fill in for her at Akpap, and stated its unanimous conclusion that Itu should be made a medical station due to its strategic location at the threshold of this newly-opened territory.

She was not at all troubled by the Council's further stipulation that it would not be able to underwrite any additional expenses for her itinerating or for the building projects she would promote in the towns along Enyong Creek. All those expenses would need to be covered out of her own salary or by private donations from her supporters in Britain. Of her perspectives on that situation she said, 'It seems strange to be starting with a family on a gypsy life in a canoe, but God will take care of us. ... I have no object on earth but to get my food and raiment, which are of the plainest, and to bring up my bairns.'

In July, 1904, after also resigning her judicial responsibilities in Okoyong, she was able to settle in Itu as her base. Urgent pleas for Christian teachers immediately came to her from Ibo, Ibibio and back at Okoyong. 'Oh Britain,' she lamented, 'surfeited with privilege! Tired of Sabbath and Church, would that you could send over to us what you are throwing away!'

By November she was able to report incredible progress to the Mission Council. In Itu a church and a house for a teacher had been built, regular Sunday services were being held, forty candidates for church membership were attending a catechumens' class, and a day-school was being conducted. At Amasu ground had been donated by the chiefs and a good school was built. Congregations had formed and work on buildings had started at four other points along the Enyong – at Akani Obio (where Onoyom Iya Nya was chief), Okpo, Odot and Asang. The Council gave her permission to extend this itinerating ministry for six more months under the same financial conditions as before.

Ibibio on the south side of the Enyong also beckoned. Her advance into that territory was aided by the fact that the British government was building roads and establishing courts in it. 'Get a bicycle, Ma,' government officials said, pointing to the road, 'and come as far as you can. We will soon have a motor car service for you.' At fifty-seven years of age she gamely learned to ride a bicycle after another government official presented her with a brand new model from England.

In the middle of 1905 Mary set forth with a twelve-year-old boy named Etim and traveled five and a half miles inland, south and west of Itu, to Ikotobong. Despite his youth, the lad proved to be an excellent teacher and disciplinarian, and soon a school of fifty children had gathered around him. Before long Mary was involved in a new building project there.

Meanwhile, the Foreign Mission Committee in Scotland approved Itu as a medical base, and a Dr Robertson was transferred from Creek Town to oversee the work. It was decided to name the hospital and dispensary the Mary Slessor Mission Hospital. To this news she responded: 'It seems like a fairy tale. I don't know what to say. I can just look up into the blue sky and say, "Even so, Father; in good and ill, let me live and be worthy of it all." It is a grand gift, and I am glad for my people.'

When the year for her intended travels ended in April, 1906, the mission desired Mary to resume her responsibilities at Akpap in Okoyong. But she could not reconcile herself to that prospect:

> There is an impelling power behind me, and I dare not look backward. Even if it cost me my connection with the Church of my heart's love, I feel I must go forward. I am not enthusiastic over Church methods. I would not mind cutting the rope and going adrift with my bairns, and I can earn our bite and something more.

To the Foreign Mission Committee she wrote:

> Okoyong and its people are very dear to me. No place on earth now is quite as dear, but to leave these hordes of untamed, unwashed, unlovely savages [in Ibo and Ibibio] and withdraw the little sunlight that has begun to flicker out over its darkness! I dare not think of it. Whether the Church permits it or not, I feel I must stay here and even go on farther as the roads are made. I cannot walk now, nor dare I do anything to trifle with my health, which is very queer now and then, but if the roads are all the easy gradient of those already made I can get four wheels made and set a box on them, and the children can draw me about. ... With such facts pressing on me at every point you will understand my saying *I dare not go back*.[5]

She was greatly relieved when the Mission decided to free her from normal responsibilities at a base so from that point forward she could act as a pioneer missionary.

Mary continued to feel strongly that Arochuku, former guardian city of the Long Juju shrine, was strategic for reaching the Aros tribes in Ibo. She offered to build a house there at no expense to the Mission if the committee would make it an official station and appoint two missionaries to serve there. At first the Mission demurred, indicating

---

5 Livingstone, *Mary Slessor of Calabar*, pp. 225-6. See also Miller, *Mary Slessor*, pp. 113-4.

it lacked the necessary personnel and finances to carry out such expansion at that time. But after John Rankin conducted a fact-finding mission to the region, he provided the committee with such an enthusiastic report of the area's potential that he himself was charged with the responsibility of opening the Arochuku station.

The British government approached Mary about serving as a court magistrate once again, this time for Ibibio. It was agreed that the court for that district could be moved to Ikotobong where she was then living. She did assume those responsibilities but refused the salary the government offered her for doing so. She was known to blend kindness and severity in the discharge of her judicial responsibilities. Her court was popular with the local people because they knew she fully understood their language and customs and were confident she would treat them fairly.

For some time Mary had desired to build a secluded, though accessible, home where ladies of the Mission, when discouraged or in poor health, could come to rest and recuperate without the concern of being a burden or expense to others. After receiving an unexpected donation of £20 in support of her ministry, Mary determined to use it for that purpose. She discovered an ideal property on a high hill at Use, between Ikotobong and Itu, and just two miles from the landing beach. From that prominence one could enjoy expansive vistas in various directions. The ground was cleared and a small semi-European cottage was erected with the intention that other cottages would follow. Before long, however, the Mission committee sent two lady agents to minister in Ikotobong so this house at Use became Mary's new base of operation.

SEVEN

Throughout 1906 Mary suffered from diarrhea and boils. By the beginning of the following year she could not walk a half dozen consecutive steps and needed to be carried wherever she went. To others and at last to herself it became apparent that she must return to Scotland if she hoped to recoup her health. Mary left Africa in May and, for a few months, enjoyed times of rest and relaxation with devoted friends and supporters in her homeland. Letters, speaking invitations and packages arrived in such profusion that she could not keep pace in responding to them.

People were astonished when Mary suddenly announced her intentions to return to Africa in October. To some who protested her plan to return so quickly, she stated simply, 'My heart yearns for my bairns – they are more to me than myself.' She was secretly and deeply concerned over troubling rumors she had received in letters concerning Jean, one of her foster daughters, and felt she could not rest till she returned to determine whether or not they were valid. Rather against her inclination, especially under such distracted circumstances, she needed to give a trio of addresses in large cities before leaving. At the meeting in Glasgow she told her audience that in all probability she would never be back to Scotland again.

Arriving back in Africa, she was relieved beyond words to learn that the unsettling report she had received about her beloved Jean was a patent lie. She immediately plunged back into her exhausting, endless round of responsibilities. On Sundays she ministered at between six and twelve meetings in various villages and wayside locations. Through the week, long days were devoted to court hearings and helping provide needy Africans who had traveled from a distance with food and lodging. Mary continued to care for a number of children, and they assisted her with the never-ending building maintenance projects that needed to be carried out at her station and other ministry locations.

These activities, and the fact that her last furlough had not been long or restful enough to restore her health and strength, soon left the missionary worn out. The early months of 1909 found her covered with painful boils from head to foot. 'Only sleeping draughts keep me from going off my head,' she related. She later became severely ill from blood poisoning. Her health and nerves shattered, Mary resigned from her court duties that November. The middle of the following year, while once again carrying out 'regular station work' by teaching, preaching and building up the congregation at Use, she was suddenly laid very low by what she described as 'one of the funniest illnesses' she had ever had. She was transported first to Itu and later to Duke Town, and at both locations members of the Mission attentively nursed her back to health. After five weeks of such care, she was eager to return to her charge in Use, and did so before some officials and doctors thought it fully advisable.

More than once Mary had been approached at Use by delegations of young men from the town of Ikpe, a two-day journey by canoe up the Enyong Creek. They stated that over forty people from their town, an old slave-trading center, were ready to become Christians, and they begged her to come and share God's truth with them. Eventually she made three trips to the region. Ikpe was larger and more prosperous but also more degraded than she had anticipated. Girls wore only a string of beads and married women a thin strip of loincloth. Even the children were foul-mouthed. But a number of young men seemed genuinely interested in becoming Christians and had begun to build a small church. Another potential congregation began to form as well at Nkanga, three miles below Ikpe on the Enyong.

Finally, after being repeatedly reproached by the Ikpe people for not having sent them a teacher for years, Mary determined to go herself, despite her now chronic weariness. A short while later she returned there with fifty sheets of corrugated iron and other materials to be used in the construction of a mission house. She did not favor the low-lying area that had been granted for the building as such a location might foster disease. But she had faith that the Lord would watch over her health.

Mary soon had 250 locals involved in clearing the land of brush and trees. She conducted Sunday services, held palavers to resolve disputes, and nursed babies and adults alike through a variety of sicknesses and diseases. Smallpox was rampant, and the British government sent African agents to vaccinate the people. But the townspeople were suspicious of the 'white man's Juju' and could only be persuaded to accept the inoculations if Mary herself would administer them.

Eventually her health declined to the point that the missionary's doctor forbad her to travel by bicycle. Hearing of her need for an alternative means of transportation, a group of ladies in Scotland sent her a Cape cart, a basket-chair on wheels capable of being maneuvered along quite easily by two boys or girls.

Concerns over Mary's continued precarious health increased on the part of friends both in Calabar and Scotland. A Miss Cook, one of the Board members of the Women's Foreign Mission Committee, wrote as 1912 progressed, urging her to take a holiday to the Canary Islands and requesting the privilege of covering the expenses herself. Her missionary colleagues strongly encouraged her to do the same and pointed out that such a break would better fit her to carry on her ministry.

Despite real misgivings about experiencing such extravagance herself, Mary finally agreed to the proposal. Typically, she commented during the holiday, the only one she ever had in her entire life: 'Oh, if I only get another day in which to work! I hope it will be more full of earnestness and blessing than the past.' She spent one month at the islands and a second month voyaging to and from them and then returned with her health greatly restored.

During the next two years she continued her active ministries in both Use and Ikpe. Sometimes she shuttled between the two points by canoe. But more often she traveled in the government motor car as it followed the road's roundabout path to its terminus at Odoro Ikpe, just five miles south of Ikpe.

In the summer of 1913, Mary received a singular honor. A series of British government officials, impressed with her heroic record of service, recommended her for special recognition. This culminated in her being inducted as a Member in the Order of the Hospital of St John of Jerusalem in England and receiving its distinguished Silver Cross medal. She received a formal letter informing her that her selection for this honor 'received the sanction and approval of His Most Gracious Majesty King George

V', the Order's sovereign head. The honor was conferred only on 'persons professing the Christian faith, who are eminently distinguished for philanthropy, or who have specially devoted their exertions or professional skill in aid of the objects of the Order'.[6]

Mary intended to keep the honor secret but it became known to her governmental acquaintances and missionary colleagues in Duke Town. When the Silver Cross medal arrived there, her friends sent her a letter stating that it would not be appropriate for such an important award to be given surreptitiously and that it was her duty to come to Calabar to receive it.

The actual presentation took place on a Wednesday in a large hall filled with Europeans as well as the students of the Mission's boys' and girls' schools. As her ministry and influence were extolled, she sat with her hands over her face. When it was her turn to speak, she hardly knew what to say. After gaining her courage by addressing the students in Efik, she then spoke to her European audience in English. She stated her sincere belief that others deserved such recognition more than she did, and gave God all the glory for anything she had been able to accomplish. 'If I have done anything in my life it has been easy because the Master has gone before.'

Afterwards she wrote to friends back home:

> Don't think that there is any difference in my designation. I am Mary Mitchell Slessor, nothing more and none other than the unworthy, unprofitable, but most willing, servant of the King of Kings. May this be an incentive to work, and to be better than ever I have been in the past.

---

6   Livingstone, *Mary Slessor of Calabar*, p. 305.

In Britain the honor was publicized primarily through Mary's denomination's missionary publication, *The Record*, which also included an abbreviated account of her fascinating missionary career. Congratulations poured in from all parts of the world. Troubled by such acclaim, she fled for a time to Ikpe, where she stated: 'I shall never look the world in the face again until all this blarney and publicity is over. I feel so glad that I can hide here quietly where no one knows about newspapers and *Records*, and do my small portion of work out of sight.'[7]

Ever the pioneer missionary, to the end of her life Mary was always concerned with actively advancing the Mission's reach. For that purpose she met with tribal leaders in various locations around Ikpe but found them resistant to permitting Christian teaching in their communities. Finally she took a stand at Odoro Ikpe, where the government road ended and a 'Rest House' was located for officials traveling through the area. The simple shelter had a doorway but no door, a dirt floor and no furnishings. It stood atop a hill that commanded a view of the town and the vast surrounding forest region. Knowing the government would not mind, she temporarily moved into the house with the girls who accompanied her.

Mary persuaded the reluctant leaders of Odoro Ikpe to allow her to begin a school and to start having church services in their town. When the Christians at Ikpe saw her devoting so much attention to the new work, they approached her with a concern, 'Ma, we are glad you have got a footing out here, but are you forsaking us?' She assured them that when she was not away at Use she

---

7   Ibid., p. 307. See also Miller, *Mary Slessor*, pp. 133-4.

would alternate her weeks of ministry at Ikpe and Odoro Ikpe. For the remainder of her life she carried out ministry at those three locations unaided by other missionaries. To her deep disappointment, the Mission had already concluded that health conditions were not safe enough at Ikpe to place other missionaries there.

The town leaders at Odoro Ikpe asked Mary to survey the land and choose a site for a station. She selected a location on top of a hill that overlooked 'a magnificent stretch of country' and that provided a constant cooling breeze. This proved to be the final and most trying building project of her career. She was no longer able to carry out such labor herself and the available workers proved to be the most lazy, greedy and inefficient group she had ever dealt with in such an undertaking. She had to supervise them constantly, often sitting in the fierce sun all day to do so. In two or three months, however, the simple house was completed and she was able to occupy it with her children.

Shortly after that, in August, 1914, she was stunned to learn that Europe was at war. The European firms in Calabar immediately stopped trading with the indigenous people, and crucial supplies were no longer available. The shock of all this proved too much for her. For two weeks she battled a high fever and diarrhea until she was finally reduced to a stupor. The young people of Odoro Ikpe carried her to Ikpe, and from there she was transported down the Enyong and, at her insistence, to her home in Use.

Mary gradually recovered and began to resume her ministerial responsibilities. But the second week of January, 1915, she was again overtaken by fever, diarrhea and vomiting. Miss Peacock, one of the single missionary ladies stationed at nearby Ikotobong, was summoned and came immediately. Dr Robertson also hastened from Itu, bringing medicine and ice for her dehydration.

Miss Peacock and the five African girls then living with Mary stayed with her through her final days and nights. At first she was very restless and could not gain a comfortable position either lying down or sitting up. Once she prayed, 'O Abasi, sana mi yok' ('O God, release me'). For a time she slept more peacefully but as her end neared her breathing became labored. All the girls and Miss Peacock were gathered around her bed when she gradually stopped breathing around 3:30 in the morning on Wednesday, January 13. She was sixty-six years old at her passing. Thirty-eight of those years had been devoted to service in Africa.

Mary Slessor's body was transported downriver to Duke Town that evening. The next morning her coffin, draped with the Union Jack, was carried from Government Beach to the cemetery on Mission Hill. A large procession made up of government officials, merchants, missionaries and students from the Mission schools followed along in silence while great crowds looked on. A short, simple graveside service was conducted by two of the Mission's leaders, and some of the indigenous church members led the singing of two hymns. As the coffin was lowered into the grave, a senior member of the mission murmured gratefully, 'Safe.'

5

Corrie ten Boom

ONE

Corrie ten Boom is best known through the movie *The Hiding Place* for the courage, faith and love she and her family members manifested by harboring Jews from the Nazis during World War 2 and while, consequently, being imprisoned in a German concentration camp. Most people know little about the first half century of her life – formative decades filled with active, fruitful service of others. Many are unacquainted with her final thirty-three years that saw her carry out tireless evangelistic ministry in sixty-four countries around the globe. Her entire life of faith-filled service of the Lord and loving ministry to others is an inspiring and instructive record worthy of consideration.

On April 15, 1892, a weak, pathetic-looking baby girl was born prematurely into the family of an impoverished young jeweler and his wife in Amsterdam, Holland. She joined three young siblings but it was feared she might not live for long, as had been the case with one of the couple's other infants. 'Oh, what a poor little thing she was,' the mother recorded in a diary of the arrival of her newest child. 'Nearly dead, she looked bluish white, and I never saw anything so pitiful. Nobody thought she would live.'

The newborn was named Cornelia ten Boom. To her family, friends and eventually millions of people worldwide she was commonly known as Corrie. At the time of her birth, likely none of her family members ever would have imagined that she would live to the ripe old age of ninety-one and that she would have the strength to carry out itinerant Christian ministry around the world.

Corrie's grandfather, Willem ten Boom, operated a watch shop on the ground floor of his narrow, three-storied home on one of Haarlem's busiest streets, the Barteljorisstraat. The house was located just half a block from the central town square, the Grote Markt. Willem remarried after the death of his first wife, and by his two wives he had ten children who survived to adulthood. (At least eight other children died in infancy.)

Willem was an elder in the Reformed Church of Haarlem and fiercely battled the modernism and rationalism that threatened many churches in that era. He was also committed to Christian outreach, having founded The Society for Christian Home Visitation. He had a strong respect and concern for Jewish people and was one of the founders of the Society for Israel in Haarlem.

Willem's first child by his second wife, Elisabeth, was a son named Casper. At age eighteen Casper left home to establish a jewelry business in Amsterdam. There he made many lasting friendships with people in the Jewish community, sharing in their celebrations and holidays. He also participated in a Christian outreach to the poor through a ministry called For the Salvation of the People.

Casper met and promptly fell in love with a soft-spoken Sunday School teacher named Cor Luitingh. Her father had died when she was still very young. Her mother had raised her eight children while managing a small store in Amsterdam. Late in her teens Cor began teaching in a kindergarten run by two of her older sisters, Jans and Anna.

Casper and Cor were married in 1884. Before Corrie, the three surviving children born to them were Betsie (1885), Willem (1887) and Nollie (1890). Cor started experiencing recurring sickness and weakness during her childbearing years, and throughout the remainder of her life her health would not be strong.

When Corrie was six months old, Casper moved his family back to Haarlem. His father had died, and he needed to manage the watch shop for his mother. Three or four years later he moved his wife and children into his childhood home. In the years that followed three of Cor's sisters – Bep, Jans, and Anna – came to live with them. In order to make room for everyone, Casper remodeled the house by adding five tiny bedrooms on the third floor.

With so many people to support, and with Casper's lack of attentiveness to the financial aspects of his business, the ten Booms were habitually pinched economically. But the family was rich in many other ways. Casper and Cor had a genuine love and compassionate concern for each other, their children, the live-in sisters and all variety of needy people around them. They smoothed over less than ideal household situations with unfailing patience, kindness and gentleness. The very real challenges of life were faced with unshaken trust in, and reliance on, the Lord.

Every morning and evening without fail, regardless of whatever else was on the family schedule, Casper gathered the entire household for the reading of a chapter of Scripture and prayer. He read and studied in four different languages – Dutch, German, French and English – and taught all of them to his children. Sometimes Bible study was conducted by having different family members read the same passage using those languages as well as Greek and Hebrew.

Casper put 'an almost religious importance' on education. He himself had had to stop school at an early age in order to assist his father in the watch shop. Despite that handicap, he went on to teach himself history, theology and literature in various languages, and he was determined his children would have the opportunity to gain the formal education he had been denied.

The children were also taught an appreciation for music. Classical music, especially that of Bach, and hymns were a staple of family life. The ten Booms had company and music in their home nearly every evening. Guests and family members would gather around the upright piano in the front room on the second floor with an assortment of flutes, violins and other instruments to play and sing countless songs together. The family also relished opportunities to attend concerts at the city's music hall and at St Bavo's Cathedral with its massive golden organ.

Corrie's mother 'loved guests and had a gift for hospitality that stretched a guilder until it cried'.[1] Guests were always welcome at the oval table in the dining room, even if their arrival was unexpected and it meant the soup

---

1   Carole C. Carlson, *Corrie ten Boom: Her Life, Her Faith* (Old Tappan, NJ: Spire/Revell, 1984), p. 28.

needed to be watered down in order to accommodate everyone. 'Mama', as the children called Cor, was constantly baking a loaf of bread or cooking a pot of porridge to be delivered to some pale young mother or lonesome old man. Her knitting needles were often busy making caps and baby dresses for needy individuals in the neighborhood.

Tante [Aunt] Bep, the oldest of Cor's sisters living with the family, was a spinster who had served for thirty years as a governess for the children of a succession of wealthy Dutch families. She had had a hard, unhappy life that left her short-tempered and caustic. Tante Anna, by contrast, had a big, soft heart that matched her considerable girth. Though she never married, she was a substitute mother for her sister's children when Cor was too ill to care for them. Like Cor, Anna spent much time cooking and sewing for the needy. She also had Bible studies every Wednesday and Sunday evening for the servant girls employed in the homes of wealthy Dutch merchants.

Tante Jans was childless when her pastor husband died and she moved into the ten Booms' home. She brought so much furniture and so many books that two rooms on the second floor were allotted for her living quarters. No other family member was granted such spacious accommodation. Jans was a stern, opinionated, talented and forceful woman. But she was generous toward the children and helped to provide them with new, though somewhat old-fashioned, clothes. She also helped Corrie and Nollie to develop their musical abilities by arranging for them to receive lessons.

Betsie was considered the frail beauty of the family. Born with 'pernicious anemia', she was unable to join the other children in their active outdoor games. She always dressed and acted in a ladylike manner. (Corrie, by contrast, after overcoming her weak start in life, developed into a stout, rambunctious, even tomboyish child. Her nickname from the time she was ten years old was Kees, a boy's name.) Because of Betsie's health issues, it was thought likely she would not succeed in having children. For that reason, though several young men showed interest in her, she chose never to marry.

Nollie, a year and a half older than Corrie, was the strongest of the three girls. She was like a little mother to her younger sister, holding her hand and watching out for her when they went outside. At bedtime she calmed her sister's fears by allowing her to hold on to her nightie. Their brother Willem shared his father's love of learning and his sense of Christian responsibility toward the Jews. He developed a starkly-realistic outlook on life that was not always appreciated by his youngest sister with her more romantic perspectives.

After completing secondary school in the spring of 1908, Corrie stayed at home in order to help with the household work. Tante Bep had been diagnosed with tuberculosis, for which there was then no known cure, and was confined to her bed. Corrie's mother's health had continued to decline and she was forced to spend increasing amounts of time in bed as well. Betsie worked in her father's watch shop and served as his bookkeeper. So to Corrie fell the responsibilities of cooking and cleaning for the family.

The following year, some time after her seventeenth birthday, Corrie became ill and was thought to have contracted tuberculosis. In that day tuberculosis was a dreaded affliction that could leave a person on bed rest for months or even years. Corrie, accustomed to a very active life, felt like she had been given a death sentence and been imprisoned when the doctor's diagnosis was received and she was ordered to bed indefinitely. After five seemingly-interminable months it was discovered that she had an infected appendix rather than tuberculosis. A minor operation was performed and she was able to return to normal life.

While Corrie had been happy living and working at home, she was also eager to experience more of life than she had been able to up to that point. So after she regained her strength, she took a job as the governess of a wealthy family in Zandvoort, a picturesque village by the sea ten miles from Haarlem. The family lived in a mansion and had every material comfort. But the children were unruly and the family atmosphere was filled with strife.

Once while the children were napping and the lady of the house was away, young, innocent Corrie was stunned to find herself being propositioned by her employer, a portly merchant with a fondness for whisky. She fled to her room and cried out to the Lord for help. Disillusioned as she was with the whole situation, she did not want to be a quitter. But she began to live for Thursday, her weekly day off, when she could return to Haarlem to see her family and have her catechism lesson.

One day Willem came to visit her with the news that Tante Bep had died. Furthermore, Tante Anna was exhausted from her prolonged exertions in caring for Bep. These revelations actually brought relief and even elation to Corrie. While not happy over Bep's death or Anna's exhaustion, she now had a logical reason to resign her job and return home since her family obviously needed her assistance there.

TWO

In 1910, while once again working at home, Corrie was thrilled to learn that a Bible school was opening in Haarlem. With her characteristic enthusiasm she promptly enrolled in seven classes: ethics, dogmatics, church history, Old Testament, New Testament, Old Testament history and New Testament history. As part of her final exams she needed to appear before a group of ministers in a conference room at St Bavo's Cathedral to be verbally quizzed about those subjects. It soon became apparent that two of the pastors were having a personal feud over the theological issues about which they were quizzing her. She became so nervous over the tense atmosphere in the room that she performed poorly in the oral examination, with the result that she failed all seven subjects.

When Corrie went home crestfallen over what she feared was a pattern of defeat already beginning to be manifested in her life, Betsie would have none of it. 'When you have failed an examination, Corrie,' the older sibling encouraged, 'you must take it again until you succeed and have your diploma.' Though it did not come about for eight more years, Corrie eventually did retake and pass the exam.

Willem graduated from the university at Leiden, about sixteen miles south of Haarlem, a year or two before World War 1 started in 1914. Two years after college graduation he completed seminary and was ordained as a minister in the Dutch Reformed Church. He began serving as the assistant pastor of a church and two months after his ordination Willem married Tine van Veen, a nurse who had been helping to care for Tante Jans.

The wedding held a special attraction for Corrie because of the presence of one of Willem's friends, Karel. She had first met Karel, a fellow student with Willem at the university, eight or nine years earlier when Willem brought him for a visit at the ten Boom home. When she first shook his 'long strong hand' and looked up into his deep brown eyes, she immediately 'fell irretrievably in love'. Though at that young age she had a habit of developing crushes on one boy after another at school, she felt certain that things would be different with Karel and that she would love him forever.

Just a few months before Corrie turned sixteen and graduated from secondary school, she again saw Karel, this time while visiting Willem at the university with Nollie. Corrie was thrilled when Karel readily recalled their first meeting and asked about her future plans. Likely her hopeful heart interpreted that as showing his special interest in her.

During the years that followed Corrie read many romantic novels in Dutch, German and English. She often imagined herself as the heroine in an unfolding romance in which Karel was sure to become her charming suitor. So when she met him as the guests were gathering outside the church for Willem's wedding, Corrie still held her strong infatuation for him. Now that they were both in their twenties, the five years' difference in their ages seemed much less significant than it had in the past. She was wearing a pretty silk dress and her carefully curled hair was piled high atop her head. While she could not quite conceive of herself as being truly beautiful, even on such a romantic day, she earnestly believed, as all the books suggested, that she would seem attractive to the man who she was sure loved her.

When Karel first encountered her in the crowd he seemed slightly unsure of her identity and expressed his amazement at how grown up she was. 'Forgive me, Corrie,' he stammered, recovering from his initial surprise, 'it's just that I've always thought of you as the little girl with the enormous blue eyes.' He then added softly, 'And now the little girl is a lady, and a lovely one.' He offered her his arm to lead her into the church, and, enraptured, she felt like she could soar over the peaked rooftops of Haarlem.

Less than a year later the family traveled to the village of Made in Brabant, the beautiful rural southern region of Holland. Willem had been called to pastor the congregation there and was to deliver his first sermon. 'And in the Dutch Reformed Church,' Corrie later explained, 'a minister's first sermon in his first church was the most solemn, joyous, emotional occasion that an unemotional people could conceive. Family and friends would come from great distances and stay for days.'

Karel, himself now the assistant pastor of another church, was one of the assembled guests. Throughout the days at Made he and Corrie took daily walks together. They found themselves talking about future plans of occupying a large manse and filling it with furnishings and a family, all the while never using the word 'marriage'. One day Willem and Tine tried to warn Corrie that Karel would not be able to marry her, even if he desired to, as he felt compelled to follow his family's wishes that he 'marry well'. This she refused to believe, both in light of Karel's obvious interest in her and because of how the novels uniformly depicted the working out of such situations.

After returning to Haarlem Corrie wrote him often, as he had requested, describing all the activities that were taking place in her home and family. His letters came with decreasing frequency but she attributed that to his busyness in carrying out his important ministerial responsibilities. Then one 'glorious, nippy November day' when it seemed to Corrie that all of Holland was singing with her, she heard the doorbell and ran to answer it. Throwing open the door, she was stunned to find Karel, with an elegantly dressed young lady accompanying him. 'Corrie, I want you to meet my fiancée,' he said.

Even as a blur fell over the scene for Corrie, her family realized what was happening and came to her rescue. They hastened to welcome the couple, served refreshments and carried on polite conversation so that Corrie had only to sit and listen. She managed to shake their hands and to wish them every happiness as they prepared to leave. Then fleeing to her room, she threw herself on the bed and wept for hours. She somehow knew deep inside that there would never be another prospective suitor in her life.

When Casper came quietly up the stairs to comfort his daughter, he did not speak false, idle words about her soon having another beau. Instead, he spoke of the pain of stifled love and wisely, gently encouraged her to seek God's higher love for this man. 'Lord,' she prayed after her father went back downstairs, 'I give to You the way I feel about Karel, my thoughts about our future – oh, You know! Everything! Give me Your way of seeing Karel instead. Help me to love him that way. That much.' Even as she verbalized the prayer of surrender, she fell asleep.

While Holland managed to maintain its neutrality throughout the First World War, those years, 1914-1918, were difficult ones for the small country and its inhabitants. Refugees, both civilians and soldiers, poured in from Belgium after it was invaded by Germany. In addition, heavy storms caused extensive flooding in the Netherlands. Those factors led to widespread food shortages. At times the ten Booms, like other families, made a pot of soup from a single turnip.

Another challenge came for the family in the opening year of the war when Tante Jans was diagnosed with diabetes. Like tuberculosis, in that era diabetes was incurable and considered a death sentence on a person's life. She passed away during the winter between Willem's wedding and his first sermon.

Shortly after the war drew to a close, Corrie's mother suffered a serious stroke that left her in a coma for two months. After regaining consciousness, her mind was clear and she eventually recovered partially from her paralysis to the point that she could move about with assistance. But she could say only three words: 'yes', 'no' and 'Corrie'. In order to communicate with her the family invented a little game, something like Twenty Questions, involving 'yes' and 'no' responses until they determined what she was thinking.

The following year Nollie married a fellow teacher at the school where she taught, Flip van Woerden. Cor ten Boom's favorite hymn, 'Fairest Lord Jesus', had been selected to close the wedding ceremony. As Corrie stood singing the song she suddenly heard her mother, still seated in the pew, joining in as well: 'Word after word, verse after verse, she joined in, Mama who could not speak four words, singing the beautiful lines without a stammer. Her voice which had been so high and clear was hoarse and cracked, but to me it was the voice of an angel.' Cor was never able to sing again, nor did she regain her ability to speak. Four weeks later she passed from a peaceful sleep into eternity.

Later that same year, in November of 1919, Betsie caught a bad cold and was bundled off to bed by her concerned family members. With Christmas just weeks away, it was the shop's busiest season of the year, so Corrie started helping out there as much as she could. She soon found that she thoroughly enjoyed the entire business end of running the shop, and Betsie discovered how much she relished being in charge of the household responsibilities. To their utter amazement they realized that for a decade they had divided the work exactly backwards to what would have more naturally suited them. The entire household and a renewed string of drop-in guests soon benefited from Betsie's assuming oversight of the domestic responsibilities. The shop prospered under Corrie's new system of conducting business and she found a joy in work she had never before dreamed of having.

Corrie soon realized that in addition to waiting on customers, ordering parts and keeping the books she desired to learn watch repair itself. 'Then you must have the best education,' her father responded, when she revealed that desire to him. 'When you can make something, you can repair it.' Consequently, in an era and a country where young women were not involved in the business world, the ten Booms took an uncharacteristically bold step. They allowed Corrie to go to live in Basel, Switzerland, where she could learn the watchmaking trade. As wristwatches had become fashionable, she enrolled in a school that specialized in that kind of work. Two years later she became the first licensed woman watchmaker in Holland.

Even before Tante Anna's death in the latter 1920s, the walls of the ten Boom's house began to echo once again with the voices and laughter of young children. As the years passed Willem and Tine had four children while Nollie and Flip had six. After serving a short series of congregations, Willem eventually left pastoral ministry to start a nursing home in Hilversum, some thirty miles southeast of Haarlem. Nollie's family continued to live in Haarlem, Flip having become the principal of the school where they taught. Nearly every day at least one or two of their children stopped by to visit Opa (Grandfather) and the aunts.

In addition, for more than ten years Casper, Betsie and Corrie cared for a succession of foster children in their home. After World War 1 they took in a small group of frightened and undernourished German boys and girls. Those youngsters remained under their nurturing care for several months. In 1925 the ten Booms took in the son, Hardy, and two daughters, Puck and Hans, of a missionary couple who served in Indonesia. In the years that followed eleven different foster children stayed in their home, with as many as seven living there at the same time. Betsie cared for the cooking and clothing of the children while Corrie supervised their sports and musical activities.

As Hardy, Puck and Hans had difficulty pronouncing the street, Barteljorisstraat, where the ten Booms lived, the children gave it the abbreviated nickname Beje (pronounced bay-yay). The shortened name came to be applied to the ten Booms' house, and that was the designation commonly given it in later books and films about Corrie's life.

Besides working at the watch shop and helping care for the children, Corrie taught Sunday School and Bible classes in the public schools. In time, a friend of her Tante Jans encouraged her to develop a ministry to teen girls. At first Corrie demurred, claiming she did not have the time for another responsibility. But after praying over the matter she concluded the Lord would have her to undertake such a ministry.

Her exceptional organizational and leadership abilities were soon manifested. In a short time Corrie recruited forty leaders to work with the large numbers of girls who flocked to her youth club. Club meetings consisted of games, music and a Bible study. The Teyler house, named after a prominent Haarlem philanthropist, was made available to the group for its many activities, which soon included instrumental music, singing, sewing, handcrafts, folk dancing and gymnastics.

Corrie organized a number of clubs. Before long a club meeting was being held every night. Girls who desired to learn more about spiritual matters were encouraged to join a confirmation class in one of the local Dutch Reformed congregations. All the club attendees called her by the same affectionate nickname her nieces, nephews and foster children used, Tante Kees. She was so well known by that designation that the mailman once delivered a postcard to her that was addressed simply, 'Tante Kees, Haarlem'.

Corrie carried out an idea that in that day was considered rather radical when she established the Club of Friends, made up of teenage boys and girls. She did not discourage the romances that sometimes budded between members in that club and was pleased when some of those relationships led to marriage.

Another ministry that Corrie started up during those years was a Sunday afternoon 'church' service for individuals with learning difficulties. If a disabled boy or girl wanted to join one of her clubs, or if a pastor approached her about such a person who was disrupting the normal Sunday service, she invited those individuals to her 'special' church. Corrie was burdened to share the Gospel with these people who could not understand a sermon but needed the Savior, and carried out this compassionate ministry for two decades.

A summer camp ministry that members of her various girls' clubs could attend was another of Corrie's ventures. Early outings were done with tents while later ones were held at a simple log cabin that had room for about sixty girls. The highlight of each day was the evening campfire when the girls sat around the fire, wrapped in blankets, to sing and listen to Tante Kees' meditation. They enjoyed her great sense of humor and her wonderful stories that always had a significant spiritual point.

Corrie's gymnastics club paved the way for the founding of the Girl Guide clubs in Holland, a European equivalent to the Girl Scouts of America. She promoted a definite spiritual emphasis in the Girl Guide organization, believing that girls needed to be won to Christ rather than merely taught to be good citizens. But over time Christian standards within the movement came to be replaced with mere 'moral instruction'. That led to the establishment of a new, explicitly-Christian movement, Netherlands Girls' Clubs.

All too soon the events of World War 2 swirled down upon Holland and the girls' clubs were forced to close. The last time Corrie met with her club members, the girls struggled to sing the national anthem through their tears. 'Girls, don't cry,' she encouraged them. 'We have had great fun in our clubs, but that wasn't why we came together. Jesus makes us strong, even in times of war and disaster.'

THREE

As it had throughout World War 1, Holland declared its neutrality in the opening months of the Second World War. One evening in May 1940, Holland's Prime Minister assured his fellow countrymen in a nationwide radio address that he had received assurances from high sources on both sides of the conflict that Holland's neutrality would be respected. Just five hours later, Germany launched a surprise attack against its unsuspecting neighbor. Corrie and Betsie were jolted from their sleep in the middle of that night by bombs being dropped on the airport near Haarlem. The hopelessly outmanned Dutch army was able to hold out for just five days before surrendering.

The opening months of Germany's occupation of Holland did not seem 'so very unbearable'. For the first time in decades, churches were packed and ministers who had never preached on Christ's second coming now encouraged their people with that prospect. German soldiers were everywhere. Many visited the ten Booms' watch shop and purchased women's watches for their mothers and sweethearts back home.

But restrictions soon began to tighten. A 10 p.m. curfew was imposed, later to be shifted to 6 p.m. The Haarlem police came under the direct control of the German Commandant. Each Dutch citizen was issued an identity card and had to carry it at all times in a pouch hung around the neck. Food ration cards were also distributed. Cars, radios, bicycles and various metals – including bronze church bells – were confiscated. Some people, like Corrie, were permitted to retain their bicycles but had to bump along on metal rims wrapped in cloth after the rubber tires were taken. The Dutch national anthem could not be sung and all references to the Queen or the royal house were forbidden.

The Germans repaired the bomb damage done to the Haarlem airport and began using it as a base for air strikes against England. English planes sometimes counterattacked the airfield with the result that dogfights sometimes raged directly over Haarlem. One night, after such fighting kept Corrie awake for over an hour, she heard Betsie stirring in the kitchen downstairs and joined her for tea. When at last the fighting tapered off she returned to her bedroom in the dark. Finding something hard on her pillow, her hand closed around it, a sharp edge cut through her skin and blood trickled along a finger. 'Betsie!' she called out in alarm as she carried the jagged, ten-inch shrapnel shard back downstairs.

'On your pillow,' Betsie kept saying as she bandaged her sister's hand and examined the hazardous piece of metal.

'Betsie, if I hadn't heard you in the kitchen ...'

'Don't say it,' Betsie interrupted, putting a finger on Corrie's mouth. She then continued earnestly, 'There are no "ifs" in God's world. And no places that are safer than other places. The center of His will is our only safety – O Corrie, let us pray that we may always know it!'

Germany's anti-Semitic policies were soon manifested and embraced by many Dutch people. Six months after the occupation, all Jews were removed from schools, universities and government posts. They were also barred from public parks, libraries, theaters, restaurants and other businesses. In time Jews were required to wear a yellow star on their clothing. Public arrests of Jews became more common. Sometimes entire Jewish families were rounded up, jammed on to busses and taken away to prison camps.

Beginning in the autumn of 1941, the ten Booms, assisted by Willem in Hilversum, were instrumental in finding homes in safer, rural districts for several of their Jewish acquaintances from Haarlem. That was the beginning of the family's underground work. As subsequent months and then years passed, their mission of mercy grew to the point that scores of Jews and several at-risk Dutch people were assisted through their efforts each month. In addition to safe homes being provided in the country, refugees were supplied with food ration cards and forged identification papers. The ten Booms had numerous helpful contacts throughout Haarlem, including a few strategic officials, who sympathized with their underground efforts and were willing to assist them in various ways. Over time a network of scores of individuals – teens and adults of all ages – assisted with the work carried out through the Beje.

Young Dutchmen were also unsafe in their own homeland. Munition factories in Germany were desperate for workers. In order to supply them, soldiers would suddenly surround a block of buildings and carry out a lightning search of them. All males between sixteen and thirty found in such a search-and-seizure operation (known as 'the razzia') were loaded into trucks and transported to Germany where they were put to work.

In addition, in the spring of 1943, 14,000 Dutch university students were informed they could not continue their education unless they signed a document stating they would 'refrain from any act against the German Reich and the German army'. Universities were shut down after eighty-six percent of the students refused to sign the loyalty oath. Those who had not signed were required to appear in court on May 5 and were sent to Germany as forced labor. Some evaded the court appearance and were forced into hiding. Dutchmen who went into hiding to avoid forced conscription or imprisonment were called 'underdivers'.

One such student, the son of a friend of Corrie, was the first hideaway the ten Booms took into their home. By that time there were no longer ample homes in the country for fugitives to find safe haven in, so some were being hidden in houses in the city. Over the course of the next nine and a half months, until the ten Booms themselves were arrested, the number of refugees at the Beje fluctuated. Some fugitives stayed only a few days. But a nucleus of six permanent refugees formed, composed of three Jews, two underdivers and a Dutch teacher.

A tiny secret room – two and a half feet deep, six and a half feet long and eight or nine feet tall – was built along the back of Corrie's bedroom, with access through a small concealed sliding panel under the bottom shelf of her closet. A mattress was laid on the floor and it was stocked with a supply of water and health biscuits. Dubbed the Angelcrib, this was to serve as a hiding place for the refugees when, as all supposed would inevitably happen, authorities raided the house looking for them. Periodic drills were held to give the hideaways practice in making their way – as quickly and quietly as possible, and without leaving a trace of their ever having been in the house – up the stairs and into the secret room.

Corrie's underground work confronted her with a number of moral dilemmas. She was frequently burdened and troubled by the secrecy, subterfuge and outright lies it involved. She knew of examples in the Old Testament where people practiced such deception in order to preserve life, but she could not find a single New Testament example where lying was excused. When asked later how she handled that tension, she responded: 'I just brought it to the Lord and asked forgiveness. Jesus loves sinners. Love covers a multitude of sins, and love is what brought us to do our utmost to save as many people as we could.'[2]

But there were certain lines that Corrie could not bring herself to cross. She declined when an underground worker, concerned for her safety, offered her a revolver and training in its use so she could defend herself if attacked. Even more stunning to her, three times she was approached about providing an assassin to eliminate a Dutch betrayer who was known to be secretly working with the Germans. On each of those occasions she offered, instead, to pray for the betrayer's conversion to Christ. One of those informers did become a Christian and a dedicated underground worker. But when the other two did not change their ways, she wrestled with the thought that she may have been partially responsible for the great harm they brought to others.

---

2   Ibid., p. 83.

Corrie and Betsie and their father believed that God's angels were watching over them and the occupants of their home. Some felt that the ten Booms became a bit careless in their underground operation because of this belief in angelic protection. Actually, they were well aware of the precariousness of their situation. Each day dozens of underground workers, reports and appeals arrived at the Beje. Such a volume of traffic at the shop and home of an old watchmaker and his two spinster daughters was sure to raise suspicions. Corrie afterward related:

> We knew we should stop the work, but how could we? Who would keep open the network of supplies and information on which the safety of hundreds depended? If a hideaway had to be abandoned, as happened all the time, who would coordinate the move to another address? We had to go on, but we knew that disaster could not be long in coming.[3]

On the morning of February 28, 1944, Corrie lay in bed, sick with flu. Her head throbbed and her joints felt as though they were on fire. Betsie apologetically awoke her, stating there was a man in the watch shop who insisted on talking only to her. As she made her way unsteadily downstairs Corrie heard voices in the second floor parlor and remembered that Willem was there for his weekly Wednesday morning prayer meeting with a number of people from town. (In addition to sincerely promoting prayer in those dark days, he used the meeting as a legitimate reason to visit the Beje each week.)

---

3   Corrie ten Boom, *Corrie ten Boom, Her Story: The Hiding Place; Tramp for the Lord; Jesus Is Victor* (New York: Inspirational, 1995), p. 92. Hereafter the individual works within this collective volume will be referenced in the footnotes as *The Hiding Place*, *Tramp for the Lord* or *Jesus Is Victor*.

In the watch shop she found a small, anxious man who claimed to be from another town. 'My wife has just been arrested,' he explained. 'We've been hiding Jews, you see. If she is questioned, all our lives are in danger. I need six hundred guilders. There's a policeman at the station in Ermelo who can be bribed for that amount. ... It's a matter of life and death! If I don't get it right away she'll be taken to Amsterdam and then it will be too late.'

Corrie told him to return in half an hour for the money. Leaving further instructions with an underground worker to complete the transaction, she then struggled back upstairs and collapsed into bed. She was awakened some time later by the warning buzzer that was used when they had a drill to see how quickly their refugees could escape to the secret room. People were hurrying past her bed, fear etched on their faces, and sliding into the Angelcrib at the back of her closet. Knowing that a drill had not been planned for that day, she realized that the emergency for which they had so long prepared had arrived. She shoved a briefcase filled with incriminating names and addresses into the hiding place and then dropped the sliding panel into place.

She had barely laid down on her bed again when a tall, heavyset man wearing an ordinary blue business suit burst into the room. 'What's your name?' he demanded.

'Cornelia ten Boom,' she responded as she sat up slowly, hoping she looked and sounded sleepy.

'Get up! Get dressed!' he commanded.

She had been preparing a bag which she intended to take with her if ever she was to go to prison. Corrie had stocked it with a Bible, clothing, needle and thread, toiletry articles, vitamins, aspirin and a pencil. 'It had become a kind of talisman for me,' she later testified, 'a safeguard against the terrors of prison.' Now she realized, however, that in her haste moments earlier she had pushed the bag up against the sliding door into the secret room. She dared not reach under the shelf at the back of her closet lest she draw the Gestapo agent's attention to the last place on earth she wanted him to look. Corrie afterward related, 'It was the hardest thing I had ever done to turn and walk out of that room leaving the bag behind.'

Once downstairs, the man in the blue suit pushed her into the rear of the watch shop and against the wall. 'Where are the Jews?' he demanded, his voice and face now fierce.

'There aren't any Jews here.'

He struck her hard across the face. 'Where do you hide the ration cards?'

'I don't know what you're ...'

He interrupted her with another violent blow that jerked her head back. One question and rough slap followed quickly after another till Corrie tasted blood in her mouth. Her ears rang and she thought she was about to lose consciousness. 'Lord Jesus,' she cried out in desperation, 'protect me!'

The man's hand stopped in midair. 'If you say that name again I'll kill you!' Slowly his arm dropped to his side, and he stated with a sneer, 'If you won't talk, that skinny one will.' He shoved Corrie into a chair in the nearby dining room and led Betsie away. When he brought her back several minutes later her lips were swollen and bleeding and a bruise was darkening on her cheek.

'Oh, Betsie!' Corrie said, after her sister half fell into the chair beside her. 'He hurt you!'

'Yes,' she said, dabbing at the blood on her mouth. 'I feel so sorry for him.'

From upstairs came the sounds of hammer blows and splintering wood as a group of men searched for the secret room. At last one of them reported to the Gestapo agent in charge of the raid, 'We've searched the whole place, Willemse. If there's a secret room here, the devil himself built it.'

'There's a secret room, and people are using it,' the agent said quietly. 'All right. We'll set a guard around the house till they've turned to mummies.'

The Beje became a trap for a number of underground workers that day. Hearing of other arrests taking place in the city that same day, dozens of concerned individuals rushed to the ten Booms' home to warn them of the danger. All told, thirty-five individuals were arrested at the Beje and taken to the police station just around the corner. In addition to Casper, Corrie and Betsie, Willem ten Boom, Nollie van Woerden and her son Peter were among those arrested.

FOUR

The next morning, February 29, the detainees were loaded on to a bus and transported nearly thirty miles south to The Hague. They were processed at the building that served as Gestapo headquarters for all of Holland. Late that night they were taken by truck to the nearby suburb of Scheveningen where the federal penitentiary bearing that same name was located. They were led into a large room in a long, low building and ordered to stand with their noses to a wall. When it came time for the women prisoners to be led off to their cell block, Corrie hung back, gazing desperately at her father, brother, nephew and 'our brave underground workers'. 'Father!' she suddenly cried out, 'God be with you!'

His head turned in the direction of her voice, and he called back, 'And with you, my daughters.' That would prove to be their final exchange.

Corrie was taken to a deep, narrow cell already inhabited by four other women. Since she was ill she was given the cot at the back of the cell while the others slept on straw ticks on the floor. When she was still sick two weeks later, she was taken to a medical office in town, under the watchful eye of a soldier. On entering a bathroom there, a nurse slipped in with her, shut the door and said, 'Quick! Is there any way I can help?'

'O yes! A Bible! Could you get me a Bible? And … a needle and thread. And a toothbrush and soap.'

'So many patients today and the soldier. But I'll do what I can.'

Just before Corrie was to leave the office, the nurse swished past her in the waiting room and pressed a small package into her hand. Corrie immediately slipped it into her coat pocket. Back in the prison, her cell mates crowded around as she unwrapped two bars of soap, a packet of safety pins and, most wonderful of all to Corrie, the Gospels in four small booklets. She divided the soap and pins among the five of them. When she offered to share the books as well, they refused. One of them stated, 'They catch you with those, and it's double sentence and *kalte kost* as well.'

'*Kalte kost* – the bread ration alone without the daily plate of hot food – was the punishment constantly held over our heads,' Corrie later explained. 'But even *kalte kost* would be a small price to pay,' she thought, as she stretched on the foul-smelling straw, 'for the precious books I hold in my hands.'

Two evenings later she was transferred to a solitary confinement cell. Like the other cell it was six paces deep by two wide, but had only a single cot. Being near the outside edge of the prison, the wind 'shrieked' and hammered against the wall, leaving the cell bitter cold. When she sat down on the cot, the combined odors of the reeking straw and the blanket, upon which someone had vomited, immediately made her throw up herself.

The one improved feature of this cell was that it contained a window. Though it was barred and high up in the wall, through it she could watch the variously colored clouds throughout the day and hear the sea when the wind was from the west. As spring came, it also brought a shaft of warmth-giving light that would slowly creep across one of the cell walls.

A month after entering solitary confinement, Corrie passed a lonely, cheerless fifty-second birthday there. Two days later she was permitted her first shower since arriving at the prison seven weeks earlier. Though strict silence was enforced on all the prisoners at the large communal shower room, just being near other people for a brief time was 'joy and strength'. Shortly after that she was delighted when a 'small committee' of ants began providing her with company and diversion by their repeated appearances in her cell. She encouraged their return by scattering bread crumbs near the crack in the floor where they appeared and disappeared.

A few weeks earlier, unknown to Corrie at the time, Willem, Nollie and Peter were released from prison.

Nollie sent Corrie a care package that contained a light blue embroidered sweater, a bright red towel, needle and thread, vitamins and cookies and this reached her eventually. Corrie noticed that her sister's handwriting on the outside of the package uncharacteristically slanted up toward the stamp. Loosening the stamp, she discovered a coded message written in miniature letters under it: 'All the watches in your closet are safe.' She understood at once what the cryptic message meant – the hideaways had all escaped safely from the secret room. So great was her relief that she reflexively burst into racking sobs.

On May 3, she received a letter from Nollie, informing her that their father had survived only ten days after being taken to Scheveningen. No details were known about how he died or where he was buried. In the middle of June, Corrie was granted the unspeakable joy of a brief reunion with her siblings and their spouses – Willem and Tine, Nollie and Flip, Betsie – for the reading of Casper ten Boom's simple will. They clung to each other, laughed, cried and exchanged as much news as they could in the short amount of time available to them. By then it had been learned that, after falling ill at the prison, their father was taken to the public hospital in The Hague. As no room was available for him at the time, he died in a hallway. Because he had been separated from his records and hospital authorities had no clue as to his identity, he was buried in the paupers' cemetery.

When Nollie first hugged Corrie at that reunion she pressed a small package into her hand. It was a complete, compact Bible tucked inside a small pouch with a string that could be worn around the neck. Corrie quickly slipped the string over her head and let the pouch fall down her back under her blouse. To receive this entire Bible was an immeasurable blessing and encouragement to Corrie. Realizing that she could not keep the riches of God's Word to herself, she had secretively passed her little Gospel booklets to various women when she was periodically taken to the communal shower. Just the day before, not knowing of the treasure she would receive from Nollie on the morrow, she had given away her last Gospel.

Two weeks later, Corrie and her fellow prisoners were bussed to a freight yard on the outskirts of town. She spotted Betsie a short distance away and, when the order was given to load into the waiting train cars, pressed sideways through the surging crowd until she was able to reach her. They shed tears of joy at their reuniting and again a few hours later when they determined that the train was headed south to the rural Brabant region of Holland rather than east into Germany. They were taken to Vught, a temporary concentration camp for political prisoners that was named after the nearest neighboring village.

Betsie was assigned to work in the barracks where elderly and infirm prisoners sewed prison uniforms. Corrie was sent to work in the 'Phillips factory', another large barracks where several hundred men and women sat at long plank tables assembling radios to be used in German fighter planes. After the eleven-hour work day, she returned to their sleeping barracks where Betsie always stood in the doorway awaiting her arrival.

One day early in September a series of explosions was heard in the area, drawing ever nearer to Vught. The Phillips factory foreman interpreted them as demolition work that the Germans were doing in an effort to disrupt the advance of an enemy brigade that was rumored to be approaching south Holland. Early that afternoon all prisoners were suddenly ordered back to their barracks. The loudspeaker in the men's camp sounded the signal for roll call and then lists of names were read over the speaker. A short while later, to the horror and dismay of the female prisoners (many of whom had husbands and brothers in the men's camp), one volley after another of rifle fire began to split the air. The firing squads continued for two hours, and an estimated 700 male prisoners perished that day.

About noon the next day the remaining prisoners, men and women, were marched out to a single set of railroad tracks some distance from the camp and crammed into waiting boxcars. The women in Corrie and Betsie's car worked out a system whereby they could all sit down, each person's torso being wedged between the legs of the individual behind them. For three days and nights the train lumbered along with no provisions being made for basic sanitation purposes. Two or three times when the train stopped, a pail of water was passed in but only those near the door got any. Occasionally bread was passed around but conditions in the car were so appalling that few could stomach food.

Finally, on the morning of the fourth day, the train stopped beside a small lake in northern Germany, approximately fifty-five miles north of Berlin. The portion of the train containing male prisoners had been taken elsewhere. The women limped from the train and eagerly drank, through swollen and cracked lips, the water that the stronger prisoners carried from the lake in buckets. A short while later they were forced to march over a mile to Ravensbruck, the Germans' notorious women's extermination camp. Of over 130,000 prisoners incarcerated at Ravensbruck during World War 2, only 40,000 survived.

FIVE

At the processing center for new arrivals each woman had to surrender whatever possessions she had brought to the camp, strip off every scrap of clothes and walk naked past a dozen watchful guards into the shower room. After showering she was given nothing more than a thin prison dress and a pair of shoes to wear. Before relinquishing their possessions and clothes, Corrie and Betsie begged a guard to show them the toilets and were tersely ordered to use the drain holes in the shower room. There, behind a stack of old wooden benches piled in a far corner, they hid the Bible, vitamin bottle and blue sweater that had been received from Nollie. A while later, after showering and selecting their prison clothes from heaps on the floor just inside the shower room door, Corrie sought to hide their little bundle of precious possessions under her prison dress.

> It made a bulge you could have seen across the Grote Markt. I flattened it out as best I could ... but there was no real concealing it beneath the thin cotton dress. And all the while I had the incredible feeling that it didn't matter, that this was not my business, but God's. That all I had to do was walk straight ahead.

> As we trooped back out through the shower room door, the S.S. men ran their hands over every prisoner, front, back, and

sides. The woman ahead of me was searched three times. Behind me, Betsie was searched. No hand touched me.

At the exit door to the building was a second ordeal, a line of women guards examining each prisoner again. I slowed down as I reached them but the *Aufseherin* [officer] in charge shoved me roughly by the shoulder. 'Move along! You're holding up the line!'

And so Betsie and I arrived at Barracks 8 in the small hours of that morning, bringing not only the Bible, but a new knowledge of the power of Him whose story it was.[4]

Corrie and Betsie joined three other women in sharing a single mattress as their bed in the barracks. Morning roll call began promptly at 4:30 a.m., was held out in the predawn chill and sometimes lasted for hours. Throughout that time the prisoners were required to stand at parade attention. Immediately next to them were located the punishment barracks. Of the overwhelming nightmarish suffering they observed in those days, Corrie later wrote:

From there [the punishment barracks], all day long and often into the night, came the sounds of hell itself. They were not the sounds of anger, or of any human emotion, but of a cruelty altogether detached: blows landing in regular rhythm, screams keeping pace. We would stand [at role call] in our ten-deep ranks with our hands trembling at our sides, longing to jam them against our ears, to make the sounds stop. ...

It grew harder and harder. Even within these four walls [of Barracks 8] there was too much misery, too much seemingly pointless suffering. Every day something else failed to make sense, something else grew too heavy. 'Will You carry this too, Lord Jesus?'[5]

---

4   Ten Boom, *The Hiding Place*, pp. 142-3.

5   Ibid., p. 143.

However, Corrie also testified of a redemptive spiritual reality that God brought about through their ministry of His word in that blackest of settings:

> But as the rest of the world grew stranger, one thing became increasingly clear. And that was the reason the two of us were here. Why others should suffer we were not shown. As for us, from morning until lights-out, whenever we were not in ranks for roll call, our Bible was the center of an ever-widening circle of help and hope. Like waifs clustered around a blazing fire, we gathered about it, holding out our hearts to its warmth and light. The blacker the night around us grew, the brighter and truer and more beautiful burned the word of God. 'Who shall separate us from the love of Christ? Shall tribulation, or distress, or persecution, or famine, or nakedness, or peril, or sword? ... Nay, in all these things we are more than conquerors through Him that loved us' [Rom. 8:35, 37].
>
> I would look about us as Betsie read, watching the light leap from face to face. More than conquerors. ... It was not a wish. It was a fact. We knew it, we experienced it minute by minute – poor, hated, hungry. We are more than conquerors. Not 'we shall be'. We are! Life in Ravensbruck took place on two separate levels, mutually impossible. One, the observable, external life, grew every day more horrible. The other, the life we lived with God, grew daily better, truth upon truth, glory upon glory.[6]

About a month after arriving at Ravensbruck, Corrie and Betsie were transferred to Barracks 28. There 1,400 women from several European countries shared quarters originally designed to accommodate 400. Eight 'acrid and overflowing' toilets served the entire facility. 'There were no individual beds at all, but great square piers stacked three high, and wedged side by side and end to end with

6   Ibid., pp. 143-4.

only an occasional narrow aisle slicing through.' The sleeping platforms were covered with rancid, flea-infested straw. Corrie and Betsie shared their particular square, designed for four, with seven other women.

For three or four weeks the two sisters joined several thousand other prisoners in doing heavy manual labor at a factory over a mile from the camp. Midway through their grueling eleven-hour workday they were given a boiled potato and a bowl of thin soup. Back at their barracks the evening meal consisted of a ladle of turnip soup.

Immediately after supper each night Corrie and Betsie held a worship service at the back of the dormitory where a small light bulb cast a pale yellow circle on the wall. At first they were timid about holding such meetings. But when night after night passed and no guard ever came near them, they became bolder. They were puzzled by that lack of interference until it was eventually discovered that the guards would not venture into the dormitory portion of the barracks due to the fleas. In time so many prisoners wanted to join the time of worship that Corrie and Betsie started holding a second service after evening roll call.

Early in November, Corrie and Betsie were put on a work crew leveling rough ground just inside the camp wall. Betsie's strength was soon exhausted and Corrie's was severely taxed. Heavy rains started to fall in the middle of that month, making the back-breaking work even more difficult. Betsie developed a fever and began coughing up blood. After several days her fever reached 104 degrees, high enough to be admitted to the camp hospital. When she returned to the barracks a few days later, she still had a fever, having received no medical examination or medicine at the hospital. But she was assigned to the 'knitting brigade', a group of enfeebled women who remained in the barracks during the day to knit gray-wool army socks.

Corrie and Betsie discussed and prayed about what God's will for them would be after the war:

> Betsie was always very clear about the answer for her and me. We were to have a house, a large one – much larger than the Beje to which people who had been damaged by concentration-camp life would come until they felt ready to live again in the normal world.

> 'It's such a beautiful house, Corrie! The floors are all inlaid wood, with statues set in the walls and a broad staircase sweeping down. And gardens! Gardens all around it where they can plant flowers. It will do them such good, Corrie, to care for flowers!'[7]

As December temperatures fell, the twice-daily roll calls became true endurance contests. The prisoners were permitted to stamp their feet while standing in formation in order to promote the circulation of blood to their numb feet and legs. Betsie, however, had become so weak she had to be carried to roll call, where she stood unable to move her feet.

One morning after roll call Corrie and another woman carried Betsie back to the barracks and got her back to her bed. 'A camp, Corrie – a concentration camp,' Betsie was trying to tell her sister something, though her speech was slow and slurred. 'But we're ... in charge.'

Corrie bent close to hear what Betsie was describing. 'It was no longer a prison,' Corrie afterward related, 'but a home where people who had been warped by this

---

7   Ibid., p. 155.

philosophy of hate and force could come to learn another way. There were no walls, no barbed wire, and the barracks had windowboxes.'

'It will be so good for them ... watching things grow,' stated Betsie. 'People can learn to love, from flowers.'

'We are to have this camp in Germany instead, Betsie? Instead of the big house in Holland?'

'Oh no!' the older sister responded, seeming shocked. 'You know we have the house first! It's ready and waiting for us ... such tall, tall windows. The sun is streaming in ...' After a coughing fit interrupted her, she fell into a restless sleep. Throughout the remainder of that day and the night that followed, Betsie awakened several times to relate enthusiastically some new detail about their future ministries in Holland or Germany. 'The barracks are gray, Corrie, but we'll paint them green! Bright, light green, like springtime!'

'We'll be together, Betsie? We're doing all this together? You're sure about that?'

'Always together, Corrie! You and I ... always together.'

The next morning Corrie was permitted to accompany Betsie as she was carried by two orderlies to the hospital. There Betsie further related, '... must tell people what we have learned here. We must tell them that there is no pit so deep that He is not deeper still. They will listen to us, Corrie, because we have been here.'

'But when will all this happen, Betsie?'

'Now. Right away. Oh, very soon! By the first of the year, Corrie, we will be out of prison!'

Betsie exchanged the horrors of Ravensbruck for the glories of heaven when she died in the hospital the next day. At morning roll call three days later Corrie was called out by name rather than number and told to stand to the side of the formation. When the other prisoners were dismissed, a guard led her to the camp's administration barracks. There to her astonishment she was issued a certificate of discharge and a railway pass for transportation through Germany to the border of Holland. But due to edema in her legs and feet, she failed to pass the physical exam that was mandatory to be released.

After a long week spent at the hospital Corrie was finally in good enough condition to be discharged from the camp. She was provided with a set of nice clothes and a day's bread ration plus food coupons for three additional days. Corrie signed a form stating that while at Ravensbruck she had never been ill or had an accident and that she had been treated well. Then, along with about a dozen other released prisoners, she was led by a guard out through the iron gate of the camp and to a small train station nearby. An interminable day of travel delays and complications, including the loss of her bread ration and food coupons, followed. By the time she reached the cavernous, bomb-gutted terminal in Berlin some time after midnight, it was New Year's Day, 1945.

Two days later Corrie reached Groningen, a Dutch city not far from the border. There she spent ten days at a Christian hospital called the Deaconess House. She was overwhelmed by the kind, attentive care of the staff and by the experiencing of normal, everyday pleasures that had been absent from her life throughout most of the previous year – delicious and nourishing food, a hot bath, clean clothes complete with undergarments, a brush for her hair, a private bedroom full of color, a soft bed, a shelf full of books, the merry sound of children playing outdoors and a Bach trio being played on the radio. As she listened to the music: 'The organ tones flowed about and enveloped me. I sat on the floor beside a chair and sobbed, unashamedly. It was too much joy. I had rarely cried during all those months of suffering. Now I could not control myself. My life had been given back as a gift. Harmony, beauty, colors, and music.'[8]

From Groningen, Corrie was able to ride on a food truck to her brother Willem's home in Hilversum. Two weeks later she continued on to Haarlem where she was reunited with Nollie. Only eleven months had passed since the ten Booms had been arrested in their home and taken to prison but to Corrie it seemed like centuries.

SIX

Corrie promptly took up residence in the Beje and began working mornings in the watch shop. She invited a number of individuals with learning difficulties who, under the Nazi regime, were always at risk of being arrested and eliminated, to live with her at the Beje. That spring she started sharing at meetings in churches, club rooms and private homes around Haarlem about the spiritual lessons she and Betsie had learned through their prison experiences.

She always shared Betsie's vision of establishing a home in Holland where those who had been hurt by the war could recover from their wounds and fears. As a result, Mrs Bierens de Haan, an aristocratic widow with five sons who had served in the Dutch Resistance, donated her fifty-six room mansion in the suburb of Bloemendaal to be

---

8   Ten Boom, *Tramp for the Lord*, p. 198.

used for that purpose. It matched perfectly the description Betsie had given Corrie at Ravensbruck of their future ministry home, including the inlaid wood floors, a broad staircase that descended to a central hall, bas-relief statues set along the walls and elaborate outdoor gardens.

The Allies liberated Holland the first week of May, and hurting people began arriving at the recovery home the following month. There they shared their stories of woe with each other and were reminded that they were not the only ones who had suffered deeply. 'And for all these people alike,' Corrie related insightfully, 'the key to healing turned out to be the same. Each had a hurt he had to forgive: the neighbor who had reported him, the brutal guard, the sadistic soldier.'

Even harder than forgiving the Germans, the Dutch found it most difficult to forgive their fellow countrymen who had sided with the enemy during the war. Those former collaborators now found themselves in desperate straits, turned out of their homes and apartments, unable to find work and ridiculed in the streets. Twice Corrie tried to bring them to the recovery home in Bloemendaal, but open fights erupted between them and the other occupants who could not yet bring themselves to forgive them. As homes and schools reopened around the country for those with learning difficulties, they vacated the Beje and she turned its use over to the former traitors.

Corrie began traveling throughout Holland, sharing her hope-filled message of God's love, forgiveness, healing and joy even in the darkest, most desperate circumstances. She believed the Lord would have her take that same message to other countries as well and before long sensed God's definite leading to go to America. She traveled there by freighter early in 1946, arriving in New York with but fifty dollars, the maximum amount she was allowed to take into the country.

Her only speaking opportunity that first week was to a group of Jewish-Christian immigrants from Germany. A lady who was at that meeting invited Corrie to stay in her apartment as long as she was in New York, an offer she gratefully accepted. But as the next five weeks passed and speaking opportunities continued to be non-existent, her funds dwindled down and then ran out entirely. Americans were polite and some even seemed interested, but none wanted her to speak at their churches or other organizations. Some questioned her claim to have been directly guided by God in coming to America or even suggested that she should have stayed in Holland.

Finally one evening Corrie knelt by her bed and poured out her heart to the Lord. She was so distressed, she fell weeping across the bed. Slowly a reassurance came to her heart that God was indeed guiding her, that He would honor Himself and care for Corrie through this situation and that in days to come she would give thanks for these challenging, faith-building days in New York.

That seemed to be the turning point. The very next day she met a Dutch pastor who invited her to speak to his congregation on Staten Island. A week or so later she was introduced to the editor of a Christian magazine who affirmed her belief in the Lord's direct guidance of her ministry steps and who invited her to write an article for his publication. He also put her in touch with a prominent Christian leader in Washington D.C. who, in turn, invited her to come there as his guest. Based on his recommendation of her to various individuals, calls began to pour in from everywhere, asking her to come and share her testimony. For the next ten months she was kept busy traveling and speaking in churches, prisons, universities, schools and clubs in American cities and towns of all sizes.

As the year drew to a close Corrie began sensing that God would have her return to Europe. Only this time, rather than directing her steps back to Holland, she became convinced the Lord was guiding her to return to the one country she dreaded, Germany. Much of that country still lay in ruins and some nine million people were said to be homeless. People lived in tumbled down buildings and in deserted army trucks. Corrie was invited to speak to a hundred families living in an abandoned factory. Sheets and blankets were hung as the only available dividers between the living quarters of the various families. She accepted the speaking invitation but not until she had lived among those families for a time.

During those months in the factory the director of a relief organization, having heard of her recovery work in Holland, came to see her. She was just about to say that she had no professional training in such matters, when she was silenced by the director's next words: 'We've located a place for the work. It was a former concentration camp that's just been released to the government.'

They drove to Darmstadt, not quite twenty miles south of Frankfurt, to survey the deserted camp, which was still surrounded by rolls of rusting barbed wire. As she had at Ravensbruck, Corrie walked up a cinder path between drab gray barracks. Entering and looking around one, she stated: 'Windowboxes – we'll have them at every window. The barbed wire must come down, of course. And then we'll need paint. Green paint. Bright yellow-green, the color of things coming up new in the spring.'

And thus the second phase of the ministry to wartime victims that Betsie had envisioned for them while still at Ravensbruck came into being. A committee of the German Lutheran Church worked with Corrie in reopening the small camp as a home and place of renewal for about 160 refugees.

After speaking on the theme of God's forgiveness at a church service in Munich in 1947, Corrie saw a balding, heavyset man in a gray overcoat making his way toward her. She instantly recognized him as one of the cruel, mocking guards she and the other prisoners had been forced to walk past naked at the Ravensbruck processing center. Now he came up to her, beaming and bowing, and with his hand extended to shake hers. 'How grateful I am for your message, Fraulein,' he stated. 'To think that, as you say, He has washed my sins away!'

Angry, vengeful thoughts boiled up in her, and Corrie kept her hand at her side. Even as she did, she saw the sin of her own thoughts and silently prayed, 'Lord Jesus, forgive me, and help me to forgive him.'

'You mentioned Ravensbruck in your talk,' the man continued. 'I was a guard there. But since that time I have become a Christian. I know that God has forgiven me for the cruel things I did there, but I would like to hear it from your lips as well.' Again he extended his hand toward her, and asked, 'Fraulein, will you forgive me?'

For what seemed like hours to Corrie he stood there with his hand held out as the emotional and spiritual conflict raged within her. She tried to smile and struggled to raise her hand but could not. She felt not the slightest spark of warmth or charity for him. Again she silently cried out to the Lord, 'Jesus, I cannot forgive him. Give me Your forgiveness.'

At last she 'woodenly, mechanically' reached out and grasped his hand. As she did, a current started in her shoulder, raced down her arm and seemed to pass between their hands. A healing warmth flooded her entire being and brought tears to her eyes. 'I forgive you, brother,' she cried out, 'with all my heart!'[9]

That was not the only time such an event took place involving Corrie. On a handful of other occasions during her ministries in Germany through the years she had the opportunity to interact with, and extend forgiveness to, one or another of her former captors. More than once it was not an easy process.

Corrie's ministry travels throughout the 1950s took her to numerous countries and nearly every continent. While it was rewarding to minister around the world, it certainly was not an easy life. She normally soldiered through the challenges and hardships of itinerant ministry with remarkable willingness and selflessness. But occasionally the difficulties and sacrifices took a toll on her, and she was tempted to give in to self-pity or to give up altogether. Invariably at those times, the Lord brought circumstances into her life that helped her through the discouragements and renewed her determination to carry on in the ministry He had for her.

Once while ministering in Japan Corrie arrived at an evening church service feeling thoroughly sorry for herself.

---

9   Ten Boom, *The Hiding Place*, p. 174; ten Boom, *Tramp for the Lord*, pp. 217-8.

She was very tired and her stomach was upset from the unusual food she had been eating. Corrie longed for a good European meal back in Holland, a table where she would not have to sit cross-legged on the floor and a soft bed rather than the hard mats on which the Japanese slept.

At the church service that night Corrie spotted a bent little man in a wheelchair. His face wore the happiest expression she could imagine. After the service her interpreter introduced her to the man. When she inquired about several small packets wrapped in brown paper and tied with string on his lap, he smiled broadly. Carefully unwrapping one of the packages to show Corrie its contents, he explained, 'This is the Gospel of John, written in Braille. I have just finished it.' He went on to explain that this was the fifteenth time he had written the Gospel of John in Braille. He had also written other Gospels as well as many shorter portions of the Bible for the blind.

'How did you come to do this?' she inquired.

The man proceeded to tell Corrie about the Bible women in Japan who travel from village to village, taking copies of the Bible as well as Christian books and pamphlets to those who are hungry for God. 'Our Bible woman is very ill with tuberculosis,' he explained, 'but she travels every week to sixteen villages, even though she will soon die.'

'When I heard about it,' he continued, 'I asked the Lord what I could do to help her. Although my legs are paralyzed, and I cannot get out of the wheelchair, in many ways I am healthier than she. God showed me that though her hands are shaky and my legs paralyzed, I could be the hands, and she the legs. I punch out the pages of Braille, and she takes the Bible around to the villages and gives them to the blind people, who miss so much because they cannot see.'

Corrie left the church that evening filled with shame. 'Here was I,' she later divulged, 'with two good legs for traveling all over the world, two good lungs and two good eyes, complaining because I didn't like the food!' She also shared the valuable lesson she learned through that incident: 'These precious people had discovered a sure cure for self-pity – service to others. ... The best antidote I know for self-pity is to help someone else who is worse off than you.'[10]

SEVEN

In 1960 the Lord provided a full-time traveling companion for Corrie in the person of Conny van Hoogstraten, a thirty-one year old Dutch woman. Early on in their working relationship, Corrie told Conny that the Lord had shown her they were next to visit Denmark, Austria, Israel and India. 'Buy our tickets to Tel Aviv,' Corrie instructed. 'I have the money for the plane that far.' When Conny reported back from the travel office that a visa to Israel could only be obtained if tickets were purchased to another destination after that country, Corrie said, 'Then order the tickets to Calcutta.'

'Do we have the money?' Conny asked.

'No, not yet. But don't forget, God is our treasurer. He has the cattle on a thousand hills, and He will perhaps sell some cows and give us the money. Our work is His business, and He always provides the money just in time.' And so it proved. When the tickets arrived, the needed funds were in hand.

---

10 Ten Boom, *Jesus Is Victor*, pp. 438-9.

In 1965 Corrie and Conny spent three months ministering behind the Iron Curtain in Russia, Hungary, Czechoslovakia and Poland. One morning while in Russia they left their hotel room to have breakfast. Corrie tried to give a Russian Gospel tract entitled 'The Way of Salvation' to a cleaning woman in the hallway. But she pushed it away while looking furtively down the hall, fearful lest someone report her for being receptive to religious propaganda. As the two Dutch women entered the elevator, Corrie prayed aloud, 'Father, I can't reach this woman. Do bring her in contact with someone who can tell her the Gospel in her own language. Lord, I claim her soul for eternity.'

Back in their room after breakfast, a knock came at the door. It was the cleaning woman who a short while earlier had refused the tract. Entering the room and closing the door, she spoke in Russian and pointed at Corrie's handbag. Realizing her intent, Corrie nearly shouted, 'Conny, she wants to have "The Way of Salvation".' Fishing it from her bag, Corrie smiled and handed it to her. The woman's face beamed joyously. She nodded appreciatively and backed out of the room. A short while later she returned with a token of her appreciation by presenting Corrie and Conny with a long loaf of fresh white bread.

Due to the fear that people had of being reported, Corrie found very few individuals who were willing to talk with her about spiritual matters on that Eastern European trip. On more than one occasion, having discovered an electronic bugging device in her hotel room, she spoke a clear Gospel message into it for the benefit of anyone who might happen to be spying on her.

Conny was eventually engaged to a missionary named Lykle Hoogerzeil. When he raised concerns over his fiancée accompanying Corrie to war-torn Vietnam, it was decided that another traveling companion should be found for that trip. She was able to team up with Andrew van der Byl, better known as Brother Andrew, God's Smuggler. Through his ministry thousands of Bibles have been smuggled behind the Iron and Bamboo Curtains.

While Brother Andrew was away ministering in various dangerous locations, the U. S. Army provided Corrie with transportation so she could get out and minister to American soldiers. One day a sergeant took her so close to the front lines in a jeep that shooting could be heard. 'The soldiers were very happy that I came,' she afterward related, 'because the only women they saw around there were prostitutes. But here comes an old lady from Holland to the battle line, and they thought that was great.'

Corrie joined Sao, a courageous indigenous evangelist, in ministering in a number of remote mountain villages. She and Brother Andrew were also able to ransom 'many' children from slavery during that trip. When the Vietnamese had a debt they were unable to pay, they commonly sold their children as servants to fulfill their financial obligation. The two missionaries located the funds to place a number of such children in responsible Christian orphanages.

Around that time the Lord supplied another Dutch traveling companion for Corrie in a registered nurse named Ellen de Kroon. God's providence in providing a nurse as Corrie's companion soon became evident. Shortly after they teamed up Corrie was involved in an automobile accident in which she was knocked out and her right arm was broken. Ellen nursed her through that recovery. In the next few years Corrie needed greater physical care as her strength and health began to decline noticeably.

Some time earlier, a Dutch baroness, Elisabeth van Heemstra, had provided Corrie with an attractive apartment in Soestdijk, near the royal palace, to use as her home base between journeys. On a number of occasions Corrie spoke at Bible studies for young society people, including Princess Margriet. After Peter van Vollenhoven married the princess, he desired to have a Bible study on Christ's Second Coming at the palace, and proceeded to invite an eminent university professor, a pastor and Corrie. Not knowing if the views of the two men would coincide with her own on that subject, she prayed, 'Lord, I want to testify, but I do not want the professor and pastor there.'

'I am so sorry, Miss ten Boom,' Peter later phoned to say, 'but the Bible study had to be cancelled, because the others can't come.'

Barely able to contain her delight, she replied, 'Oh, there is no reason why we can't get together anyhow.'

'But just my mother-in-law [the Queen] will be there.' And so it was that on that occasion Corrie had the opportunity to provide Holland's monarch with a private Bible study on that vital subject. On other occasions she was invited to stay at the palace for a few days as a guest. She rarely spoke of her relationships with the royal family. In fact, when people asked her about it, she would often become quite evasive.

Corrie had a remarkable ability to communicate effectively to all different kinds of people in all varieties of settings. She shared the message of God's love and forgiveness with royalty in palaces, government officials in embassies, celebrities at posh social gatherings, intellectuals and students in universities and schools, illiterate local people in their villages, upstanding citizens in service clubs, criminals in prisons, patients in hospitals and beggars on the street. Corrie seemed at ease and effective whether ministering to thousands in a large crusade or church meeting or to a single individual in an airport or restaurant. She often blended the teachings of Scripture with her own life experiences to communicate spiritual truth. That approach seemed appealing and effective with all types of individuals, from the most sophisticated to the simplest.

Corrie once ministered in a small African country where a new government had come to power. Just that week the new regime had begun secretly, systematically putting Christians to death. As the people gathered at the little church where she was to speak that Sunday, fear and tension were written on every face. Corrie first read to them 1 Peter 4:12-14 (Phillips' Translation):

> And now, dear friends of mine, I beg you not to be unduly alarmed at the fiery ordeals which come to test your faith, as though this were some abnormal experience. You should be glad, because it means you are called to share Christ's sufferings. One day, when He shows Himself in full splendor to men, you will be filled with the most tremendous joy. If you are reproached for being Christ's followers, that is a great privilege, for you can be sure that God's Spirit of glory is resting upon you.

Closing her Bible, she proceeded to relate a conversation that took place between her and her father when she was a little girl. "'Daddy,' she had said one day, "I am afraid that I will never be strong enough to be a martyr for Jesus Christ."

'"Tell me," her father wisely answered, "when you take a train trip from Haarlem to Amsterdam, when do I give you the money for the ticket? Three weeks before?"

'"No, Daddy, you give me the money for the ticket just before we get on the train."

'"That is right," he responded, "and so it is with God's strength. Our wise Father in heaven knows when you are going to need things too. Today you do not need the strength to be a martyr; but as soon as you are called upon for the honor of facing death for Jesus, He will supply the strength you need – just in time."

'I took great comfort in my father's advice,' Corrie told her audience. 'Later I had to suffer for Jesus in a concentration camp. He indeed gave me all the courage and power I needed.'

'Tell us more, Tante Corrie,' one grizzled old member of the congregation spoke up. All were listening intently, seeking to store up truth that would strengthen them for the day of trial.

So she shared an incident that had taken place at Ravensbruck. A group of fellow prisoners had approached her, asking her to tell them some Bible stories. The camp guards called the Bible *das Lugenbuch* – the book of lies. Death by cruel punishment had been promised for any prisoner who was found possessing a Bible or talking about the Lord. Despite her awareness of those potential consequences, Corrie retrieved her Bible and started teaching from the Scripture.

Suddenly she was aware of a figure behind her. One of the prisoners silently mouthed the words, 'Hide your Bible. It's Lony.'

Corrie knew Lony well. She was among the cruelest of all the women guards. Corrie, however, felt she had to obey God who had so clearly guided her to bring a Bible message to the prisoners that morning. Lony remained motionless behind her as she finished her teaching.

Corrie then said, 'Let's now sing a hymn of praise.' She could see the worried, anxious looks on the faces of the prisoners. Before it had been only her speaking but now they, too, were being asked to join her in singing. But Corrie believed God wanted them to be bold, even in the face of the enemy. So they sang.

When the hymn came to an end, Lony instructed, 'Another song like that one.' She had enjoyed the singing and wanted to hear more. Heartened, the prisoners sang song after song. Afterwards Corrie even went to Lony and spoke to her about her need for Christ as her Savior.

'Let me tell you what I learned from that experience,' she now told her African audience. 'I knew that every word I said could mean death. Yet never before had I felt such peace and joy in my heart as while I was giving the Bible message in the presence of mine enemy. God gave me the grace and power I needed — the money for the train ticket arrived just the moment I was to step on the train.'

As the meeting ended, the fear and anxiety were gone from the peoples' faces. Joy shown on their countenances and their hearts seemed filled with peace. Corrie later learned that more than half the Christians who attended that service subsequently met a martyr's death.

In the early 1970s, as Corrie neared then surpassed her eightieth birthday, she suddenly found herself gaining worldwide fame through books and movies that were produced about her life. She herself had earlier written a number of books about her life experiences that had been read by thousands. But her books *The Hiding Place* (written with John and Elizabeth Sherrill, published 1971) and *Tramp for the Lord* (coauthored with Jamie Buckingham, published 1974) both became bestsellers that were read by millions. The former related the story of her formative years and her experiences throughout the Second World War while the latter chronicled the fascinating story of her subsequent ministries around the globe.

In addition, in 1975 World Wide Pictures, the motion picture branch of the Billy Graham Evangelistic Association, released a top-quality movie about Corrie's World War 2 experiences that also bore the title *The Hiding Place*. As a result of the film playing across the United States and in many other countries, she became the most sought after woman speaker in the world. Hundreds of speaking invitations began to pour in and television programs vied to interview her. Billy Graham had her share her testimony at his crusades and thousands crowded into stadiums to hear her.

In the midst of that tidal wave of popularity and ministry opportunity, Ellen (Corrie's aide) met the man who would become her husband, Bob Stamps, the chaplain at Oral Roberts University. As a result, Corrie contacted Pam Rosewell, a young, soft-spoken English woman whom she already knew, about becoming her next full-time traveling companion. Pam had worked for Brother Andrew for seven years. With her British efficiency, she was the perfect person to help Corrie continue to carry out her demanding schedule.

In 1976 Corrie moved into a beautiful California home where she had a bed of her own, a settled place to work on her books, a dining room for entertaining friends, an organ and a garden full of flowers and birds. Dubbed Shalom House, Corrie hardly viewed it as a retirement home. 'The Lord has told me I will write five books and do five movies here,' she asserted. While some were skeptical, as it turned out she was exactly right about the five films but underestimated the number of books by one. The films were biographical and testimonial in nature. One of them was especially geared for reaching people in prison.

One day her heart started beating more and more slowly, sometimes only twenty beats a minute. Thinking that her life might be about to draw to a close she wrote: 'The best is yet to be. Now I must go Home, to see Jesus face to face. From service good to service best. What joyful work there would be for me in heaven!' Instead, she underwent an operation to have a pacemaker put in and her life of service on earth was extended.

After completing a final book of daily devotions, *Each New Day*, Corrie was scheduled to attend the 1978 Christian Booksellers Convention in Denver. Completely unknown to her, her publisher and World Wide Pictures planned to film a program there before an audience of two thousand entitled *Corrie: The Lives She's Touched*. Cliff Barrows, Billy Graham's songleader and a longtime friend of Corrie, served as master of ceremonies. At the close of the program, a beautiful bouquet of flowers was presented to her. She deflected any praise she had received that evening to the Lord by looking up to heaven with a face full of devotion as she raised her bouquet to Him.

A few weeks later, in August of 1978, Corrie had a severe stroke that left her unable to move or speak. She was hospitalized for three weeks and then was able to return home. After undergoing physical and speech therapy, she still could not speak in complete sentences or write but she was able to communicate through single words and various hand signals. Pam Rosewell and other faithful ladies provided her with around-the-clock care and company.

Many originally thought that God, having blessed Corrie as one of the premiere Christian communicators of her generation, would not leave her incapacitated for long. But in one of the imponderable determinations of Providence, such proved not to be the case. Rather than gradually recovering, or being taken home to heaven in timely fashion, Corrie lingered on more than four years as her physical health and capabilities continued to erode due to advancing age and subsequent strokes.

Numerous people who visited her during those years testified that God's love, joy and peace continued to shine through her to others. On several occasions her caretakers heard her 'laughing with pure joy'. One of her acquaintances recorded: 'The visitors who left Corrie's bedside saw a peace that "passes all understanding" [Phil. 4:7]. Many said that if she could be joyful in the Lord in her circumstances, then they surely could be in theirs.'[11] Thus, even in her final protracted trial of life, she was able, though silenced, to bear a strong testimony to others.

At last, on April 15, 1983, her ninety-first birthday, God mercifully released His faithful servant to her heavenly restoration and reward.

---

11 Carlson, *Corrie ten Boom*, p. 206.

Conclusion

The lives and ministries of the women featured in this book differed significantly from one another. But common themes and lessons can be drawn from their varied life experiences for the benefit of present-day Christians.

Their lives show that God has different ministries for each of His servants to fulfill. Believers are not all given the same kind of ministry and normally the Lord has more than one major ministry for each servant to discharge. Susanna Wesley's ministries centered on her children in her home and, to a lesser degree, on the people in her husband's parish. Fanny Crosby's primary ministry was hymnwriting, but she also used that as a platform for speaking ministries in missions, YMCAs and other public settings. In addition to placing a priority on the spiritual upbringing of her children, Catherine Booth carried out a powerful preaching ministry, especially emphasizing evangelism and a proper Christian response to the down-and-out of society.

For years, while providing the primary source of financial support for her own family, Mary Slessor was also actively involved in youth ministry at her local church and neighborhood missions. Her career of missionary service in Calabar involved school teaching, itinerant evangelism, church planting, foster care and judicial responsibilities. For nearly fifty years Corrie ten Boom's life revolved around household responsibilities and ministries to the young people and those with learning difficulties in her community. The final four decades of her life involved altogether different ministries, including the harboring of fugitives from the Nazi regime, providing a bright Christian witness in the darkness of German concentration camps and, after the war, heralding the message of God's love and forgiveness throughout the world.

Their examples remind believers to identify and fulfill the unique ministries that the Lord has for them to fulfill rather than thinking they need to have the same ministry emphasis as someone else. Christians should also remain sensitive to new ministries that God may desire to lead them into as they go along in their service of Him.

Each of these women experienced marked hardships in life. For most, if not all of them, difficulties were regular rather than periodic occurrences. How they processed those trials was crucial. Instead of turning away from God because of marked adversity, they drew near to Him for His help and strength in getting through the trials. As a result, their faith was progressively strengthened rather than gradually weakened and ultimately destroyed. Doubtless those hardships were one of the primary means God used to develop their stalwart faith and character. The principles of James 1:2-4 concerning the faith-building effects of enduring various trials are readily observable in their lives. As it was with them, so it is with contemporary believers: hardships tend to be part and parcel of the Christian life; God uses those difficulties to strengthen the faith and develop the character of His children.

These women were characterized by selfless service of the Lord and others. Their lives were all about serving Christ and benefiting others, not at all about living for self. They sacrificed many personal conveniences and comforts in order to serve faithfully. Their lives fulfilled such service-related scriptural injunctions as Matthew 16:24-25 and Philippians 2:3-8, 20-21. Periodically they were tempted to feel sorry for themselves in light of the constant and sometimes heavy sacrifices their service required of them. But the vast majority of the time they bore their self-sacrificial service willingly and without complaint. Their example is a necessary corrective to many modern Christians who are absorbed with their own interests and comforts while manifesting little inclination or willingness to expend their lives in serving Christ and those around them.

Susanna, Fanny, Catherine, Mary and Corrie also shared a zeal for evangelism and Christian missions. For Susanna and Catherine with their biological children, as for Mary with her adopted bairns, earnest evangelistic endeavor began at home. Sharing the Gospel, whether one-on-one or in public settings, was a pronounced emphasis for Fanny, Catherine, Mary and Corrie throughout their ministry careers.

Susanna shared her husband's fervent desire to see the American Indians brought to Christ and happily released two of her sons, John and Charles, to serve in a missionary venture to that end. Fanny promoted missions through many of her hymns, Catherine through the Salvation Army's advance to numerous countries, Mary through her decades of service in Africa and Corrie through her worldwide travels.

Contemporary Christians do well to share in their fervor for evangelism and missions. Those were obvious emphases in the early church and have always been evident features in healthy churches and believers.

Another commendable characteristic of these women was their proper balancing of family and ministry responsibilities. Mary and Corrie were both extremely devoted to helping, caring and providing for their family members. In addition, for many years Mary served as a loving foster mother and Corrie as an affectionate adopted aunt to numbers of children. Neither of them married, though they had that fond desire for a season. They were content to remain single and thus be freer to carry out the specialized ministries the Lord had for them to fulfill for Him (Matt. 19:12; 1 Cor. 7:32-35).

Susanna and Catherine were loyal to, and supportive of, their husbands' ministries. At times that would have required some effort on their part due to ministry demands, straitened finances or, in Susanna's case, having a domineering and insensitive husband. Susanna and Catherine also dedicated a great deal of time and effort to the training of their several children. They raised their children with strict but loving discipline. Their primary concern with their children was that they would develop into devout Christians. Instead of allowing their children to be self-centered, they impressed upon them the conviction that their purpose in life was to serve God and their fellow human beings.

The positive examples and high principles of these women with regard to fulfilling one's family responsibilities, deciding whether or not to marry, and raising children for the Lord are worthy of emulation by Christian singles, spouses and parents today.

About the Author

Vance Christie is a pastor and author of *Timeless Stories: God's Incredible Work in the Lives of Inspiring Christians*, a collection of narratives from the daily lives of Christian heroes like George Müller, Charles Spurgeon, Dwight Moody, Corrie ten Boom, Billy Graham and others. Best known for vivid retelling of missionary stories, he is the author of recent 'History Makers' biographies *David Brainerd: A Flame for God* and *John and Betty Stam: Missionary Martyrs*. He has previously written for the 'Heroes of the Faith' series. He and his wife, Leeta, live in Aurora, Nebraska and have three daughters.

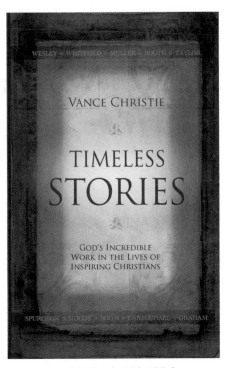

ISBN 978-1-84550-557-8

Timeless Stories
God's incredible work in the lives of inspiring Christians

VANCE CHRISTIE

They were, much like us, ordinary citizens of their time. Yet their extraordinary lives resound through the generations for the glory of God, pointing us to a higher way of life today. *Timeless Stories* is an exceptional collection of narratives from the daily lives of Christian heroes like George Muller, Charles Spurgeon, Dwight Moody, Corrie ten Boom, Billy Graham and others.

ISBN 978-1-84550-640-7

Feminine Threads
Women in the Tapestry of Christian History

DIANA SEVERANCE

From commoner to queen, the women in this book embraced the freedom and the power of the Gospel in making their unique contributions to the unfolding of history. Wherever possible, the women here speak for themselves, from their letters, diaries or published works. The true story of women in Christian history inspires, challenges and demonstrates the grace of God producing much fruit throughout time.

Diana Severance (PhD, Rice University) is an historian with broad experience teaching in universities and seminaries.

Christian Focus Publications
publishes books for all ages

Our mission statement –

STAYING FAITHFUL
In dependence upon God we seek to impact the world through literature faithful to His infallible Word, the Bible. Our aim is to ensure that the Lord Jesus Christ is presented as the only hope to obtain forgiveness of sin, live a useful life and look forward to heaven with Him.

REACHING OUT
Christ's last command requires us to reach out to our world with His gospel. We seek to help fulfil that by publishing books that point people towards Jesus and help them develop a Christ-like maturity. We aim to equip all levels of readers for life, work, ministry and mission.

Books in our adult range are published in three imprints:

Christian Focus contains popular works including biographies, commentaries, basic doctrine and Christian living. Our children's books are also published in this imprint.

Mentor focuses on books written at a level suitable for Bible College and seminary students, pastors, and other serious readers. The imprint includes commentaries, doctrinal studies, examination of current issues and church history.

Christian Heritage contains classic writings from the past.

Christian Focus Publications Ltd,
Geanies House, Fearn, Ross-shire,
IV20 1TW, Scotland, United Kingdom
www.christianfocus.com